SHL ITEM BARCODE

19 1778175 9

SENATE HOUSE LI
UNIVERSITY OF LONDO

Tel: 0207 862 8437/8 http://www.shl.lon.ac.uk
Please note that this book is due back on the latest date stamped below.
It may be requested if required by another reader in which
case it will not be possible to renew the loan.
Fines are payable on books returned after the due date.

0 5 NOV 2012 3/1/13.		
.		

A Child for Keeps

Also by Jenny Keating

THE DROUGHT WALKED THROUGH: A History of Water Shortage in Victoria

PEOPLE'S PLAYGROUND: A History of the Albert Park (*with Jill Barnard*)

A Child for Keeps

The History of Adoption in England, 1918–45

Jenny Keating

© Jenny Keating 2009

All rights reserved. No reproduction, copy or transmission of this publication may be made without written permission.

No portion of this publication may be reproduced, copied or transmitted save with written permission or in accordance with the provisions of the Copyright, Designs and Patents Act 1988, or under the terms of any licence permitting limited copying issued by the Copyright Licensing Agency, Saffron House, 6-10 Kirby Street, London EC1N 8TS.

Any person who does any unauthorized act in relation to this publication may be liable to criminal prosecution and civil claims for damages.

The author has asserted her right to be identified as the author of this work in accordance with the Copyright, Designs and Patents Act 1988.

First published 2009 by
PALGRAVE MACMILLAN

Palgrave Macmillan in the UK is an imprint of Macmillan Publishers Limited, registered in England, company number 785998, of Houndmills, Basingstoke, Hampshire RG21 6XS.

Palgrave Macmillan in the US is a division of St Martin's Press LLC, 175 Fifth Avenue, New York, NY 10010.

Palgrave Macmillan is the global academic imprint of the above companies and has companies and representatives throughout the world.

Palgrave® and Macmillan® are registered trademarks in the United States, the United Kingdom, Europe and other countries

ISBN-13: 978-0-230-51788-2   hardback
ISBN-10: 0-230-51788-9   hardback

This book is printed on paper suitable for recycling and made from fully managed and sustained forest sources. Logging, pulping and manufacturing processes are expected to conform to the environmental regulations of the country of origin.

A catalogue record for this book is available from the British Library.

Library of Congress Cataloging-in-Publication Data

Keating, Jenny.
  A child for keeps? : the history of adoption in England, 1918-1945 / Jenny Keating.
    p. cm.
Includes bibliographical references and index.
ISBN 978-0-230-51788-2 (alk. paper)
  1. Adoption—England—History. 2. Adoption—Law and legislation—Great Britain—History. I. Title.
HV875.58.G72E5446 2008
362.7340942'09041—dc22   2008025121

10 9 8 7 6 5 4 3 2 1
18 17 16 15 14 13 12 11 10 09

Printed and bound in Great Britain by
CPI Antony Rowe, Chippenham and Eastbourne

Contents

List of Illustrations	vii
Acknowledgements	viii
List of Abbreviations	ix
Introduction	1
Secrecy	3
Attitudes to adoption	6
Adoption histories	8
1 Setting the Scene: The Historical and Legal Background	11
Changing families	11
New views of childhood	18
The development of child protection legislation	22
Parental rights before 1926	27
Marriage breakdown and custody	28
Illegitimate children and unmarried mothers	30
2 Developments in the Voluntary Sector	39
The beginning of organised adoption	39
The formation of the first adoption societies	42
The establishment of the National Council for the Unmarried Mother and Her Child	62
3 Pressure for Government Action	67
The first conference on adoption	67
The Hopkinson Committee	71
The Hopkinson Report	83
The 1920s – an era of legislative reform	87
The years after the Hopkinson Report	89
4 Legislation Takes Shape	94
The Tomlin Committee's report	95
Parliamentary debates on adoption	103
The Adoption of Children Act 1926	113
5 The First Years of Legally Sanctioned Adoption	117
Initial reactions	117
Court procedures	120
In re Carroll	126

	Other legal issues	128
	Adoption of Children (Scotland) Act 1930	129
	The London County Council	130
	Who were the adopters, the adopted, and the relinquishing parents in the early years?	137
6	Action on the Adoption Societies	144
	Concern about the role of adoption societies	144
	The Horsbrugh Committee	153
	Report of the Departmental Committee on Adoption Societies and Agencies	154
	The Adoption of Children (Regulation) Act 1939	167
	The death of Miss Clara Andrew	172
7	The Second World War and Its Aftermath	175
	Implementing the Adoption of Children (Regulation) Act	177
	Servicemen's wives and adoption	180
	Unmarried mothers	182
	Renewed pressure for adoption reform	185
	Adoption legislation	190
8	Conclusions – And Later Developments	195
	Attitudes to adoption	195
	The rise of adoption	197
	Who was adoption for?	199
	Secrecy	201
	Adoption and women	203
	Adoption since 1950	205
	Final conclusions	208

Notes	213
Biographical Notes	244
Bibliography	252
Index	266

Illustrations

Figure 2.1	Miss Clara Andrew and an adopted child (from the London Metropolitan Archives)	44
Figure 2.2	Tower Cressy, the NCAA hostel, Campden Hill, Kensington (from an NCAA leaflet, The National Archives)	49
Figure 2.3	'Two little girls some months after adoption' (from an NCAA leaflet, The National Archives)	56
Figure 2.4	Day nursery, Tower Cressy (from an NCAA leaflet, The National Archives)	59
Figure 2.5	Princess Alice, Countess of Athlone, with an adopted child (from the London Metropolitan Archives)	61
Figure 3.1	Sir Alfred Hopkinson, 1928 (from the ©National Portrait Gallery, London)	73
Figure 5.1	Adoption order, 1928 (from a private collection)	124
Figure 6.1	Miss Florence Horsbrugh, 1931 (from the ©National Portrait Gallery, London)	154

Acknowledgements

Ultimately the person responsible for this book is my grandmother, Bridie Moran, who signed a relinquishing form for my father in 1928 when he was three-and-a-half-years old and then disappeared from his life forever. I know nothing whatever of her story; who she was, why she gave up my father, and what happened to her afterwards, but the little I knew of my father's early years led me to a wider interest in the history of adoption, and nine years ago, returning from Australia to the UK, and trying to think of a subject for a thesis, I came up with adoption.

So this book started life as a DPhil, and I must thank the supervisors I had over the years – Professors Eileen Yeo, Pat Thane and Carol Dyhouse – whose support and positive challenging of my ideas was so helpful. I would also like to thank my examiners Professor George Behlmer and Dr Claire Langhamer who, far from being the terrifying interrogators I envisaged, were enthusiastic, and encouraged me to publish the thesis. I am grateful for the help given to me by all the staff of the libraries and archives I visited, in particular the University of Sussex Library, but also those at the National Archives (formerly the PRO); the London Metropolitan Archive; the London School of Economics Library; the Women's Library; the Family Records Centre; the British Library Newspaper rooms; the Elizabeth Roberts Archive at the Centre for North-West Regional Studies, Lancaster University; and the Records Offices of Bath, Exeter, Bristol and East Sussex. I would also like to thank the Royal Historical Society who gave me a grant for travel and copying.

Thanks to all the people – strangers and friends – who helped in so many ways, responding to email enquiries, reading and commenting, and checking for errors. Special thanks to Patricia Wreford King, who contacted me out of the blue and shared her fascinating papers relating to Miss Clara Andrew, Princess Alice and the National Children Adoption Association with me. Finally, my thanks to Andy, Robin, Lily and Rosa for enduring the adoption saga for so many years.

Jenny Keating

Abbreviations

ASCMI	Associated Societies for the Care and Maintenance of Infants
COS	Charity Organisation Society
CWC	Child Welfare Council
HCAAS	Homeless Children's Aid and Adoption Society
HO	Home Office
LCC	London County Council
LCO	Lord Chancellor's Office
MH	Ministry of Health
MOH	Medical Officer of Health
NAS	National Adoption Society
NCAA	National Children Adoption Association
NCH	National Children's Home & Orphanage
NCUMC	National Council for the Unmarried Mother and Her Child
NCSS	National Council of Social Service
NCVO	National Council for Voluntary Organisations
NCW	National Council of Women
NSPCC	National Society for the Prevention of Cruelty to Children
NUSEC	National Union of Societies for Equal Citizenship

Introduction

> A man came a little while ago to us and said he and his wife wanted to adopt a child and had we one for adoption? I said No, I had not. The next day he came back and said he had been to a bureau which had forty children, all of whom could have been adopted, and he could have picked out one and taken it away, but there was not one which happened to suit him. That is really putting it on a par with being able to buy a domestic pet of any kind.
> (Lady Henry Somerset, witness before the Hopkinson Committee, 2 November 1920, see Chapter 3)

> Overall the adoption system – including the courts – is too slow and bureaucratic, too opaque and too unfair. Children should not be left waiting indefinitely for the perfect family on spurious grounds or a perverse sense of what is and what is not politically correct.
> (Alan Milburn, the then Secretary of State for Health, quoted in the *Guardian*, 30 October 2001)

My father was adopted when he was nearly four, in early 1928, a year after the first English adoption law came into force. His childhood was unhappy, his relations with his adoptive father strained, and I was not surprised when my mother eventually told me that the grandfather we all called 'Pop' was not his real father. At some point it became family lore that he had been picked out from the other children in the orphanage because of his pretty looks but soon afterwards returned when his first adopting parents found him difficult. He was chosen again and this time the adopting parents kept him. I was always intrigued by this casual process, which seemed to have more in common with choosing a dog from a rescue home than the rigorous selection procedure now faced by potential adopters.

Child adoption is the process of transferring a child from its natural parent or parents, on a permanent basis, to another person who then takes on the rights and responsibilities formerly held by the natural parent. The child effectively becomes the son or daughter of the adopting parent or parents. Until 1926 there was no such thing as legal adoption in the United Kingdom, even though by the early 1920s most English-speaking countries and states, including those of the then British Empire and the United States of America, had enacted legislation to give the process legal standing. There were ways for the wealthy in Britain to establish some kind of legal entitlement to children who were not their offspring but the vast majority of people who looked after other people's children on a permanent basis had no legal right to them and in theory the natural parents might at any point return to claim them. Equally, there were no regulations about adoption; anyone could obtain a child from an adoption society or take on someone's unwanted baby with no questions asked.

My father was one of these children: he was born illegitimate in 1924. There is no father's name on his birth certificate but his mother was 'a domestic help'. She remains a mystery; there is nothing about her in any of the obvious sources and no trace of her but her signature on the relinquishing form. My father never talked about being adopted or revealed to anyone that he was illegitimate. When I spoke at his funeral I mentioned a little of his early background and was surprised when people he had worked with for years told me afterwards they knew nothing about it. The stigma of illegitimacy went deep in him; he equated it with humiliation, failure and abandonment. When I had my first child without being married he was devastated and refused to speak to my partner. For him the shame he felt about his background was one of the driving forces in his life, obsessively compelling him to succeed in the world. In later years he realised I was curious about his natural parents and told me to make no effort to trace them until after his death; he wanted nothing to do with people he felt had rejected him.

A number of the themes in this thesis are touched on in my father's story. The fear and revulsion illegitimacy inspired, and the corresponding obsession with secrecy among those involved in the process of adoption; the emphasis on the immediate desires of the adopting parents with a contrasting lack of interest in a child's individual personality and the disregard by the adoption system for the relinquishing parent's needs. And my father's adoptive parents exemplified the aspiration for 'respectability' among the upwardly mobile lower and middle classes, which was embodied in the creation of a family with the necessary one or two children. They also demonstrated the increasing awareness that families did not need to grow randomly but could be shaped by contraception or adoption; even a middle-aged widow with adult children, and the younger man she had recently married, could create their own family. In the 1920s they faced no questions about their motives, their relationship, their inability or lack of desire to conceive a baby themselves; they simply went along to the children's home, picked out a child and took it home.

Nowadays there is continual criticism from many quarters of the lengthy procedures and constraints faced by people wishing to adopt children.[1] Looking back at how things were in the early days of legalised adoption perhaps provides a useful counterbalance to these views. Similarly, although there are still advocates of anonymous donor insemination, cloning and other high-tech fertilisation processes which obliterate or muddle the identity of the biological parents, there is a growing consciousness that children conceived in these ways may face problems and confusion similar to that of adopted children whose past has been covered up. The shadow of secrecy lasts a long time; I am not the only child of an adoptee who would like to know more about my grandparents. In the growing literature on adoptees' searching and reunion there are often stories of children persuading or helping their parents to search for their birthparents, and since I wrote an article on the early years of legalised adoption in an online university journal I have received a number of emails from people searching for more information about their parents' original parents.[2] They and their parents are the legatees of the passion for secrecy which drove so many of those involved in the early years of adoption.

Secrecy

This is the issue which overshadows every aspect of the adoption discourse in the interwar years, through the Second World War and into the 1960s and beyond; the perceived need to preserve secrecy about every part of the adoption process. Not everyone, as we will see, felt that secrecy was important but most of those directly involved in the process did. Indeed some potential adopters claimed that they would not adopt if there was any chance of their action becoming public knowledge.

The adoption societies supported the adopters in this and campaigned throughout the period, with considerable success, for increasing secrecy in adoption procedures. If adopted children had all been orphans, the desire for secrecy would inevitably have been less urgent; the awareness that most adopted children were illegitimate led some adopters to feel that their respectability and social standing would be directly threatened if people knew their child was adopted. Adopting couples would also have to deal with a presumption that they were unable to conceive their own child, which many found embarrassing. And for many of the birth mothers it was important that they were able to start again with a clean slate, with their reputation untarnished.

For those who believe that adoption has run a steady course from complete secrecy to today's much more open system the following chapters show the reality was much more complex. Those running the newly formed adoption societies in the 1920s believed that there should be a complete break between the adopted child and its natural parents so that the latter knew nothing about the adopting family and the child started life afresh. But in the interwar years there was also a considerable body of informed opinion which felt this was unnecessary – and undesirable – once an adoption had been given legal security. In the 1920s and 1930s the process of enforced secrecy was, at least in theory, not complete, and adoptees retained a right to see their original birth certificate (a right not easily accessed and unfortunately there are no figures on how many ever managed to obtain the requisite court order – one would imagine very few).[3] In 1930 the National Children Adoption Association's petition for a Royal Charter was turned down because the Home Office believed its great emphasis on secrecy was at variance with government policy.[4]

Murray Ryburn looked at the historical development of secrecy in English adoption.[5] Looking at the three parliamentary committees reporting on adoption during the interwar period, he felt attitudes changed between the interwar years and after the Second World War when secrecy was accepted across the board. Ryburn attributed the desire for secrecy not just to the fear of the reappearance of birth parents but also the fear of adopted children searching out those parents in later life. This was especially pertinent during the Second World War when the large rise in adoptions was widely assumed to be partly attributable to the babies born to married women whose husbands were away in the armed forces. Those women would be desperate to keep the births secret. The post-war feeling was about starting again, moving on from a difficult past, not looking back. Nurture rather than nature became the emphasis, 'a crucial part of helping a child to become "adoptable" through a new environment and care regime lay in the creation of a divide between this new life and what was seen to be the disabling influence of her or his original circumstances'.[6]

The issue of secrecy will emerge through later chapters but I would suggest that although 'establishment' attitudes to secrecy may have changed pre– and post-Second World War the difference in practice was probably less marked. Long before the 1949 Act there were ways of evading 'openness', the most common being the practice of obtaining the relinquishing parent's signature on a blank form so she never saw the name of the person adopting her child and then ensuring that she was never aware of the subsequent court hearing. The adoption societies were quite open about these practices which were really part of their marketing strategy to potential adopters. By the 1950s and 1960s secrecy in adoption was clearly a dominating doctrine among adoption professionals although the issue never sparked as passionate an ideological battle here as it appears to have done in the States. There was some vociferous opposition in the Parliamentary debates on the access clauses in the 1975 Children Act but they were passed and have proved relatively uncontroversial since.[7]

In his history of adoption in the United States,[8] E. Wayne Carp looked in some detail at the issue of secrecy and has charted changing attitudes towards it. Inevitably there are similarities and differences. Adoption was legalised much earlier in America than in the United Kingdom. Massachusetts enacted a 'modern' adoption law in 1851 and in the next half century the majority of states passed similar legislation. Large-scale transfer of children to remote western settlements (analogous to the child emigration from the United Kingdom to Canada, Australia and South Africa) in the late nineteenth century eventually provoked a very negative reaction from the public. Not until the 1950s did adoption become a widespread phenomenon. Carp considered the major emphasis on confidentiality and secrecy emerged at this point. After the Second World War illegitimacy in the USA rapidly increased and many more children offered for adoption were illegitimate rather than from married or divorced mothers who could not support them (the pre-war illegitimacy rate in the United States appears to have been considerably lower than here). To encourage these mothers to come to the regulated professional adoption agencies in the 1950s, rather than to private, amateur ones which asked no questions, social workers felt it necessary to promise secrecy.

Carp described the American social work profession as increasingly embracing psychoanalytic theories which suggested that unmarried mothers were neurotic, emotionally immature and irresponsible people for whom the baby was an attempt to find an answer to their unmet needs. The inescapable conclusion appeared to be that the best treatment was to sever the mother completely from her child and withhold all information from her about its subsequent fate.[9] Similarly, adult adoptees seeking information about their original family were now seen as disturbed victims of Freud's 'family romance' theory. This is the common practice of children fantasising that they are adopted which normally ends as children come to accept that their parents have a sexual relationship.

In reaction, adoption rights movements started, springing out of the radical movements of the 1960s and the sexual liberation of the same period, which meant unmarried motherhood and illegitimacy became less shameful. However, Carp considered that the social work profession in America has been relatively reluctant to welcome more open access to adoption records, and although some states have passed helpful legislation and some agencies have cooperated with adoptees' search for their natural parents, there is no equivalent to the 1975 Children Act which made access a right in England and Wales.[10]

Looking briefly at other countries where adoption followed a similar pattern to the United Kingdom: in New Zealand the identity of birth parents was only concealed with legislation in 1955.[11] In Australia the legal position varied from state to state but attitudes to secrecy appear to have followed a similar pattern to those in England[12] and access to birth information has been gradually granted on a state by state basis.

Attitudes to adoption

As well as secrecy there runs through this whole narrative the question of attitudes towards adoption during this period – and whether they changed? And for whose main benefit was adoption? Throughout the interwar years there was a strong underlying debate about the merits of encouraging adoption, particularly in relation to relinquishing unmarried mothers. On the whole, war orphans were seen as acceptable beneficiaries of the practice, but fears were frequently expressed about the danger of encouraging recurrent immorality if it was too easy for unmarried mothers to dispose of their illegitimate children. Clara Andrew, who founded the National Children Adoption Association, spoke of how in the early years when she spoke about adoption around the country: 'At every meeting of a public character I was heckled by one or two organised bodies. All thought it a dangerous movement and in the case of the illegitimate child, subversive of public morals.'[13] There was also concern about the severing of the mother-child relationship, and the way in which relinquishing parents were treated by some of the adoption societies. However others were impatient with unnecessary bureaucracy which might hinder unwanted children from finding families.

In whose main interests was adoption carried out during this period—birth parents, adoptive parents or the children involved? Ideally their interests harmonise with each other for the benefit of all. In practice they often do not, and at different points throughout the history of adoption different weight has attached to the interests of child or adopter – sometimes one seems to be considered most important, sometimes the other. The interests of the relinquishing parent are usually the least considered of the three. Then, as now, it was almost always stated by everyone involved in the adoption process that the child's interests were paramount, but this was not necessarily the case. Writing as an adopted person, the novelist A. M. Homes said, 'adoptees don't really have any rights, their lives are about supporting the secrets, the needs and desires of others'.[14] Defining the 'best' interests of the child was anyway problematic: this continues to be an area that is controversial and was even more difficult at a time when a change of home circumstances could offer such enormous material benefit to a child and when relatively little was known about the emotional and psychological damage which could result from removing a child from its family.

In fact the concept of three interests is simplistic: a book about adoption in Australia is entitled *The Many-Sided Triangle*. It is explained in the preface that the triangle represents the three interests involved in adoption but it 'falls short of the complexity of adoption. It says nothing of other family members, siblings, uncles and aunts, grandparents, children'. The 'many-sided triangle' image has been chosen because it suggests 'that there are more sides, and more angles, to adoption than one might think'.[15] Similarly, one of the many books on the process of adoption reunion of adopted children and their birth parents is subtitled *Experiences from the Adoption Circle* and illustrates how many people are affected by the reunion experience – and indeed the whole process of adoption – beyond the immediate mother and child.[16]

Current political thought appears to take it for granted that for children in need, adoption is a better solution than institutional or foster care or inadequate parents. The adoption societies in the inter-war years certainly thought this and the Curtis Committee, reporting in 1946, did too. Within social work circles over the years there has been considerable debate about this. An enormous literature has been generated but for obvious reasons there has never been a large controlled research study done on outcomes of equivalent groups of children, adopted and kept with one or other parents. There are now many (mainly post-Second World War) accounts and anthologies of people's experiences of being adopted, relinquishing their child, and adopting a child – and stories of reunions and attempts at reunions.[17] But it is still hard to make generalisations about the success or otherwise of adoption because so many variables are involved; in a sense every account is no more than anecdotal evidence. Until the 1980s the vast majority of 'stranger adoptions' (i.e. adoption of a non-relative) involved a child who was given up at birth or soon after, and it is impossible to know what might have happened if they had stayed with their mother or been chosen by another family.

Adoption histories

I wrote this book as a historical narrative discussing the development of adoption because as I began my research I was surprised to find how little had been published about the early history of adoption in the United Kingdom. One of the few accounts of it is included in a detailed chapter in George Behlmer's account of the history of intervention in what is often portrayed as the private sanctum of the family before the intrusion of the welfare state. This placed adoption in the context of middle-class involvement in working-class families, ranging from the infant life protection campaigners reacting to the mid-century baby farming scandals through to the great children's rescue charities' boarding out and fostering at the end of the century, and offered an overview of the work of the adoption societies and the campaigns for legalised adoption during the interwar period.[18] A few unpublished theses have also touched on the history of adoption but mainly from a social work or social policy point of view.[19]

Most writing on adoption in England has been from a social work perspective and there is now a vast body of literature on all aspects of current practice and policy. However in the interwar period social work as a profession was in its very early stages and social workers had little involvement with adoption.[20] Social work teachers and practitioners began to write about adoption after the Second World War as official attitudes towards adoption became encouraging rather than merely regulatory or enabling. Adoption became a much more established part of local authority work and social workers considerably more involved with it. Many of these books in the 1950s and 1960s contain a chapter or two on the history of adoption as background to their comments, often tracing it all the way from the Greeks and Romans to the developments of the 1950s. Prominent examples are Margaret Kornitzer's succinct introduction to the state of adoption practice in the early 1950s,[21] and Alexina McWhinnie's study of the emotional and social development or 'adjustment' of fifty eight adults living in South East Scotland in the early 1950s who had been adopted as children.[22] J. P. Triseliotis similarly included some analysis of the historical background to adoption in his early work and provided a brief but useful discussion of changing attitudes to illegitimacy.[23] In 1971 the Home Office produced its own survey of the subject which has a few statistics from the pre-war period but mainly concentrated on the period after the Second World War.[24]

When I started my research on adoption I envisaged going through the records of a couple of adoption agencies – perhaps a society and a local authority. I would see who gave away their children and why, and who wanted to adopt – and what happened to the children. But I soon discovered that this was impossible; even when records still exist the data protection laws and confidentiality rules are strict and rigorous, and, if anything, seem to be getting tighter. Even my own father's records were unobtainable; they turned out to be among the many that are lost or destroyed. At one point I thought one of the major children's charities which arranged some adoptions in the interwar years would let me into its archive but in the end the privacy rules were again insurmountable. So the emphasis of this history is perhaps a little different than was originally intended – but such is the nature of books, they change and evolve. Adoption turned out to have been a controversial issue from when it was first begun on an organised basis, and much of this book looks at the debates and arguments that surrounded it and how adoption developed out of them.

As a historian I feel passionately that nothing in the present can be understood without reference to the past and I hope that in some small way this book will give people an insight into why modern adoption practice and policy have developed in the way they have. I know from the experience of friends how infuriating, even soul-destroying, the current adoption vetting procedures can be, and many people have written heart-felt, angry accounts of the process. But permanently taking away children from their parents and relatives is an enormous step which resonates throughout the adoptees' lives. One of the reasons for introducing access to birth records was because the first surveys of adopted people's experiences were beginning to show that a number of them suffered psychological problems from their confused sense of self and identity.[25] The process of adoption can probably be improved but it needs to be about thoughtful care, not attention-grabbing headlines. Do people really want to return to a system where babies are swapped between complete strangers at railway stations?

1
Setting the Scene: The Historical and Legal Background

The campaign for legalised adoption after the First World War and during the 1920s emerged against a background of considerable change in the shape of the family and in public and private attitudes towards children and their upbringing and protection. This chapter looks at these changes and also offers a brief historical account of the legal position of children prior to the Adoption of Children Act 1926. Finally the legal and social position of illegitimate children and their mothers at the beginning of the twentieth century is considered.

Changing families

The English family was changing. The average number of children per family had nearly halved (from six to just over three) between 1860 and 1911, and nearly a third of families now had only one or two children. The Fertility of Marriage Census, produced in 1911 although its publication was delayed until 1917, confirmed that the average number of children born to successive marriage cohorts had fallen by nearly half since the 1860s (from about six children to little more than three). 'Furthermore, since the 1870s the percentage of large families with nine or ten offspring had fallen from nearly 14 per cent to 4 per cent, while those with only one or two children had risen from 12.5 per cent to nearly one third.'[1]

The birth rate was falling across all classes, although initially it was falling at a more pronounced rate in the middle and upper classes. Among the working classes the position was more complicated: using a detailed analysis of the 1911 Fertility Census and a comprehensive overview of historical sources, Simon Szreter described the many 'diverse fertility regimes' in the late nineteenth and early twentieth centuries which were strongly marked 'by a variety of regional, local and industrial sectoral variations'.[2] However, it does appear that by the end of the 1920s 'the differences in fertility of various occupational groups and social classes were narrowing ... it was increasingly clear ... that the birth rate was down for all classes.'[3] During the interwar period these figures declined further, and with the accompanying decrease in infant and maternal mortality (the latter to a lesser degree) there was an associated change in the value placed upon each individual child, which will be discussed later.

There has been considerable historiographical discussion about the changing nature of the family and its members. Philippe Ariès sketched a rough picture of this change, which he sees as the family retreating from sociability into a private world of its own. He depicted this change as a long process commencing in the eighteenth century but his description was particularly appropriate to this period. He considered it a phenomenon initially of the middle classes that inevitably drew in upper and lower classes as well.[4] Since Ariès wrote in the 1960s, historians have written a great deal about the development of the family in the interwar period and much of this writing relates to his ideas. Writers such as Jane Lewis have described a trend towards increasing privatisation of the respectable working-class family. Men in regular employment found their real wages rising and many families moved out to the new housing estates, where evidence of female depression arising primarily from physical isolation rapidly came to light.[5]

The keynote of this period is the importance of child rearing and, by implication, domesticity in women's roles. Ellen Ross suggested that the assumption by the state and by society 'that children belonged with and to their mothers rather than to their fathers' grew up after the introduction of compulsory state education in 1870. From then on the child's dependency on its family lengthened and the expectation of maternal care increased.[6] Lewis proposed that during this period the middle-class pattern of a family with a male breadwinner was also adopted as an ideal by working-class families, and the trade union movement took on with enthusiasm the idea of 'the family wage' – a wage sufficient for the male to support his dependent family so his wife need not take paid employment. Lewis argued that the ideal of a male breadwinner family model was shared by both men and women of the working classes, with the accompanying acceptance of primary responsibility for home and children resting with the wife. 'By the 1890s it was uncommon for the wives of skilled men to work and the ability to keep a wife had become a measure of working-class male respectability,'[7] albeit with considerable regional variability.

By 1931 the number of married women in paid employment had declined from 6.3 per cent in 1901 to 4.8 per cent, although the percentage of all women working had risen marginally from 29.1 per cent in 1901 to 29.7 per cent in 1931,[8] and the census figures omit the 'unofficial' part-time and casual employment of married women. Wives were particularly affected by high unemployment and by marriage bars in a number of areas, such as the civil service, teaching, and even some factory employment. A number of writers have discussed the emphasis in popular culture on domestic virtues and companionate marriage to encourage women based at home on the often-isolated new estates looking after their small families.[9] Martin Pugh suggested that there was a definite attempt 'to elevate the status and prestige of housekeeping, and it was now extended across the social scale to middle-class women just as much as to working-class ones',[10] because middle-class women had to manage their houses with less help than before as the number of servants declined. Although by the early 1930s this decline had been largely reversed, even if domestic service was now seen as a last resort by most young working-class women.

There was the possibility for leisure in many people's lives in the interwar period in a way there had never been before – it was partly filled by cinema, radio, books and a great many new magazines for women. How far these magazines really 'imposed' an ideal of domesticity is difficult to say. Diana Gittins suggested that those aimed at a middle-class readership contained all kinds of information as well as entertainment news, and said that 'it is impossible to gauge whether they were a response to, or a reflection of, an existing ideology, or whether they actually helped to create one.'[11] Cynthia White described 'the reorientation of women's journalism away from the servant-keeping leisured classes, and towards the middle ranks', and noted that 'the new periodicals dedicated themselves to upholding the traditional sphere of feminine interests and were united in recommending a purely domestic role for women.'[12] However, when both White and Gittins turned to those magazines aimed specifically at working-class readers they found the majority, such as *Peg's Paper*, were dedicated to fictional escapism, with 'virtually no emphasis put on home, family or children'.[13]

Whatever the merits of the debate about the imposition of domestic values, the interwar years were clearly a period when relatively few married middle-class women worked at all, and working-class women's employment was mainly prior to marriage and subsequently on a casual and part-time basis. This, plus a number of other factors, encouraged the construction of women's identity as wives, and particularly as mothers.

For example, Gittins showed how little emphasis there was on health care or welfare for women – all the attention was given to the children. The implicit message was that women's primary importance was as mothers. 'Successful womanhood was becoming virtually synonymous with successful motherhood.'[14]

Adoption fitted in well with the emphasis in popular culture during the interwar years on domesticity, skilled motherhood and home-based activities. Many lower-middle- and working-class families now aspired to an ordered, domesticated lifestyle not dissimilar to that of the middle class, if more modest in scale, in a way which would have been unthinkable for many people before the First World War. Michael Anderson has written of the increasing 'homogeneity of experience ... of the majority of the population', which occurred as life events happened at increasingly similar stages in people's lives.[15] The large families of the nineteenth century with their uncertain survival rates and remarriage and widowhood were a thing of the past. By the 1930s even maternal mortality was beginning to come down and, as divorce was still difficult and socially unacceptable, the norm in this era, possibly more than at any other period in history, was two parents living together in a home with between one and three children, all of whom would survive into middle age and beyond. The pressure on couples to conform to this norm must have been considerable.

Many historians have stressed the importance of the enormous growth in house building by the end of the interwar years[16] in encouraging 'a certain version of family life that insisted on privacy, seclusion and intimacy'.[17] By 1939 approximately a third of all homes were new, a quarter of them were subsidised, mainly 'council housing'. Apart from a relatively few blocks of flats with shared bathrooms, these were all self-contained dwellings, mostly with gardens. Writing about the middle classes during the first half of the twentieth century, Alan A. Jackson considered that

> privacy was of course basic to the vision of the home as a means of withdrawal from the harsh realities of the outside world into a familiar, controllable and secure environment. It was also important in relation to the need to demonstrate outward decorum, respectability and perceived social status, whatever the state of affairs within.[18]

Jackson was writing about the middle, especially the lower-middle, classes, but the desire for privacy was not limited to them. In his history of housing, John Burnett analysed the Mass Observation survey about housing satisfaction carried out just before the Second World War. Of working-class housing he said, 'the desire for gardens and for "privacy" (interpreted as not sharing accommodation or facilities and not being overlooked) came out as overwhelmingly important.'[19] As the upper-class Naomi Mitchison wrote ruefully, after canvassing for Labour in the early 1930s:

> We have been going all out on housing. Schemes for clearing up slums and building decent homes. These are always envisaged as nice little home-nests, brick houses with every convenience for the housewife and home-lover, all separated so that no-one need know what her neighbour is doing or saying, each with a little garden. These are the kind of houses which are going to encourage the feeling of the close family group, the comfortable feeling of male ownership, the house-pride in the woman, all the things which those of us who hate ownership in all forms must be up against. But these are the houses which as a matter of fact almost all working men and women do want.[20]

Mitchison alluded to the perceived desire to be separate from the neighbours. Judy Giles singled this out as well: 'One of the potential rewards of a home of their own was a degree of freedom from the critical surveillance of authority, whether in the form of parents, "experts" or local gossip.'[21] Joanna Bourke, considering working-class cultures, commented that 'changing patterns in working-class housing and spatial mobility encouraged a view of the homes as a secluded, self-contained domain, or, in the words of a popular saying, a respectable external front had to be maintained because "there's more pass by than comes in"'.[22]

Respectability is a crucial concept in the study of adoption in the interwar years. If asked for a picture of typical adopters, the adoption societies would have described a 'respectable' lower-middle-class childless couple in a new house in a suburb who wanted a child to complete their dream of a family. The need to nurture and preserve the respectability of the adopting parents permeated the work of the adoption societies and lay behind the desire for secrecy which dominated so much of the way they operated. Respectability is above all a desire to be untainted, unconnected with anything which might bring shame or embarrassment. For many people it appears that it was of profound importance in the way they approached the whole of their working lives, their social relationships, their homes and their families.

A dictionary definition of respectability is 'honest and decent in character or conduct, without reference to social position. Similarly of appearance, character etc.'[23] However this does not convey the essence of the idea, which includes a need to present an appearance of order and decency and to maintain distance from the disorder and messiness of what were seen as the 'rough' sectors of society. Geoffrey Crossick described how maintaining standards was a substitute for 'genuine social mobility',[24] a way in which those with unfulfilled aspirations to higher social status might feel some satisfaction. He was writing about the Edwardian period, but during the post-war years and the Depression there were probably even more people in the lower-middle class who clung on to notions of respectability and status as a way of differentiating themselves from skilled manual workers whose income, at least when they were in work, was little different from theirs, albeit usually less secure.

It was not just white-collar workers to whom respectability was important. Using the oral history evidence gathered in North West England by Elizabeth Roberts and herself, Lucinda McCray Beier looked at working-class attitudes towards sexual knowledge. She considered that:

> It is difficult to exaggerate the importance of respectability in early- and mid-twentieth century working-class communities. ... The effort to keep an out-of-wedlock pregnancy secret was motivated both by family shame and by the hope of preserving the girl's chance of a respectable future.[25]

Beier suggested that social mores possibly became more restrictive, and respectability more important, in the first half of the twentieth century than they were before that period and afterwards. Anderson also proposed that the interwar period 'had particularly high incidences of at least outwardly stable conventional Christian family morality' although he was unclear why this was so.[26] Beier considered that 'respectability was the key to important social and mutual aid networks,' so it was necessary for most working-class people, as well as for the socially aspiring who might need the networks less but needed to keep a pristine reputation. She commented that 'a typical phrase for a socially aspiring working-class woman of the mid-twentieth century was "I kept myself to myself", which implied distance and independence from neighbours.'[27]

So when 'respectable' people, of whatever class background, adopted a child they had no wish to have any reminder of the confused and troubled background it very likely came from – and certainly not of the fact that the child was probably illegitimate. It was not so much the idea of sex without marriage which seems to have appalled people – clearly this was relatively common by the 1930s (as illustrated by the Registrar General who calculated that in 1939 'nearly 30 per cent of all mothers today conceive their first borns out of wedlock,' although nearly 70 per cent of these women married before the birth[28]). It was perhaps more that the idea of children being born without marriage threatened the accepted ideas of the way society operated through work, marriage and the nuclear family. This is borne out by a comment from one of the men Elizabeth Roberts interviewed when he was asked if any girls had to get married because they were pregnant:

> That was a regular thing in those days. When they did talk about it they didn't talk about her with any disrespect. ... They hadn't any disrespect for them because there were too many of them to have disrespect for. ... The main thing was always, well, as long as he has married her what's the difference?[29]

Not all Roberts's interviewees agreed with this viewpoint but it reflected a not uncommon pragmatic approach. So as long as the couple married it was alright – if not, it made people feel particularly vulnerable because children were involved. Hugh McLeod suggests that

> in one area nearly everyone felt the pressure of [respectable] values: the bringing up of their children. The protection of the children from corrupting or vulgarising influences, or simply from physical danger, provided the strongest motive for maintaining the unity and isolation of the household.[30]

So far I have essentially been considering what for convenience is called the nuclear family. However, as the authors of a book on the development of the modern family pointed out, long before the late twentieth century families were more complex than this in terms not only of their composition, which might draw in outside relatives or friends or even work relationships, but also the way in which they interacted and transferred property, stories and secrets between their members.[31] One of these historians, Katherine Holden,[32] has written extensively about the role played in the family by the unmarried woman, or spinster, during the interwar years. In the first third of the twentieth century over 14 per cent of women never married – one in seven – and only in the late 1930s did this percentage begin to decline.[33] As unmarried mothers, single women obviously played a large (if usually non-speaking) part in the story of adoption, but unmarried women also had an active role through their involvement with the adoption societies and on the parliamentary adoption committees and in the civil service. They also adopted children themselves during this period, in perhaps larger numbers than has previously been realised, although unfortunately few figures for the interwar years about the marital status of adopters are available, and accounts of single women adopting remain anecdotal (see Chapter 5).

New views of childhood

Inseparable from the discussion of the increasingly small, private family with its emphasis on respectability is the way in which the value placed on children was changing. In the early decades of the nineteenth century, children had still been viewed as younger adults, responsible for their actions and their conditions. By the end of the century a sentimental view was taking hold. Christina Hardyment described a softer approach to child care and pointed to the publication of books like *Peter Pan* (J. M. Barrie) and *A Child's Garden of Verses* (Robert Louis Stevenson), which portrayed an idealised portrait of childhood.[34] There was growing interest in children's development; the Child Study Movement was set up; specialist teacher-training colleges were established and books and journals were devoted to the topic.[35]

A number of historians have analysed this change in the way childhood was valued. The American writer Viviana A. Zelizer argued that there was 'a cultural process of "sacralization" of children's lives'; 'sacralization' meaning a 'sense of objects being invested with sentimental or religious meaning'.[36] She suggested that by the mid-nineteenth century the middle class had in large part constructed an 'economically worthless child' who produced nothing and was expensive to educate and provide for but whose emotional and sentimental value was increasingly high. Writing from an American historical perspective she described, in contrast, the working-class child's growing economic value in the late nineteenth century as economic opportunities opened up in new industries for poor children.[37] In England the process of transition to a state of relative 'economic worthlessness' for working-class children ran in a smoother trajectory as the growth of jobs for children had come much earlier in the nineteenth century. Changing economic patterns, legislation restricting child labour and, crucially, compulsory primary education meant that by the end of the nineteenth century even working-class children were losing their economic value.

Although adoption in America has not followed the same pattern as in England,[38] Zelizer's argument about the way adoptive children were viewed is pertinent to adoption. Children came to be assessed for their emotional rather than economic value so that 'the priceless child was judged by new criteria; its physical appeal and personality replaced earlier economic yardsticks.'[39] Babies also became desirable as environmental theories of development became increasingly accepted in the 1920s and those considering adoption were reassured that heredity had little to do with character. Increasing use of intelligence tests and improved methods of determining children's physical health allayed adopters' concerns about taking on children of unknown parentage.

Writing about English childhood, Harry Hendrick considered that throughout the nineteenth century there was a developing consensus among the middle class and 'respectable working class' about the nature of childhood. At the beginning of the century this consensus had been non-existent – the meaning of childhood was ambiguous and there was no popular demand to clarify it. Hendrick believed that by the end of the century 'childhood was being legally, legislatively, socially, medically, psychologically, educationally and politically institutionalised.' He went on to describe the process:

> During the nineteenth century the making of childhood into a very specific kind of age-graded and age-related condition went through several stages, involving several different processes. Each new construction, one often overlapping with the other, has been described here in approximate chronological order as: the natural child, the Romantic child, the evangelical child, the factory child, the delinquent child, the schooled child and the psycho-medical child.[40]

He suggested that the child who emerged into the twentieth century was 'a distinctive being characterised by ignorance, incapacity and innocence'.[41] George Behlmer similarly saw 'a progressive lengthening of childhood' by the end of the nineteenth century, which was made inevitable by the advent of compulsory education which confirmed children's lack of 'intellectual and physical powers to cope with the adult world'.[42]

Gradually there developed what Gittins described as an 'elaborate "ideology of childhood"', which was a result of 'the development of psychological theories related to the importance of childhood, of medical opinion emphasising the need for better standards of nutrition, health and hygiene during childhood'.[43] Jean Heywood cited the declining birth rate and high infant mortality rate of this period as changing the emphasis away from individual cases of child neglect or murder to a significant movement concerning itself with general infant welfare.[44] As has been well documented, there was widespread shock at the poor physical state of many of the potential recruits for service during the Boer War in the late 1890s. During the early 1900s there was considerable debate over the causes and solutions for this state of affairs. A government Interdepartmental Committee on Physical Deterioration, which reported in 1904, concentrated on making recommendations about improving child health through public health measures and educational practices, which was, as Deborah Dwork commented

> an indication of what was then considered possible or practicable. It was easier to teach cookery, hygiene, and domestic economy to women and girls, to advise physical exercise for children of both sexes; it was even easier to provide health visiting of infants and sterilized milk for them, than to address radically the causes which made all of this necessary: to improve wages, housing, and the terms of employment.[45]

The poor health of adults was coupled with a very high infant mortality rate, which had actually slightly increased during the last quarter of the nineteenth century.[46] A number of ameliorative measures were taken in the years before the First World War, such as ensuring the purity of milk, and in some areas supplying sterilised milk for young babies. Mothers were increasingly seen as the crucial factor in any improvement in infant mortality. Dwork quoted the socialist John Burns opening the first national conference on the issue with an initial explanation of its causes as being jointly 'the mother, society and industry', but concluding that: 'I believe at the bottom of infant mortality, high or low, is good or bad motherhood.'[47] Most labour activists and many other commentators continued to believe strongly that poverty was the primary cause of infant deaths but increasingly it became accepted that, at least for the time being, maternal education was 'the best alternative available within the English political and economic structure at the time'.[48]

Attempts to improve mothering skills led to an expansion of the health visiting system which had started in some parts of the country during the latter part of the nineteenth century, whereby mothers would be visited by women who were either working for charitable societies in a voluntary or paid capacity or employed as sanitary inspectors by the local authorities. These ladies gave the mothers instruction about how to improve the care and nutrition of their children and the management of their homes. As well as home visits, maternity and child welfare centres were organised where mothers could go for advice and classes to learn about their children's development. By 1913 'in a significant number of towns 90 to 100 per cent' of all new babies were visited, meaning that 'health visiting (the basis of the maternal education system) which had been started as a class-oriented measure was increasingly brought to bear upon the entire spectrum of society.'[49]

The years leading up to the First World War also saw the beginning of the eugenics movement (the Eugenics Education Society was formed in 1907, renamed the Eugenics Society in 1926), which was concerned with the falling birth rate, the 'degeneration' and the mental and physical condition of the nation. The eugenicists regarded the larger families of the poor as something to be severely discouraged. They took issue with the infant welfare movement's campaigns and measures to improve the conditions of poor children, believing it encouraged the survival of weak and sickly children who could only bring down the overall health and well-being of the general population. They tried to devise ways of encouraging the upper classes to have more children, and at the beginning of the First World War they established the Professional Classes War Relief Fund to help the families of professional and creative men at the front on the basis that they were used to a higher standard of living than other soldiers and 'according to eugenic analysis, already inclined to sacrifice marriage and parenthood to maintain this standard'.[50] The eugenicists hoped to ensure that this sacrifice would not happen.

Concern about falling population rates and high infant mortality rates was increased by the advent of war. As the death toll at the front mounted, the need to conserve the infants at home became an emotive issue and

> for the immediate future at least, prudence and patriotism required the preservation of quantity as well as the promotion of equality ... The result was an uneasy, tenuous alliance of the eugenics movement with the diverse reform elements comprising the maternal and child welfare movement.[51]

Both eugenicists and child welfare campaigners agreed on the importance of the mother in the successful production of children. From the eugenic point of view, a healthy, educated and devoted mother was much more likely to produce a healthy, physically and mentally fit child; so the Eugenics Education Society joined the alliance lobbying for the Notification of Births (Extension) Act 1915, the Maternal and Child Welfare Act 1918 and the establishment of the Ministry of Health (1919). It was one of the 90 groups supporting the first National Baby Week in 1917.

National Baby Week was modelled on a similar campaign which had started in the United States the previous year and it went on to be a nationwide feature of the interwar period every summer. The slogan in 1917 was 'It is more dangerous to be a baby in Britain than it is to be a soldier.' Across the country there was an annual week of baby shows, parades, 'mothercraft' examinations and exhibitions, handicraft classes and competitions, cookery classes and lectures and later films on child welfare and hygiene. School children were regularly given half-day holidays to attend some of the events. 'The purpose of the campaign was, in part, to give women the education that the Government thought they needed in order to be mothers.'[52] In general the war years saw a great expansion of government expenditure on services for children[53] and an accompanying increase in official control over the programmes being provided. Infant mortality nearly halved in 20 years – from c150 per thousand births in each year of the 1890s to c80 by 1920–2, although, as Pat Thane commented, historians have differed as to whether environmental health improvements or the infant welfare provision 'had the greatest impact upon infant survival and health'.[54] As the First World War ended, a significant piece of legislation was passed, the Maternity and Child Welfare Act, which 'signified the explicit recognition of the responsibility of the State to protect the health of its citizens regardless of socio-economic status, albeit for one age group only.'[55]

Thus by the beginning of the interwar period, motherhood, helped by the state, was viewed not just in sentimental terms but as a vital element in the survival of the nation's children, and 'mothercraft', a term invented in 1910,[56] was a necessary skill to be learnt and applied by all mothers. And if mothercraft was a skill that must be learnt, it followed that the person doing the mothering did not have to be biologically related to the child.

The development of child protection legislation

As well as a general involvement in the care and welfare of all children by the early twentieth century the state was also taking an increasingly active role in managing the lives of individual children considered to be at risk of physical abuse from parents or carers. Prior to the second half of the nineteenth century the state had taken no role in the protection of such children. Even destitute children had received little help. Under the old Poor Laws (the first major one was passed in 1597), children who were without effective parents or guardians to take care of them became the responsibility of the parish. How they were treated depended largely on the local board, and the individual officials who dealt with them. The Poor Relief Act of 1601 obligated those responsible for the care of deprived children – churchwardens and parish overseers – to take measures to set the children to work or bind them as apprentices. The Poor Law Amendment Act 1834 which introduced workhouses for the able-bodied poor placed some responsibility on the authorities to provide for deprived children who presented themselves – but not to search them out, which became the role of philanthropy.

A great deal of legislation in the nineteenth century affected children's welfare, including factory acts and compulsory schooling, but the first major legislation dealing with how children were looked after was the Infant Life Protection Act 1872, which followed major 'baby farming' scandals.[57] 'Baby farming', or 'professional adoption', was the practice whereby the parents (generally unmarried mothers) of children whom they could not afford or manage to look after, paid someone, usually a middle-aged woman, a lump sum to look after the child. There was a tacit assumption that the mother would not be returning to reclaim the child and that the baby farmer would not overly strive to keep it alive. Probably some of those looking after the babies did their best to care for them but naturally the cases which hit the headlines were the scandals, such as the one in Brixton in 1870. Sixteen dead babies were found in a few weeks in streets and open spaces in Brixton and Peckham. Every year many babies were found dead in the London streets (276 in 1870, the majority less than a week old[58]) but so many in one area was unusual. A keen policeman followed up the case and eventually ten drugged and emaciated babies were found in a house in Brixton run by two sisters. Five of the babies subsequently died and one of the sisters, a widow, Margaret Waters, was found guilty of murder and executed. An advertisement which Mrs Waters had been regularly inserting in a weekly newspaper stated:

> Adoption—A good home, with a mother's love and care, is offered to any respectable person wishing her child to be entirely adopted. Premium £5, which sum includes everything.[59]

It is little wonder that 'adoption' gained slightly sinister overtones.

This case, and other contemporary baby farming cases, received a great deal of publicity and the movement for legislation to prevent the practice, led by concerned doctors, gained momentum. The campaigning activities of the Infant Life Protection Society which they established led to the setting up of the Select Committee on the Protection of Infant Life whose report on baby farming in 1872 resulted in the passing of the first Infant Life Protection Act. Under its provisions, all those receiving two or more infants under the age of one 'for hire or reward' had to register with the local authority. It was neither effective nor enforced.[60]

Two years later what sounds like a minor piece of legislation but was in fact an important step in the campaign against baby farming and infanticide was passed – the Births and Deaths Registration Act which imposed fines for failing to report births (within 42 days) and deaths (within eight days). In 1897 a second Infant Life Protection Act raised the relevant age to five. This was incorporated into the Children Act 1908, which took the age of supervision for children kept for hire or reward to seven, and prohibited life insurance for children (a controversial issue).

Adoption at this time was often seen as either a synonym for baby farming or as akin to fostering, a form of social service for children from very difficult backgrounds, carried out by the rescue societies[61] and the Poor Law Guardians (see below). In 1889 the Earl of Meath introduced an Adoption of Children Bill in the House of Lords 'to prevent parents or other guardians from recovering their children after they have consented to their adoption, unless they can satisfy the Justices that their claim is legitimately made for the benefit of the children'.[62] The Earl ended his speech proposing the bill with a suggestion 'that there are a large number of people in this country who are very desirous to obtain children, having no children of their own, and who would be glad to adopt children if only they felt they had a legal claim upon them when they had adopted them'. The Lord Chancellor was scathing about the inadequacies of the Bill. A couple of years later, after some court cases about children being removed from voluntary homes by their natural parents, the Earl of Meath was involved in the enactment of the Custody of Children Act, which was designed to make this more difficult for 'vicious parents', but as it necessitated recourse to the High Court it was little used.

The National Society for the Prevention of Cruelty to Children (NSPCC), which had already begun to wield considerable influence, became increasingly concerned about baby farming and fostering. It was formed in 1889 from some of the societies for the prevention of cruelty to children, which were set up from 1883. Their agitation had already led to the passing of the Prevention of Cruelty to, and Better Protection of, Children Act 1889. This established for the first time that the State could interfere in the family in order to prevent hardship or danger to children. Ill treatment of boys to the age of fourteen and girls to age sixteen was now a punishable offence. Although parents were already compelled to send their children to school, until the 1880s their rights to deal with their children in their own home as they wished had remained sacrosanct, except in the most exceptional circumstances. Now the state was beginning to intervene. Hendrick suggested that 'in the closing decades of the nineteenth century parental authority was substantially reduced as it found itself in conflict with that of the state'.[63] In the five years following the 1889 Act, 5792 people were prosecuted for cruelty.[64] Further legislation was pushed through by the NSPCC in 1894, making the penalties for ill-treatment more severe and empowering the police to remove suspected victims of child cruelty from their homes without a court order. Further child protection measures followed throughout the 1890s and they were incorporated in the Children Act 1908, which extended the law to cover not just 'wilful' cruelty to children but also that arising from negligence.

Legal adoption began during this period, in the sense of the assumption of parental rights by the Poor Law Guardians to give them more powers to direct the fate of the children in their care. It was an extension of the policy of 'boarding out' workhouse children and involved substantial numbers by the turn of the twentieth century. Rather than putting them in the workhouse, from the late 1870s some Poor Law Unions had either placed children in their care in 'cottage homes', where a number of children lived with a resident housemother or boarded individual children with private families.[65] The Poor Law Amendment Acts of 1889 and 1899 gave Guardians the right to assume parental rights and responsibilities over a child in care until he or she was eighteen, in effect the right to 'adopt' certain boys and girls. Initially this right applied only to deserted children, but in 1899 it was widened to include orphans and children whose parents were disabled, or judged impaired or unfit to have control of them.[66] Parents had the right of appeal to a magistrates' court but presumably not many did so, or their pleas were dismissed, because in 1908 alone 12,417 children were adopted by Boards of Guardians. However this was not adoption as it is understood now; as Lionel Rose explained, it 'did not connote the lifelong acquisition of a quasi-blood tie; the Poor Law could revoke the adoption and transfer the child back to the parent if it saw fit'.[67]

Behlmer described how the Poor Law authorities used their powers of adoption mainly to protect children at risk from neglect or abuse within their family, quoting evidence from Poor Law Union minute books in the north of England showing that most children were taken into care following gross 'neglect by parents' – for example, less than 10 per cent of the children adopted in Carlisle by the Guardians were orphans or illegitimate.[68] Most of these children were boarded out with foster parents on a long-term basis but in theory they remained under the care of the Guardians who, at least in the more organised areas, continued to inspect them on a regular basis. In a minority of cases permanent situations with the foster families resulted, but this was not an intended consequence. In evidence to the Hopkinson Committee on Child Adoption in 1920, clerks to the Guardians of Southwark and Tynemouth Unions said that the practice of 'boarding out' and 'adoption' (which they used in a fairly interchangeable way) had gone out of favour with Boards of Guardians, and finding suitable foster parents was difficult. Mr Stanwell Smith of Southwark said there was no uniform practice across the country as to when children should be taken into care and when adopted, despite the seriousness of the action, which meant no more parental visiting or even correspondence with their child.[69] Mr Percival of the Tynemouth Guardians explained that

> [e]xperience of Guardians generally is, I believe, that the placing out by adoption of children chargeable to them, is, on the whole, unsatisfactory. Evidence given before the Royal Commission 1908 showed that the Bradford Guardians had largely used adoption as a means of disposing of their children, but had had to give it up, as they found the adopters only kept the children until they were tired of them and then returned them in an unsatisfactory condition.
>
> The casual fashion in which persons take such responsibilities is illustrated by the number of applications received to adopt any abandoned baby to which attention has been called in the newspapers, and our experience is that in the majority of cases the foster parents tire of the child after a time, because it does not turn out to be quite so attractive as anticipated, or simply because they cannot be bothered with it, and it is dumped back on the Guardians very often in need of strict discipline, on account of the bad training.[70]

However Nigel Middleton suggested that the practice continued during the interwar years, with a considerable number of children boarded out not just by the Poor Law Guardians (and then the local authorities after the transfer of functions in 1929) but also the Ministry of Pensions, fulfilling its responsibilities towards ex-servicemen's dependants who were being neglected, or facing family breakdown of some kind.[71] In fact, boarding out does not appear to have been used consistently across the country – the Lambeth Board of Guardians' Adoption Register shows that the great majority of children 'adopted' by them up to 1929 were sent to residential schools, mainly Norwood School. A few were 'adopted for service' or to the army or 'emigration' and a very few to foster parents.[72]

Although adoption had no legal standing apart from the measures affecting these Poor Law children, a curious clause was included in the Infant Life Protection Act 1897, which allowed adoptions of children up to two years old to go unnotified to the local authority if the sum paid for the adoption was more than £20. Hendrick pointed out that 'the intention was to control cheap, low-class and therefore potentially dangerous adoptions … [and] leaving aside the class-discriminatory nature of this clause, the rule could obviously be evaded with ease'.[73] This clause was abolished in the Children Act of 1908, which also established the principle that homes where just one child was being looked after for payment should (except in a few exempted situations) be inspected by local authorities. This measure was contested by a number of the children's charities as they used fostering and boarding out for some of the children they looked after and feared that they would lose their 'nursemothers' if they were subject to inspection and regulation.

The Children Act also raised the age of children protected by the boarding-out regulations to seven and dealt with the whole spectrum of children's care as well as infant life protection: cruelty and neglect of children and young people; reformatories and industrial schools; the establishment of a separate system of juvenile courts; juvenile smoking; and miscellaneous provisions mainly dealing with children and intoxicating liquor. It was mainly a consolidating act but its breadth highlighted the state's now major role in regulating and protecting the child.

Parental rights before 1926

To clarify the situation, I will briefly describe the legal situation before 1926 as far as parents' rights to their own children and 'adopted' children were concerned, including the legal, social and economic position of children whose parents were not married. Legislation around the care of children had developed over the centuries in several ways – the concept closest to legal adoption was 'wardship' under which a guardian was given effective custody of a child by the Chancery Court. The second strand of legislation was related to the custody of children where married parents were separated or divorced. The third was the infant protection legislation dealing with abandoned, neglected or abused children described in the previous section of this chapter.

Apart from the little-used wardship provision, people had virtually no parental rights in relation to other people's children they might be looking after as part of their family even though adoption had always existed informally, and children were described as being 'adopted' from at least the nineteenth century.[74] The term had no legal standing: in common law the paternal right to custody was inalienable.

The concept of wardship derived from the medieval king's role as liegelord, the *parens patriae*, obliged to maintain and defend his people in return for service and obedience. This role included his prerogative right to protect persons and estates of infants, idiots and persons of unsound mind. Initially he carried out this role directly and received petitions and made orders himself. These powers and duties were later exercised by the Lord Chancellor, until in 1660 his Court of Wards and Liveries was abolished and its prerogative transferred to the Court of Chancery. (It is now exercised by the judges of the Chancery Division of the High Court.)

In theory the monarch was parent of all his or her children but in practice the Chancery Court tended to deal only with those with property or some means. Lord Eldon LC explained in 1827[75] that this was because the Court could only act when it had the means to do so, that is, by being able to apply resources for the use and maintenance of the infants in its care. However, the sums involved eventually became relatively small – it became customary that if a small amount was settled on the child, proceedings could be brought for its administration. The Court of Chancery would then act on the child's behalf, especially if all that was required was the removal or appointment of a guardian. The procedure involved the Court making an infant a Ward of Court and then, if necessary, appointing a guardian for the child who would have to follow the scheme of education and upbringing drawn up by the court for the child. A Ward might not marry or leave the jurisdiction without the consent of the Court.

In practice, wardship proceedings only involved a very small number of children and it seems unlikely that they were used by any but a small minority of the wealthier members of society.

Marriage breakdown and custody

Prior to 1857 under Common Law there were very few circumstances in which any court would interfere with a father's custody of his infant children when a marriage ended. Courts did not even have the jurisdiction to grant a right of access to the mother. The first legislation amending the Common Law came with the 1839 Custody of Infants Act. This allowed for an order to be made giving a mother access to her children where the father had sole custody or control, provided she had not been judged adulterous. However, in practice this did not encourage radical change. Case law established the principle that the Court should decide in favour of paternal rights where possible.

Before 1857, the only likelihood of a mother recovering custody was either by writ of *habeas corpus* if the father's behaviour could be proved to be grossly immoral, or by Petition in the Court of Chancery. Death of the father also affected maternal rights; if he appointed a testamentary guardian this took priority over the mother's rights to custody. Where there was no such person the mother was seen 'in equity as guardian for nurture and had the right to custody of infants up to the age of fourteen'.[76]

In 1857 the first major legislation around marriage, separation and custody – the Matrimonial Causes Act – was passed. This empowered the court to make interim orders before the final decree, and orders after it, for judicial separation, nullity of marriage and dissolution of marriage, with respect to the custody, maintenance and education of the children of the marriage. The act could also set in motion proceedings to place children under the Court of Chancery. Other legislation relating to custody and marital breakdown included the Custody of Infants Act 1873, which repealed the earlier 1839 Act and gave the Court of Chancery power to give access, custody and control to the mother of an infant under 16 (and then make arrangements for access by the father or guardian). It also removed the bar to petitions by mothers whose adultery had been established. The Custody of Children Act 1891 allowed the High Court to refuse custody to a parent who had abandoned a child or who was deemed 'unfit'.

In 1886, the Guardianship of Infants Act laid down that on the death of the father of an infant the mother alone should be the guardian unless the father had appointed a guardian, in which case they would act jointly. It also stated that the court could, on application by the mother, make an order re custody and right to access as it thought fit 'having regard to the welfare of the infant and to the conduct of the parents, and to the wishes as well of the mother as of the father'; that is, the court was given full jurisdiction to override the Common Law rights of the father in relation to the custody of his infant children.

One of the important pieces of domestic legislation passed during the 1920s was the 1925 Guardianship of Infants Act, which was notable for two statements. Its preamble mentioned the Sex Disqualification (Removal) Act of 1919 and 'various other enactments [which] sought to establish equality in law between the sexes' and said that 'it is expedient that this principle should obtain with respect to the guardianship of infants and the rights and responsibilities conferred thereby'. In its first clause the act also stated that in any proceedings before any court relating to the custody or upbringing of an infant or the administration of any property or income relating to a child 'the court, in deciding that question, shall regard the welfare of the infant as the first and paramount consideration' – rather than any claims by either parent or common law rights of the father. As the preamble suggested, this Act evened up the rights of each parent to guardianship after the death of the other parent. Now either parent could appoint a guardian who would act jointly with the surviving parent.

Illegitimate children and unmarried mothers

Traditionally the life of an illegitimate child was difficult and precarious. Although the individual illegitimate child had occasionally prospered, in general the position of unmarried mothers and their children had been dire:

> Illegitimacy was an offence against Christian morality and the institution of marriage; because of the cost which was laid upon the parish and public charity, it was an offence against the well-being of society. The combination of moral failing with lack of financial responsibility was thus a sin from which the righteous might properly recoil.[77]

Poor Law practice discriminated against them, judging them to be a particularly wanton example of self-induced poverty. Unmarried mothers were sometimes given less food in workhouses than married women, and if they had a second illegitimate child they might be forced to wear distinguishing gowns as part of their disgrace.[78] As with other paupers, many were forcibly returned to their original home area under the settlement laws. In desperation the babies were often abandoned, sold or even murdered. There were few options open to unmarried mothers during the nineteenth and early twentieth centuries; if they were in domestic service they would be dismissed, and the low wages for other jobs open to women made it impossible for most unmarried mothers to carry on a job and pay for childcare. The few homes for mothers and babies were harsh and judgemental, and putting the child in an orphanage such as the Foundling Hospital meant giving up all contact with it. This was the background to the many dead babies found in the big cities every year and to the widespread baby farming discussed above.[79]

The public reaction to unmarried mothers remained punitive and fearful, although Kiernan, Land and Lewis showed how 'unmarried mothers enjoyed a brief period of sympathetic consideration during the [First World War] as the mothers of the babies of service men who might die for their country'.[80] However, by the end of the War the slight relaxation in punitive judgement was over, and if anything the perceived loosening up of sexual mores during the interwar period meant that there was more vigilance for overt immorality. The writers bleakly summed up the practice towards unmarried mothers in the 1920s and 1930s:

> [B]etween the wars unmarried mothers were more rigorously classified [than during the War]. Voluntary organisations took mainly 'first offenders' and tried to place them in domestic service. The poor law authorities took 'repeaters' and from 1927 had sweeping powers to detain girls who were classified as mentally defective and who were in receipt of poor relief at the time of their child's birth.[81]

One of the men Elizabeth Roberts interviewed worked for nearly forty years in a hospital, which was still a workhouse when he went there in 1924. He described the regime for unmarried mothers and their children in the 1920s. Women would be sent there by their parents when they became pregnant:

> The ladies came ... into the workhouse and did domestic work, cleaning up and washing and they did that until such time as the baby was due and then they were moved into another section to have the baby. Whilst they were with the baby and providing they were feeding the baby they stayed there looking after the babies in the nursery. They came back again, if they had nowhere to go, back into the workhouse to do ordinary domestic work. The children were taken care of by the Cottage Homes which was ... under the care of ... the Master and Matron and there they remained until such times as they were leaving school when the Board of Guardians or the Councillors as the case may be found them employment.[82]

For the unmarried mother the problem was not just the shame imposed upon her by society, it was also the sheer difficulty of surviving on her own with a child and no income, child care or accommodation.[83]

Not all gave their children up. It is impossible to make even a rough estimate of how many kept their children but the number of illegitimate births was always much greater than those legally adopted after 1926. Even allowing for informal adoptions and infant mortality (which remained higher than for legitimate births although it was halved during the interwar period) there must have been a considerable number of illegitimate children who remained with their mother or her immediate family. The only evidence during the interwar years is anecdotal. In her work on the Elizabeth Roberts collection, Ginger Frost looked at attitudes to illegitimacy, and found that when Roberts asked her interviewees if they knew anyone who had a child out of wedlock 'most claimed to know only one or two, and almost all recorded that the maternal families cared for illegitimate children as a matter of course.'[84] She suggested that a kind of informal adoption was practised because 'the horror of the workhouse was so strong that even the poorest people would take in abandoned children rather than let them go to such a place.' She concluded that 'the most typical situation for an illegitimate child was to remain in a private family, usually the maternal home'.[85]

Carl Chinn suggested that attitudes were class related, with 'lower working-class' families offering far more support, although he suggested that even these families would cover up the truth, ensuring that even in these poorest of families, secrecy about illegitimacy was maintained: 'the child would be raised believing its grandmother to be its mother, and its natural mother to be its sister. The successful maintenance of this fiction depended on the tacit support of the local community.'[86] Chinn considered that maintaining 'respectability' was as important an aim in most of these lower working-class communities as in upper working-class and middle- and upper-class families but that the sense of familial loyalty was strong enough to ensure that the pregnant woman would be supported. He also suggests that as some of the poorer communities became more settled from the 1880s onwards, the stabilising influence of married women, in providing support and continuity was immense:

> It was this, together with the practice of a courting couple marrying if a girl became pregnant, which was as great an influence in the decline of the national rate of illegitimacy as was the increased use of contraceptives. In 1870 this rate had stood at seventeen per 1000 unmarried women aged fifteen to forty five; by 1904 it had dropped to 8.4 and by 1920 to 3.6. The fall corresponds too closely to the establishment of settled communities amongst the poor and to the rise of a matriarchy within them to dismiss their significance.[87]

In fact, the fall in illegitimacy rates was less consistent than this implies, although overall the trend into the 1930s was certainly down. The numbers of illegitimate births were actually at their highest in 1918 (and close to this in 1919) since 1887 in real terms, (c. 42,000 in 1918 and 41,000 in 1919). They would not reach these levels again till 1943 when they jumped from 36,000 in 1942 to 43,000. In contrast, the general birth rate was at its lowest in 1918 (663,000 births) since 1858, and did not drop to that level again till 1927. During the earlier years of the First World War, the real numbers of illegitimate births had remained stable – as they had since the 1890s – at around 38,000 per year with occasional variations plus or minus 1000. As the general birth rate declined, the ratio of illegitimate to legitimate births obviously went up—from 4.54 per cent in 1915 to 6.33 per cent in 1918 (and nearly as high in 1919, 5.92 per cent). In 1920 there was a vast drop in the actual number of illegitimate births to 15,000. As there was a steep rise in the general birth rate to 943,000 (from 651,000 in 1919) the ratio of illegitimate to legitimate births plummeted that year to 1.57 per cent.[88]

Family support and the covering up of illegitimacy provided some protection for young unmarried mothers in poor but stable communities against being placed in a mental hospital under the Mental Deficiency Act of 1913. This legislation gave powers to local authorities to certify pregnant women who were homeless, destitute or deemed 'immoral' and detain them indefinitely. In the early years of the twentieth century 'the rather diffuse debate over degeneration [of the British race] found a sharper focus as mental defectives became defined as the central eugenic threat facing the nation'.[89] It fitted in with the concerns of the eugenics campaigners, the Social Purity and Hygiene Movement (whose aim was to protect innocent young women), the churches, youth groups such as Guides and Scouts, Boys' Brigades, Young Men's Christian Association and the Band of Hope, who all 'were involved in a civilising mission to instil values of patriotic and religious duty, discipline and higher moral standards into young people, and in particular working-class youth'.[90]

The Mental Deficiency Act came about, as Matthew Thomson described, because of the increasing linkage between 'immorality' and 'imbecility':

> In the last quarter of the [nineteenth] century an increasing number of the women in rescue homes were reported as being feeble-minded. Mental defect provided both a convincing biological explanation for the plight of these women – their mental defect left them with no restraint over their sexual instincts and unprotected against abuse by

men – and a powerful justification to place then under protection and control in refuges and houses. Gradually, mental defect and immorality became so closely associated that it was not uncommon for immorality to be viewed as evidence, rather than the consequence, of mental defect.[91]

Steve Humphries interviewed an old lady who had spent most of her life in a local mental hospital. She had been placed there from the workhouse where she had gone after becoming pregnant following rape. She herself had been illegitimate, which made her particularly vulnerable to the provisions of the Act which 'fell most keenly on destitute young women who were themselves illegitimate ... for according to fashionable eugenic theories of the time, they and their children were thought to be hereditarily feeble-minded'.[92] Thomson has looked at some case papers of those confined under the Act and confirmed that 'control of sexuality could ... lead to long-term institutionalisation of women whose mental defect was only minor, if it existed at all'[93] (the diagnosis of eleven of the thirteen women certified at age eighteen or over whose papers he saw was 'linked to sexual concerns'), but he specifically took issue with Humphries that having an illegitimate child was enough on its own to lead to placement in a mental deficiency institution.[94] He concluded that the

> [l]ack of thorough research has led to a series of confusions in the historiography. When we go beyond the rhetoric of debate, it is clear that the popular myth that the Mental Deficiency Act was simply a tool to control young women with illegitimate children is a gross caricature: such women – if they could also be proved to be intellectually defective – were a critical concern, but in total, women did not outnumber men disproportionately.[95]

The number of unmarried mothers placed in mental institutions remains unknown. It is not clear how far the practice was publicised but it seems to have become part of a general anxiety about the potential consequences of 'illicit' sex and the danger of 'falling' from respectability, which was so deeply ingrained in almost all layers of society up to the 1950s and into the 1960s. Many of Elizabeth Roberts's interviewees spoke of the dread of illegitimacy: 'It was such a catastrophe to get yourself pregnant when you were unmarried ... it was a terrible thing.'[96] And, 'We always had that fear, me and my mate. When you get to 16 or 17 you start talking and she said, "Don't let a lad touch you".

I used to say my Dad would kill me.'[97] On the other hand, an interviewee who was illegitimate said that she never felt any stigma at all: 'It's never weighed upon me that I am what you would call illegitimate at all. It's what you are that counts ... [People] just accepted me.'[98]

In 1986 the National Council for One Parent Families (formerly the National Council for the Unmarried Mother and Her Child [NCUMC] and now renamed One Parent Families) invited unmarried mothers and their children to write about their experiences of illegitimacy. The booklet the Council compiled showed feelings of humiliation which persisted even into the 1980s. One correspondent wrote, 'I am so ashamed of being illegitimate myself – I am in my sixties now – that I have never had any kind of social life, or friends ever at all, in case it should be revealed by chance'. Others worried about how to tell their children that their parent was illegitimate, or spoke of the pain of always lying about their family.[99]

Writing for *The Clarion* in 1913 about the pregnant girlfriend of a convicted murderer who had been refused permission by the Home Secretary to marry her as he awaited execution, the young feminist and free-thinker Rebecca West said that 'an unmarried mother is the most outcast thing on earth. We, as socialists ... know that this is nonsense ... But the fact remains that most people do not think like that. They will treat [her] as an unclean person who has been meddling with important things in an unpleasant manner'. And, following correspondence from politically correct *Clarion* readers who declared marriage an old-fashioned and dangerous irrelevance, she recommended:

> [E]very correspondent who asserts that an unmarried mother suffers no social discredit to announce casually before a few friends that he and his wife are not legally married. My arguments would then be enforced by his wife. If he required any further conviction, let him consider that a servant who has an illegitimate child loses her situation, that the Board of Education suspends the certificate of a schoolmistress, that no hospital nurse or typist would expect for a second to keep her position ... And the social stigma [of the illegitimate child] is an indefensible but quite real consequence of the degradation of the unmarried mother. The child sees its mother shunned by the godly, associates itself with her disgrace and grows up to think of itself as a pariah.[100]

Eighteen months later Rebecca West herself became the unmarried mother of a son by H. G. Wells, and although she kept her son and never denied she was his mother (in contrast to the writer Dorothy L. Sayers, who, in a similar situation a decade or so later, pretended to be her son's cousin and left him in the foster care of her own cousin – see Chapter 5), she secluded herself from society for several years and certainly did not publicise his birth.

In 1970, the historian Constance Rover suggested that there was a movement among some feminists in Britain, Australia and the USA after the First World War towards 'bachelor motherhood' or 'the right to motherhood without marriage'. She believed it was motivated by the lack of potential husbands following the slaughter of the war, the eugenic advantage of choosing a suitable father without the need to marry him and the opportunity to combine career and marriage at a time when they were seen as alternatives.[101] However, her sole English example was Sylvia Pankhurst, who at forty-five had her only child without being married, gave it her surname and announced it in the *News of the World* as a 'eugenic baby', but she was living with the child's father so does not really fit the description.[102] Others either moved in very permissive circles or kept a very low profile.[103]

In the next chapter I will look at the formation of the NCUMC in 1918 to help unmarried mothers, using a dual strategy of political campaigning and encouraging practical measures such as hostels. Throughout this period the Council remained convinced that if possible it was better for a child to stay with its mother than to be adopted. However despite all its efforts, together with those of the moral welfare workers who organised hostels and services for unmarried mothers in need, provision for them remained piecemeal and inadequate. In their detailed survey of social services during the Second World War, Sheila Ferguson and Hilda Fitzgerald reviewed the provision before the war:

> In large areas of Britain there were neither voluntary nor public homes for unmarried mothers ... Nobody knew exactly the size, type and quality of the existing voluntary services for unmarried mothers. Local grants of varying size were given to a limited number of voluntary homes but otherwise the local welfare authorities made little use of their increased powers to help unmarried mothers and their babies.[104]

If a woman produced a second illegitimate child she was deemed irremediably 'fallen' and there was no alternative to what had until recently been called the workhouse, or a few Salvation Army hostels. Most adoption societies also refused to take second or subsequent illegitimate children.

Legally an illegitimate child was officially *filius nullius* – child of no one. As the child of no one, prior to 1926 they could only inherit if they were specifically named; that is, they would not be included if their parent left property to 'my children' or their grandfather to his 'grandchildren', or if these relatives died intestate. If an illegitimate person died intestate without spouse or issue their personal property, at least in theory, passed to the Crown.

Under the Bastardy Laws Amendment Act 1872, the mother of an illegitimate child could obtain an order for maintenance against the putative father before the child was born. This also extended the father's liability to support his child until the age of 16 and enabled Boards of Guardians to assist mothers in recovering maintenance costs. It fixed the maximum weekly amount payable under affiliation orders at five shillings a week. In 1918 the Affiliation Orders (Increase of Maximum Payment) Act raised this amount to ten shillings and the 1923 Bastardy Act doubled the amount to twenty shillings.

As far as the custody of illegitimate children was concerned in the 1920s, one of the twenty-two women called to the Bar by the middle of 1923, Monica Mary Geikie Cobb, described the position:

> An illegitimate child, being at law filius nullius, has no legal guardians, but the mother has a right of custody, though this is more limited than the corresponding right of a father over a legitimate child. But the mother's right is recognised as against the father's, and if the child is of tender years and the father obtains possession of the child from the mother by force or fraud, the mother can regain possession by means of a writ of habeas corpus. She is responsible so long as unmarried or a widow, and correlatively she has the right to its custody and to determine questions concerned with its upbringing, such, for example, as its religious training, even as against the father.

Further:

> Should the mother of a bastard child marry, her husband is then responsible, during her lifetime, for the maintenance of that child until it reaches the age of sixteen, whether he be the father or no.[105]

In 1926, the Legitimacy Act, one of the decade's pieces of reforming legislation, was passed. It was not as radical as its supporters had hoped for but it introduced the principle of legitimation *per subsequens matrimonium* into English law if a man married the mother of his illegitimate child. The provisos were that he must be domiciled in England or Wales at the date of the marriage and both parties must have been free to marry at the time of the child's birth (i.e. the child was not the issue of an adulterous union). Previous attempts to introduce this legislation had proposed to legitimise all illegitimate children whose parents subsequently married but this was seen as condoning adultery. This Act also gave the legitimised person various rights to inherit property on the same terms as a legitimate person but not to inherit titles. The Act also gave mothers the right to succeed to their illegitimate child's intestacy as though the relationship was legitimate and they were the only surviving parents, and it gave illegitimate children the right to take on their mother's intestacy if she left no surviving legitimate issue.

This Act was immediately used extensively. In its first year the births of 5495 children were re-registered as legitimate, and although the numbers gradually declined as the backlog of eligible cases was dealt with, even in 1936 nearly three thousand births were legitimised.[106]

2
Developments in the Voluntary Sector

Informal adoption had always existed in all social classes. Neighbours might take in the children next door when they were left orphans to save them from the workhouse. Or relatives would look after children left motherless, while their father went off to look for work. Medieval pages and Tudor apprentices grew up in families not their own; aunts, uncles, grandparents and neighbours brought up orphaned relatives and friends' children. Middle- and upper-class families might assimilate nieces and nephews whose parents died or simply could not afford to give them a good start in life – one of Jane Austen's brothers was adopted by a distant cousin and his wife who were wealthy and had no children.[1] Nineteenth- and early twentieth-century literature abounds with 'adoption' stories – Silas Marner and Eppie, Miss Havisham and Estella, Mr Carrisford and Sara Crewe to mention but a few.[2] But with the exception of the Poor Law adoptions described in the last chapter, there were no organised programmes of widespread domestic adoption prior to the First World War except for the limited examples described here.

The beginning of organised adoption

Adoption was probably too closely associated with baby farming for the practice to meet with much enthusiasm among those involved with children's welfare. However the main children's charities did quietly organise some adoptions. The National Children's Home and Orphanage organised a limited form of adoption from 1869. Although they concentrated mainly on bringing children up in residential homes, by 1892 they were 'boarding out' or fostering younger children with 'approved families'. Usually these children returned to residential homes when they were seven or eight but some were adopted by their foster parents; by 1920 over 260 adoptions had taken place.[3] The Salvation Army's witness to the Hopkinson Committee in 1920, Commissioner Adelaide Cox, said that the Army had arranged about five hundred adoptions in the previous thirty years. The witness for Dr Barnardo's, Dr Margaret Hudson, was adamant that the only form of adoption occurring through her organisation was where the foster parents with whom they had placed children grew so fond of their charges that they decided to maintain them without pay from Dr Barnardo's, but both she and Commissioner Cox also described the wide-scale emigration of children to the colonies, mainly Canada and Australia, organised through their agencies.

The emigration of 'unwanted' British children to the colonies had been going on since the early nineteenth century (indeed even earlier in the sense that children were 'transported' as criminals and delinquents). In general the process was organised by voluntary societies and individuals. Most of the children were apprenticed or worked as servants or farmhands but some younger ones do appear to have been 'adopted' in the sense we understand it. They usually still had to work hard[4] but, as discussed in the previous chapter, working-class children were only beginning to be valued for their sentimental rather than economic worth in the late nineteenth century, so this would have been the case for most working-class children.

Dr Barnardo had begun his emigration operation in 1882, and by the beginning of the First World War this had arranged for over twenty-four thousand children to be sent to Canada. Joy Parr described a three-stage indenture system in operation for the Barnardo's migrants (with similar arrangements in other organisations): younger children (six- to ten-year-olds) were boarded out with families for a monthly fee; eleven- to fourteen-year-olds received board and lodging but like similar age family members were expected to do a fair amount of work; after fourteen they were employed for wages. Parr saw a purely business arrangement for the Canadian farmers:

> The children's placements were determined by economic criteria. They were moved as their economic worth increased. They were not placed to meet the emotional needs of Canadian homes nor monitored by guardians who allowed emotional considerations to be paramount.

She described the child immigrants moving frequently during their indentures; girls an average of four times during their first five years in Canada, boys three times.[5] Parr considered that the indenture system protected the British children from exploitation (as it was designed to do), 'but in the process destroyed the illusion, the warm and welcome illusion of being "like family", which every child immigrant must have at some time entertained'.[6] Those few rescue homes who did not use indentures 'pandered to the vain illusion of equality' which 'left their young wards in an ambivalent position in Canadian households which occasionally might turn to their advantage but usually made them into drudges'.[7] This was not, in any sense of the term, adoption, and in 1924 after the Canadian authorities became increasingly concerned about the practice, the Federal Canadian Government placed a temporary ban on the entry of unaccompanied children under fourteen to Canada, which was made permanent in 1928.[8] Barnardo's and the Fairbridge Society continued to send children to Australia, and New Zealand had its own programme. Indeed towards the end of the Second World War the Australian government declared its desire for a vastly enhanced programme of child migration from Britain.[9]

In the United Kingdom, prior to 1947 (when it became a registered adoption society) Barnardo's as an organisation saw itself as the adopter, not the families with whom it sometimes boarded out children. For all intents and purposes it took for itself the custody and control of the children in its care. This usually appears to have been accepted by the children's relatives, although in 1891 Barnardo's was involved in two key cases[10], in both of which a mother had agreed to give up her child to the Society but had then changed her mind. On appeal the courts ruled in both cases that the mother's wishes for her child were paramount unless they were detrimental to the interests of the child. During the interwar years Barnardo's portrayed itself as a 'family': June Rose described its powerful emotional appeal as 'the Barnardo family, the largest family in the world'.[11]

So the major children's welfare organisations had had a limited involvement with adoption and they were wary of it. They saw themselves as having continuing responsibility for the children they rescued and cared for. Adoption, by its nature, meant relinquishing control to someone else. Even if children were boarded out for many years, they were still ultimately under the control of the society arranging the foster parents. Within the United Kingdom, Barnardo's in particular maintained a strict regime of random inspections of the boarded-out children throughout their childhood, even those who were 'adopted' (prior to the 1926 Act) by the families who had fostered them.

Apart from the profession of concern for unwanted children, the major child welfare societies had very little in common with the adoption societies which started during the First World War. Although the adoption societies described their work in flowery and sentimental terms and were mostly run by dedicated volunteers, their work arose from a more pragmatic base than that of the big children's charities. During the War they saw two needy parties whose needs could simultaneously be fulfilled for the benefit and convenience of both – unwanted children, generally orphaned or illegitimate, deprived of satisfactory family life – and bereaved parents, childless couples, and lonely spinsters and widows in need of infant companionship. All that was necessary was to bring the two elements together.

Evidence given to the Hopkinson Committee in 1920 showed that by the beginning of the First World War a number of upper-middle-class ladies were already arranging adoptions informally. Miss R. S. M. Peto told how she had adopted seven children herself since 1908, and during the years after 1915 had arranged about twenty permanent adoptions for other families. She had confined herself to dealing with illegitimate 'children of the better classes' and all had gone to families of similar background. Initially she and two friends had set up a society calling themselves 'The Storks', and had advertised for babies in *The Times* but had found the response (40–50 replies to each advert) too overwhelming, and had ended the society after a few months. She now did limited work on a very small scale.[12] Another witness was Lady Henry Somerset who looked after a hundred children in her own homes but also arranged for workhouse foundling babies to be adopted.[13]

Miss Peto told the Hopkinson Committee that she was now winding up her adoption work because there were 'two real adoption societies' on the scene so there was no need for private individuals to do adoption work. The two societies she referred to were the National Children Adoption Association (NCAA) and the National Adoption Society (NAS). Other societies appeared during the 1920s but these were the first substantial ones whose sole purpose was adoption. The NCAA was particularly influential in publicising the idea of adoption, and successful at fundraising for its activities.

The formation of the first adoption societies

The founder of the NCAA was Miss Clara Andrew.[14] She was born in May 1862 into a professional family in Exeter; her father Thomas was then High Bailiff of the Exeter County Court and subsequently an official at the Board of Trade, and her brothers Sidney and Henry became respectively a solicitor and surgeon. She went to Maynards School in

Exeter and studied in Germany.[15] It is unclear what exactly she did in the decades after that but she appears to have devoted herself energetically to 'good works' and committees. In a letter in 1918 she described her career as follows:

> I was one of two original women members of the Exeter National Insurance Committee.
>
> The chief responsibility of equipping the first tuberculosis hospital and selecting the staff in the district was left to me, as [was] also the care of tubercular children.
>
> At the beginning of the War I became Organising Secretary & Vice President for the Devon and Cornwall War Refugees Committee, giving evidence at the Parliamentary Commission of the L.G.B [Local Government Board] on the work.
>
> After eighteen months, when the organisation was completed, I went to the Arsenal at Woolwich as Asst. Lady Supervisor, subsequently holding the head post as Lady Superintendent at Newbury & Swindon Munitions Works.
>
> Whilst in these positions, I... held myself personally responsible for the welfare of neglected and unwanted children whose birth was kept secret, or who for various reasons, had not been brought before welfare organisations.
>
> I have placed children in homes and got one or two adopted in families well known to me and where I am allowed access; in fact I am 'godmother' to the children.[16]

Miss Andrew appears to have been forceful and persistent, and sometimes perceived as impatient with those she considered her social or intellectual inferiors. Her work with Belgian war refugees in Exeter revealed all these traits, and her brother Sidney had considerable correspondence with the Lord Lieutenant of Devon, Lord Fortescue, sorting out a new committee structure for the project after she fell out with the city's Mayor who was also involved with the refugee work. A new Committee was established; the Devon County War Refugees Committee, with Exeter retaining a separate committee for looking after the refugees within the city boundaries. The Lord Lieutenant wrote to Mr Andrew that 'in order to save the Mayor's face it was desirable that Miss Andrew should not occupy on paper, too prominent a place in the new organisation, though of course it would be idiocy not to utilise fully her experience and capability, if she is still willing to continue her work'.[17]

Figure 2.1 Miss Clara Andrew and an adopted child (from the London Metropolitan Archives)

The correspondence suggests that Miss Andrew successfully set up a scheme of volunteers for providing care and accommodation for the Belgian refugees who were beginning to arrive in England during that period and were distributed to various centres across the country such as Exeter. After successful fundraising:

> Miss Andrew was sent to London, and returned to Exeter with 120 refugees, and Exeter became the first provincial centre to receive Refugees, and the first place to provide them with homes. By the end of October, it was reported that over 800 persons had been provided for in the neighbourhood. Local Sub-Committees were formed in many places, Miss Andrew being the leading spirit in these activities.[18]

The experience of Miss Andrew's war work led her to believe that there was a need for a form of broker between unwanted children and would-be parents. Adoption work would also have offered her new challenges and interests at a time when she was facing the end of her busy wartime career which had absorbed her energy, organising skills and charitable urges. It is not known whether she had gained training or qualifications or had any private income but if not the opportunities for her as an unmarried middle-class woman in her late fifties were limited – thus she had to create them for herself. The letter quoted earlier, describing her early career, was to a civil servant, Mr Stutchbury,[19] at the Local Government Board (soon afterwards the Ministry of Health). She had already had a brief meeting with him, following an introduction from Lord Rhondda, when she was seeking official recognition for her adoption work. In her follow-up letter in January 1918 she suggested that she work on a voluntary basis as 'a recognised "adoption officer"', responsible to him. She explained, 'I believe there is no one undertaking regular 'adoption work' and that it would be greatly expedited if would-be parents had some one person to whom they could apply when willing to care for a child with "full surrender"'.[20]

The civil servants were not quite sure what to do with Miss Andrew[21] but in any case a month later they received a letter from Mrs England, the wife of the Headmaster of Exeter School, announcing the launch that day in Exeter of the 'Children Adoption Association' of which she was Hon. Secretary and Miss Andrew the President. It was intended to set up local committees across the country to spread information about the Association and process applications 'from those wishing to adopt or resign children' and visit and take up references from them.[22] The formation of the Association was met with approval by local papers in Devon although the comments of the *Western Evening Herald* reflect the rather ambivalent attitude to adoption which many people held:

> In such a scheme each case must be considered an individual problem, lest the easy transfer of children should lead to an increase of one of our evils, but doubtless the organisers are well aware of this, and will guard against it. Generally speaking, it seems to us the scheme is to be welcomed and will relieve much anxiety and cause much happiness though it may not be in what one may call the main road of social reform.[23]

Much later Miss Andrew described outright hostility to the new organisation rather than ambivalence:

> I spoke during 1917 and 1918 at hundreds of meetings, organised by Churches of all denominations, Rotary Clubs and Women's Clubs and I was heckled at every meeting. I was told the orphan was for the orphanage and the illegitimate child should be kept by its mother or the State and people spoke of the danger to public morals if the illegitimate child shared in the benefits of this new movement.[24]

During the first six months of 1918, Miss Andrew visited the Local Government Board when she was up in London at least three times to make sure the officials were aware of the new Association and to ask if they could give advice and help. By July 1918 the Association had taken on the title of National Children Adoption Association. According to *The Western Morning News* whose representative talked to Miss Andrew at the NCAA stall at the Baby Week Exhibition at Central Hall Westminster, there were NCAA committees by now in Salisbury, the Isle of Wight, Plymouth and Liverpool.[25] An NCAA leaflet published during this period describes the Association's policies. It states:

> We regard as suitable for adoption, orphans, or children who, by reason of cruelty or neglect, have been removed from the care of their parents or guardians, or the illegitimate infants of girls who, in many cases may fairly be described as 'sinned against rather than sinning'. These have thrown themselves away through ignorance, or folly or love, without a thought of consequences. In many cases the girls are deceived by men to whom they have been engaged to be married – perhaps for years ...
>
> Full enquiries are always made into the character, health and history of both parents; and none of the children accepted are borne of vicious parents.
>
> Some people hold back from adopting illegitimate children, fearing what they may inherit, but it does not follow that because children are born out of wedlock they have an evil heritage ...
>
> In considering the inheritance of any child (legitimate or illegitimate) it is important to remember that good as well as evil traits are hereditary, and that it is impossible to over-rate the immeasurable forces of environment and education in shaping character. Of course these statements are open to criticism, but we write from a personal observation of a large number of cases.[26]

The Association gave adopters full particulars of the child's history and a certificate of health. References were taken from both adopter and parents, and parents were never told their child's destination unless the adopter expressly consented. Most people asked for orphans of two or three years old who were actually seldom available for adoption. The reality was that the majority of children on offer were illegitimate and in the later years of the association the proportion probably grew as maternal mortality gradually declined. The NCAA's leaflet said that orphans of 'better-class people' were 'generally in the care of guardians, who will naturally only allow them to be adopted if they may keep in touch with them – a condition which prevents the adoptive parents from ever feeling that the child is really their own'.[27] In later years babies would be more in demand, but at this stage, before the popularisation of psychoanalytic theories would encourage adopting parents to prefer a *'tabula rasa'* on which they could make their own imprint, adopters (perhaps influenced by eugenic ideas) placed more emphasis on the advantage of knowing that a child had been strong enough to survive infancy.

It was frankly admitted that when a child was adopted, although the natural parent signed a document drawn up by a solicitor giving up their child entirely and promising never to reclaim it, in fact 'no parent can legally do this'. To circumvent this, a maintenance clause was inserted into the agreement, 'binding the parent in case of a breach of faith, to pay maintenance from the date of adoption. This soon puts an impossible line between parent and child'.[28] The wording in the agreement was designed to intimidate, although whether or not it would have been enforceable in a court of law is unclear:

> The Parent will, in the event of any attempt on her (his) part to retake or regain possession of the said child, pay to the Adopter all costs, charges and expenses in respect of the maintenance, clothing and education of the said child reasonably incurred by him and appropriate to that station in life in which he intends to bring up the said child for the whole period during which such child shall have been in the custody and control or care of the said Adopter – this amount if disputed to be settled by Arbitrators.[29]

In case this sounded too ruthless the leaflet quickly goes on to say: 'the main protection, however, lies in the moral obligation, and the fact that the cases are chosen most carefully, and no pressure is ever put on the parent. It must be her own decided wish to part with the child.'[30]

And the problems facing single mothers were so difficult and the fate of many illegitimate children so dire that 'in all these cases a double good is surely affected by the adoption of babies'.³¹

In early 1919 Miss Andrew visited Miss Puxley³² at the Local Government Board (the Ministry of Health from 24 June 1919). Miss Puxley had already met Miss Andrew on a number of previous occasions and wrote:

> Miss Andrew called today with a long story of difficulties with the Committee she recently set up, and also with Miss Plows-Day [a vice-president], who was one of her original helpers.
>
> She also spoke of amalgamating with a Mr Buttle who was doing some work of the same kind in Cambridge. I did not go to it any more than I could help as it did not appear to concern the Board; but I gather Mr Buttle and Miss Plows-Day have in some way joined forces and Miss Andrew is left without either of them.³³

Whatever Miss Andrew's problems with her former colleague and Mr Buttle (Miss Plows-Day did work for his National Adoption Society for many years although he left it at the end of the 1920s and was regarded with some suspicion by the authorities in the 1930s – see Chapter 6), she appears to have recovered swiftly from the setback and within weeks a London branch, shortly to be the centre of the organisation, had been established, with a committee of worthy people and a public meeting presided over by the Bishop of Kensington.

By April 1919 the NCAA had opened permanent headquarters in London.³⁴ Its president was now Lady Northcote and by December the Association had the official patronage of Princess Alice, the Countess of Athlone (a granddaughter of Queen Victoria).³⁵ Despite being in South Africa quite frequently as her husband was its Governor-General 1924–31, Princess Alice was assiduous over the next twenty years in attending fund-raising events, opening hostels and offices, chairing committees and making speeches on the Association's behalf whenever she was in the country.³⁶ (By 1937 she was the President and Chairman of the Association, and the Queen had become the Patron). The Association had been given a large house, Tower Cressy, in Campden Hill to accommodate children accepted for placement who were awaiting adoption and could not remain in their own home. It was used as a hostel from June 1919 and formally opened by Princess Alice in December.³⁷ The Ministry of Health provided it with an annual grant after it opened (a capital grant of £114 per annum for ten years plus an annual maintenance grant³⁸), and as running the hostel was clearly an expensive undertaking, this money was very important to the NCAA. Miss Puxley reported that 'she [Miss Andrew] was horrified at the barest possibility of withdrawal of grant and begged that at least they might have long warning. She almost implied that there would be a rising throughout the country if anything of the sort were suggested.'[39]

Figure 2.2 Tower Cressy, the NCAA hostel, Campden Hill, Kensington (from an NCAA leaflet, The National Archives)

Clara Andrew was now officially the Hon. Secretary of the NCAA and had been extremely busy in using her contacts and their friends to assemble not just the patronage of Princess Alice but also an impressively titled list of thirteen Vice-Presidents who included three Countesses, one Viscountess, two Ladies, a Dowager Duchess and a Dowager Countess, a Rear Admiral, the Lord Bishop of London and the Chief Rabbi. The Association's Hon. Counsel was Thomas Inskip KC MP, later knighted and then given a peerage, and Solicitor General and Attorney General in the Conservative Governments of the 1920s and 30s.[40] Even the Executive Committee was a well-connected group, including MPs, high-ranking army men, the Bishop of Kensington, and some of their wives and other ladies. When the NCAA registered under the Companies Act in 1926 its seven subscribers included 'Lucy Baldwin (Married Woman, 10 Downing Street)'.[41]

The information booklet now produced by the NCAA for publicity and fund-raising purposes was substantial. It was lavishly illustrated with photos of the children at the Tower Cressy hostel – in their night nurseries, day nursery, bathrooms and garden. It presents a slightly conflicting picture – on the one hand it shows an organisation with a structured and efficient policy of interviews, referees, visits, application forms and Case Committees, and a register of potential adopters and children who are matched for compatibility, and on the other offers a vivid image of adopters choosing their baby. They enter

> our offices with the tremulous anxiety and excitement which are characteristic of motherly little girls going to a doll shop. They have some definite image before their eyes; most of them look for some of their own family traits in colour or form, and they want to see several children. With the establishment of the Hostels it will, of course, be possible to allow adopters a wider choice than can be given now.'[42]

A husband is cited approvingly who came with his wife 'to choose a baby' but left her 'without any say in the matter when he held out his arms to a crying baby and she had smiled at him though her tears. "That settles it; this is our baby", he said quite firmly, and he would not look at another'.[43] Another, 'most excellent adopter wrote to us: "Please send baby before the summer sales are over: it would mean a great economy of scale"'.[44]

The tone of these parts of the booklet – and the style of the photographs – is reminiscent of the illustrated children's books of the interwar period by authors such as Mabel Lucie Attwell, showing cute large-eyed doll-like infants. The photographs show neat photogenic little girls or babies. This must have served to reinforce existing consumer prejudice, because as the booklet points out, adopters were 'much more eager to take a girl' than a boy, although 75 per cent of the children offered for adoption were boys. The leaflet suggested that 'people are more willing to abandon a boy as being more difficult to educate and put out in the world. For the same reason adopters are certainly much more eager to take a girl.'[45] Miss Andrew suggested that 'they believe [girls] are cheaper and a better investment. They want them for companions in their old age'.[46]

In October 1920 Miss Andrew described the NCAA's procedure to the Hopkinson Committee on Child Adoption. Babies were assessed for health and fitness and then if suitable had three months in which to be adopted. During this period they either remained with relatives or foster parents or came to one of the Association's hostels, usually the one at Tower Cressy in Kensington. About a quarter of the children coming to them were 'derelict' or orphans and about a quarter were legitimate. The Association turned down children with financial 'complications' – if they had money or if there was a court order enforcing a settlement on the mother. They refused 'all second cases' (i.e. where the mother had already had an illegitimate child), or where the mother had 'exhibited any sort of disease' or 'is known to be leading an immoral life'. If the children were not adopted they went back to their mother or to the workhouse. If adopted they were given to the adopter on a month's probation – not for the adopter to be assessed but to ensure they really did want the child. Miss Andrew explained that 'A great many people who take children are middle-aged people who have never had a child, and it is quite possible for a woman to have developed on very narrow lines ... it gives her time to make up her mind as to whether she can stand it'.[47] Adopters 'might have ten children on probation if they liked. As a matter of fact, they have never had more than two'.[48]

Miss Andrew estimated about 15–20 per cent of the people applying to adopt were from the upper classes, about 25 per cent working class, and the rest from the middle classes which she defined as 'the professional classes, tradespeople, clerks, and sergeants in the police', and naval and army people. Many adopters were people who had lost sons in the war and came in for a daughter, or else childless couples married for ten to fifteen years who 'want to start domestic life'. About three quarters were married couples but a sizeable proportion were war widows in their forties wanting a child.[49] In describing the people approaching the Association Miss Andrew expanded on the pamphlet quoted above: 'They say they must have a child which resembles their family; they must have the right colouring and the right age. Two people have been to us and said they must have a child born on a certain date.' She appeared unworried about this approach to child selection: 'The extraordinary part is that these sentimental people have been such a great success as a rule.' However, her figures suggest that not every potential adopter was approved, although unfortunately the Hopkinson Committee did not ask her to explain the criteria for selection. Between April 1919 and October 1920, the NCAA Case Committee passed 2310 applications for adoption and refused 588. During this period 448 adoptions were completed, with many more children in adopters' homes for their probationary period.

In contrast to the emphasis of the big crusading rescue charities on reclaiming vulnerable and unwanted children, the NCAA's focus was on bringing together children and adopters to create new families. The world presented was a secular, respectable one. Secrecy and discretion were emphasised throughout. Most of the other adoption societies established during the 1920s and 30s originated to a greater or lesser degree from a religious background but despite the presence of the rabbi and bishops in the Association, the NCAA appears at this stage not just ecumenical but largely removed from religion. In the 1930s the Association apparently did introduce a rule that children should be adopted by people of British nationality and of the same religion as the natural parents[50] and by the 1940s their literature had a more overtly Christian emphasis but in the 1920s the adoption agreement provided by the association makes no mention of the religion of the child (or of the parent or adopter), and the application form requesting adoption of the child merely asks one question about baptism. At this stage there appears to have been no effort to match the religious affiliations of child and adopter, although, at least according to the stated policy of the organisation, there was some concern to match the class background of child and adopter ('as far as possible they are all placed in homes suitable to their birth'[51]). Perhaps this, together with secrecy and respectability, was perceived as more important to the majority of prospective adopters immediately after the First World War than religion. In any case, as Miss Andrew explained to the Hopkinson Committee, the NCAA saw the adopted child as starting again with the adopting family, so in a sense previous religion was irrelevant.[52]

The Association's success was helped by the fund-raising and publicity drives organised by its well-connected supporters. In March 1920 the Prime Minister's wife, Mrs Lloyd George, who 'had received continual appeals for help from unmarried mothers of the "unwanted" children born during the war',[53] arranged for a matinee performance at the Palladium, at which the money raised went to a fund to be chiefly administered by the NCAA. Not only was money raised for the Association by such events but also useful publicity; in the lead-up to the matinee 'during the last fortnight 670 people have expressed their desire to adopt babies'.[54] On the whole the Association received positive comment. Although the Ministry of Health 'was not keen on adoption in a general and wholesale way' it was complimentary about the hostel it part-funded:

> Every report on its work has been good and certainly some of the cases taken by the Society have been wonderfully benefitted [sic]. So far as we ever have any means of ascertaining, the organisation is well run and careful enquiries are made prior to adoption.[55]

However, the NCAA was not immune from controversy and, particularly in its early years, was sometimes the subject of quite critical press coverage.[56] In 1922, following the Association's denial of any negligence in its operations, the *John Bull* newspaper published a detailed account of a transfer two years earlier of babies at Durham railway station by two women working for the NCAA, and witnessed by the attendant in the waiting room:

> The two women had entered the [first class waiting room] that morning carrying a baby, and remained there for nearly two hours. About half-past eleven two other women and a girl entered. There was a short conversation, the baby was handed over to them, and they went away with it. No papers were signed.
> The two women then left the room and presently returned with a sad-eyed young woman of about twenty, carrying an infant. Some papers were placed on the table, and a few minutes later, the young mother left, sobbing bitterly, without her child. The two women asked for a taxi to Spennymoor, and went off with the baby, returning about 3.30 pm without it.[57]

The NCAA women were interviewed by the Chief Constable of Durham. He visited the woman to whom they had handed the first baby

> who said she had answered an advertisement in a Sunday paper, and received a letter from Miss Clara Andrew of the NCAA, asking for two

references. She sent these, and then received another letter, telling her to meet the two ladies at the railway station, where the baby was handed over to her without further ado.[58]

Ministry of Health officials had a meeting with Miss Andrew about this and various other problems which had arisen with individual cases. She gave them the correspondence which she had with the chief constable at the time, in which she had written strongly, complaining that one of the NCAA ladies had to spend the night in a railway carriage as she had missed her train because of the police questioning and 'had been treated with a great lack of courtesy'.[59] Miss Andrew had told the Chief Constable that her Association had made full enquiries about the woman given the baby, and asked him if there was any reason to mistrust her, in which case they would remove the child. He had replied that the lady had been twice visited and 'although she resides in a poor locality, she and her husband appear to be quite respectable, and the child appears to be well cared for. The Police on this occasion, only carried out in a courteous manner, the duties imposed upon them by the Children Act 1908'.[60] In the notes on Miss Andrew's meeting with the Ministry officials she comes over as fluent and convincing if occasionally evasive in the face of a difficult question (e.g. 'It was not quite clear from Miss Andrew's statement whether a prospective home is always actually inspected' and 'we could not ascertain clearly from Miss Andrew whether in fact the adopter's home had in this case been previously inspected.'[61]). There were other complaints in the press about the NCAA, but Miss Andrew either denied the stories completely, or, as with the above case, was adamant that everything had been checked out properly.

The NCAA and the other large adoption society operating during this period, the National Adoption Society, were often confused with each other; their names were very similar and at one point there seems to have been a possibility that they might merge (see above). The Reverend Frank Buttle apparently set up the NAS in London in late 1916 or early 1917,[62] adopting a formal charter in April 1917. According to Gwyneth Roberts, who was able to interview former staff of the NAS and the Church Adoption Society, when Mr Buttle lived in Cambridge before the War he was disturbed by the large number of illegitimate children fathered by University undergraduates[63] and he started arranging adoptions as a private individual there with the help of the Church League of Women's Suffrage.[64] Moving to London during the war he again became involved with adoption. However Clara Andrew, although she mentioned the society in Cambridge in a meeting in early 1919 with Miss Puxley of the Ministry of Health (see above), told the Hopkinson Committee in October 1920 that the NAS had been formed by people who broke away from the NCAA over 'a personal matter'. Possibly they joined up with the Rev. Buttle as he was in the process of establishing the society in London. Although the NAS managed to gain some aristocratic fund-raising support – Princess Helena Victoria gave her patronage to a children's party in its aid in January 1924[65] and the Marquess and Marchioness of Bath lent their London house for an 'at home'[66] – it never gained quite the level of establishment recognition that the NCAA achieved. The Ministry of Health were quite dubious about it in the early 1920s: 'The 'National Adoption Society' is the one we know rather doubtful things about already, and have no connection with'.[67] Although an ingenious fund-raiser, the Rev. Buttle found it difficult to work with others and his financial manipulations led him into controversies.[68] In 1931, having fallen out with members of the NAS, he left it to set up the Church of England Adoption Society (later renamed The Adoption Society and then the Church Adoption Society), which was to provoke considerable criticism during the 1930s for its financial methods and adoption practices, and was the unnamed adoption society singled out for especial criticism in the Horsbrugh Report (see Chapter 6).

A leaflet produced by the National Adoption Society (probably in 1918 or 1919) presents an interesting contrast to the material produced by the NCAA. It makes similar points about checking out the children's background, taking references from the adopters, arranging a probationary month, and the importance of secrecy: 'Experience has taught the Society the wisdom of making it a *sine qua non* that the Adopters and Guardians do not meet, and that the identity of the Adopters is not disclosed to the Guardians',[69] but, as the above sentence exemplifies, the word 'mother' is not mentioned throughout the entire document, nor is 'illegitimacy'. The NAS includes no sentimental discussion of the relinquishing mothers' plight which the NCAA displayed even in its short leaflet; it has a businesslike air about it – presumably because it is literally in the business of dealing with babies and children and its approach is more clearly revealed when it says:

> As the work of the Society depends entirely on voluntary support, Guardians are asked to give a donation to the funds of the Society and the Adopters are invited to do the same wherever possible. This donation on both sides is purely voluntary.

The Society suggests that this *voluntary* donation should be given in three installments, one when the agreement is signed, and the other two on the succeeding anniversaries of the child's birth.[70] [original italics]

The NCAA invited donations but was clear that there was no compulsion or pressure, especially on the natural mothers, and although its adoption practices were sometimes questioned it was never accused of dubious financial dealings or exploitation. The businesslike image of the National Adoption Society is reinforced by the way one of the Society's most publicised ventures (which met with some criticism) was reported in *The Times*. In 1921 the NAS arranged for a dozen babies to be sent to America for adoption by childless couples and apparently there was enormous demand for them. A couple of brief news items in *The Times* said 'the experiment has been so successful more babies are to be "imported"' and, 'The society promises another consignment of British orphans next month'.[71] The NAS leaflet concludes by describing how it attempted to find a way around the lack of adoption legislation: 'Adopted children may, if desired, be made Wards in Chancery, and Guardianship Orders can be obtained, which secure to the Adopters the legal custody of the child.'[72]

Figure 2.3 'Two little girls some months after adoption' (from an NCAA leaflet, The National Archives)

In its day-to-day work the operation of the NAS sounds similar to that of the NCAA. Both turned away infants who were not completely healthy, both found in the early years that the majority of adopters wanted female toddlers and small children rather than babies. Both ran hostels for infants awaiting adoption in which they trained student nurses. The NAS' procedure for accepting adopters was that they must attend a personal interview and provide at least two satisfactory references, one from a doctor, lawyer or minister of religion, the other a professional woman or a mother or a woman with experience in the care of children.[73] If accepted and given a child the parents then had a probationary period of not less than one month and in 1924, 35 children were returned 'for various reasons', mainly it appears because the child was over three years of age and found it difficult to adapt to its new home.[74] This is a much higher figure than was ever admitted to by the NCAA.

The confusion between the two main adoption societies continued throughout the 1920s. Even at the end of 1922 Miss Puxley at the Ministry of Health was having to clarify the situation to her colleagues.[75] The NCAA appears to have been more concerned than the National Adoption Society about the presence of the two adoption societies with similar titles and aims – or at least it was more vocal about its displeasure and keen to assert its separate identity. In early 1924 *The Times* published a 'note' saying it had been asked to state that the National Children Adoption Association had 'no connexion [sic] with any other similar organisations'.[76] Part of the distrust for the other society presumably arose from the mysterious dispute between them mentioned earlier which Miss Andrew occasionally alluded to. On a more practical note Miss Andrew explained that

> One of the evil effects of two adoption societies is that people who want to get rid of their children and are discouraged at one office immediately rush to the other, or threaten to do so, and as far as I can tell, all cases are registered at both offices ... This apparent competition, I think, is likely to increase the evil of people trying to give up their children who have no right to do so. We must try and lessen the danger in some way: probably it may be worth while to refuse to deal with any case registered in any other office.[77]

Besides the NAS, there were other, smaller, adoption societies in the interwar period and there were organisations, mainly with a religious background, such as the National Children's Home and Orphanage (started in 1869 by Methodists), which carried out some adoptions in the course of their work with children. But the NCAA was clearly the most prominent and influential adoption society in the interwar period. In 1932 Princess Alice said that the Association had arranged the adoption of nearly four thousand children since it began and had established a hostel and affiliated committees in South Africa. In the same speech she announced the establishment of another London hostel and nursery school, Castlebar in Sydenham Hill, which was opened by the Queen in 1933.[78] In 1937 Princess Alice announced that the Queen had become the patron of the Association.[79] By the end of the decade the Association said 6000 children had been adopted through its agency. As will be shown in later chapters, it pushed hard for the legalisation of adoption which it saw as a safeguard for adoptive parents against natural parents removing their child. Subsequently it campaigned successfully for the regulation of adoption practice when it saw unscrupulous individuals and societies jeopardising its work by bringing adoption into disrepute.

However, behind the scenes even the NCAA, which prided itself on its superiority to the other adoption societies, was not immune from serious problems although it proved extremely adept at keeping them quiet. At the end of 1932 the NCAA Nursing Committee, which was appointed to visit the two hostels and keep an eye on their day-to-day activities, produced an extremely critical report of the way Tower Cressy was run. Following a special meeting on 3 January 1933, its Hon. Secretary, Mrs Peacock, took this report to the NCAA Executive Committee the next day to show 'the very unsatisfactory state of affairs at Tower Cressy, particularly with regard to the health of the children'.[80] Between July and December 1932 there had been four cases of bronchial pneumonia and eleven of 'marasmus' (essentially malnutrition – the Committee defined it as 'wasting disease due to improper feeding'[81]) and three babies had died. When members of the Nursing Committee visited two days before the meeting: 'the Sick Room is filled and everyone in the hostel has a cold. With the exception of two none are doing well'.[82] The Committee said that

> it seems obvious that [the Matron] does not understand the feeding of very young and no doubt 'difficult' children most of whom, though healthy on admittance, are usually under weight and require great care and experience to handle successfully.
>
> [The Matron] has not hitherto held the post of Matron. The Nursing Committee therefore recommend that her offered resignation be accepted.[83]

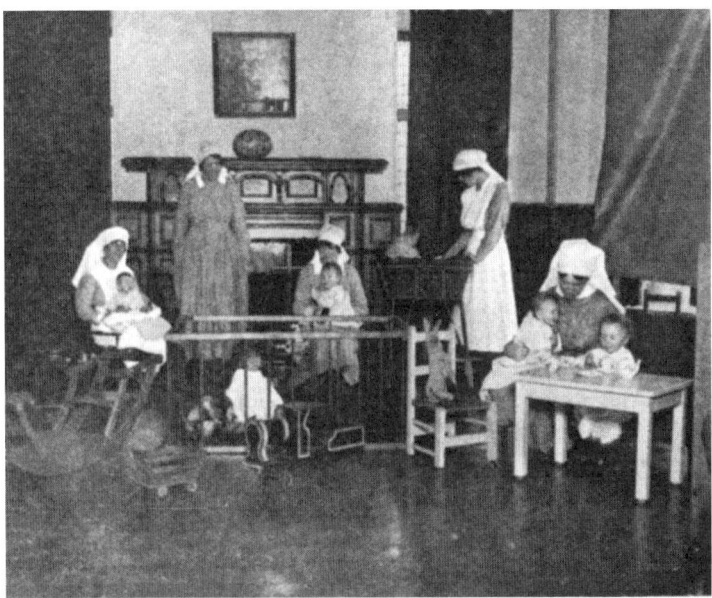

Figure 2.4 Day nursery, Tower Cressy (from an NCAA leaflet, The National Archives)

The Executive accepted the Matron's resignation and agreed that Tower Cressy be closed for a short period and thoroughly disinfected.

Miss Andrew was not present at the special meeting as she was only told of it on the 28 December and was leaving London for a short visit to Exeter the next day. She did not know about the Report and so had no reason to cancel her trip. There followed months of tension and accusations, with Tower Cressy remaining closed for a considerable time, causing some aggravation to the disgruntled student nursery nurses and their parents who were paying £80 for the privilege of training there and who had to move to Castlebar or leave. The main protagonists were Mrs Katherine Peacock, wife of a Canadian banker, and Lady Augusta Inskip, Chairman of the Nursing Committee, and wife of Sir Thomas Inskip (the then Solicitor General), who also became involved in the dispute. Princess Alice, to whom they all deferred, was not informed of the early stages of the controversy and then left for a trip to South Africa.

Miss Andrew contested all the allegations of staff incompetence and disputed doctors' reports which Lady Augusta produced, pointing out that only one of the three doctors had even visited Tower Cressy, and that after the hostel was closed. She was deeply upset by the situation:

> I have had infinite pain in the constant, almost daily blows, administered to me, following on the Report prepared by Mrs Peacock with its untrue charge of three deaths due to negligence. This hurried Report was accepted without enquiry, and is being used against me ...
> It is not the illegal aspect alone which distresses me, but the lack of appreciation of the labour of fifteen years and the want of courtesy. I find the position well nigh unbearable.[84]

Her brother, Sidney, the solicitor in Exeter, became heavily involved and took out a writ for libel against Mrs Peacock. He wrote to Clara at one point, 'this has become my battle and I trust you will leave it alone. I had rather you had been able to give up the whole thing and come home but as I know you are incapable of doing that you must ... give me a free hand.'[85] At the beginning of March, Princess Alice's husband, the Earl of Athlone, intervened. The Queen was shortly due to perform the official opening of the Castlebar hostel and it was impossible that she be embroiled in the scandal. Either the opening would have to be cancelled or 'I must ask you to withdraw unreservedly the writ against Mrs Peacock and to leave the consideration of the misunderstanding between you and the Executive Committee until the return of Princess Alice at the end of March.'[86] The writ was withdrawn.

At last Princess Alice returned: she had long talks with both Clara and her brother and wrote in a firm but pleasant fashion to Lady Inskip and said that as President of the Governing Body she was urging the hostel's immediate reopening, particularly in view of pressure from the London County Council (LCC) who gave it a 'substantial grant'. However this, the NCAA's Hon. Secretary (Lt-Col Rhys Samson) pointed out 'very respectfully', was not possible until authorised by the Executive Committee or Governing Body. So, as Princess Alice told Miss Andrew in a series of affectionate and chatty letters, they would have to wait till the meeting of the Executive Committee in May. Of her letter to Lady Inskip, Princess Alice said:

> I could have said dreadful things but I think she will be able to read through the lines & it would have been a mistake to let her think I was prejudiced. I had such a satisfactory talk with your brother & was thankful to have all my facts quite right so as to strike with effect ...
> With love, Yours affec, Alice[87]

Developments in the Voluntary Sector 61

H.R.H. PRINCESS ALICE, COUNTESS OF ATHLONE,
WITH AN ADOPTED CHILD.

Figure 2.5 Princess Alice, Countess of Athlone, with an adopted child (from the London Metropolitan Archives)

The dispute rumbled on. Sir Thomas Inskip became more involved, worried about 'irregularities' and 'most respectfully' felt that 'Your Royal Highness has not had proper advice in this matter'.[88] In a letter to Miss Andrew's brother, Princess Alice wrote: 'Did you ever know such a persistently silly man?'[89] Finally in June the Nursing Committee was split into two, one committee for each hostel. Lady Inskip and Mrs Peacock 'unselfishly tendered their resignations' for their positions on the old main Committee and received grateful thanks from the Princess at the Nursing Committee meeting. Lady Inskip's resignation speech was less gracious: She said she resigned, 'solely in deference to the wishes of the President [Princess Alice] and not because she felt that the Committee had in any way acted wrongly with regard to Tower Cressy. She desired to make it clear that she considered such action ... was fully justified'.[90]

Lady Inskip and Mrs Peacock were then among those appointed to the Castlebar Committee, with Lady Inskip being elected its Deputy Chairman and Mrs Peacock appointed its Secretary. By late July Miss Andrew felt 'convinced they know they are fighting a losing battle now. They are only spitting at me!',[91] and in January 1934 Mrs Peacock resigned both as Secretary and from the NCAA.[92] Lady Inskip stayed involved and later became Chairman of the NCAA (as Lady Caldecote, as Sir Thomas had been made a Viscount in 1939).

What is so surprising about this whole incident is that for the best part of a year the NCAA central governing group were at loggerheads and their main hostel was closed, but meanwhile they maintained their excellent public image, called for rogue adoption societies to be investigated (see Chapter 6) and let no hint of it all seep through to the general public.

The establishment of the National Council for the Unmarried Mother and Her Child

At the same time as the adoption societies were establishing themselves towards the end of the First World War a group of concerned people were setting up another organisation dealing mainly with illegitimate babies and their mothers, the National Council for the Unmarried Mother and Her Child (NCUMC). However it had a quite different approach to the women and their children. It was never in conflict with the adoption societies but had a much less enthusiastic attitude to adoption, particularly in the interwar years. It arose out of the growing concern during the War about the infant mortality rate (death in first year of life) of illegitimate children. In 1914, 37,329 illegitimate babies were born; their death rate was 207 per 1000, for legitimate births it was 100.[93] With the carnage at the Front and the declining birth rate even illegitimate births were seen as increasingly too precious to squander. There had been attempts, in particular by Joseph King MP, to introduce measures to make legitimation possible. Even if they had been passed they would not have necessarily helped the children, but their passing might have softened social attitudes and paved the way for better welfare provision. The National Society for the Prevention of Cruelty to Children, and later the magistrate, W. Clarke Hall, suggested, among other measures, making all illegitimate children wards of magistrates' courts so that the courts would watch over the future care of the child in the same way that the Chancery Court safeguarded the well-being of its usually wealthier wards.

Although attitudes to unmarried motherhood were not radically changing during the War, pragmatism made some compromise inevitable. When the Government was made aware by the National Relief Fund of how many 'common law marriages' there were it agreed to pay the same separation allowance – the extra amount paid to married soldiers – to unmarried mothers with 'an established home' where the serviceman had been the sole source of financial support. Kiernan, Land and Lewis quoted the National Relief Fund noting that this 'need not prejudice the married state after the war', and commented that 'indeed by 1927 marriage rather than motherhood had been restored as the key determinant of adult women's benefits and unmarried wives had been removed from the list of dependants eligible for benefit.'[94] Similarly, during the War places were offered to the children of unmarried mothers as well as married ones in some of the new crèche facilities set up so women could work in munitions factories. Barnardo's set up separate crèches for married and unmarried female workers at Woolwich Arsenal although these, together with virtually all their other crèches, were closed by mid-1920.[95]

Meanwhile the concern in the voluntary sector about the condition of illegitimate children had led to the Child Welfare Council (CWC) of the Social Welfare Association, which represented seventy bodies dealing with children, establishing an enquiry office in 1914 to deal with unmarried mothers. It was rapidly overwhelmed with appeals for help and advice. A consensus evolved amongst those dealing with the mothers and their children and the CWC, together with a number of other voluntary organisations involved with unmarried mothers, held a conference at the Mansion House in London on the issue, and launched the National Council for the Unmarried Mother and Her Child there on 14 February 1918.[96] Its fifty-three members represented almost every organisation connected with the welfare of women or children, together with medical people, public health officials, the National Union of Women Workers, the Women's Local Government Society and the Workers' Education Association. It remained nondenominational but worked closely with the churches, so its opinion was broadly representative of feeling in the social welfare movement and carried considerable weight.

Its official aims were relatively specific:

1. To obtain reform of the existing Bastardy Acts and Affiliation Orders Act.
2. To secure the provision of adequate accommodation to meet the varying needs of mothers and babies throughout the country; such provision to include Hostels with Day Nurseries attached, where the mother can live with her child for at least two years, whilst continuing her ordinary work.[97]

The Council's first Chairman was Lettice Fisher, wife of H. A. L. Fisher, the historian, who was then Education Minister in Lloyd George's wartime Government. She was herself an Oxford graduate and published author.[98] Despite continuing accusations of encouraging immorality Mrs Fisher managed to steer the organisation through to respectability while maintaining its strong campaigning side. By the early 1930s Vice-Presidents of the NCUMC included the Archbishops of Canterbury and York and the Bishop of Birmingham, and the future Prime Minister, Neville Chamberlain, was President from 1928 to 1931. However funding for the Council during the interwar years was always 'a constant anxiety'.[99]

The Council was established as a campaigning pressure group and initially individual cases were referred to the Child Welfare Bureau but after this closed the Council took over the work in September 1919.[100] So many unmarried mothers approached it for help that in 1920 a Case Committee was set up to deal with individual enquiries. In that first year it dealt with 600 cases and the number rose rapidly.[101] As illustrated in the last chapter, the mothers' plight was grim. Even for the minority who had court affiliation orders against the fathers of their children, the maximum payable was ten shillings a week from 1918 and twenty shillings from 1923. And although widows and separated mothers were allowed a low level of relief under the Poor Law policies, this was not given to unmarried mothers for whom it was 'felt it would provide an incentive for immoral and feckless behaviour'.[102] The only provision for them was residence in the workhouse where they would have to work for their keep under conditions which were deliberately severe as a deterrent. The child was usually sent elsewhere and the mother would be allowed to visit it every three months. The mother was not allowed to discharge herself without taking her child.[103] The NCUMC gave support and advice to organisations and individuals setting up homes and hostels for unmarried mothers and their babies and by 1926 fourteen homes and hostels in London, nine across England and one in Scotland, were affiliated to the Council.

Adoption was obviously a way out for the desperate unmarried mother but the Council maintained a policy of trying to keep mother and child together, considering adoption an option of last resort. To those who suggested that this policy might be seen as condoning immorality it retorted 'that this course affords incomparably the best hope of [the mother's] moral regeneration'.[104] The Council continually warned of the danger of encouraging too easy adoption. In a detailed statement it issued on adoption, it said:

> A number of those who become unmarried mothers, do so from a lack of sense of responsibility. The advent of the children gives an opportunity of developing that sense of responsibility, and, provided social conditions can be adjusted, mother and child can, and do, in many cases, lead a normal existence resulting in useful citizenship for both, whereas the removal of the child before the sense of responsibility is developed in the mother acts as a direct encouragement for a continuation of the line of conduct which has led to the birth of the first child.[105]

Despite its reservations about adoption in the interwar period the NCUMC was always a strong advocate of its legalisation, on the basis that since it was happening anyway there should be effective legal safeguards for all parties involved, and its original manifesto said: 'the provision for legal adoption is greatly needed. This would tend to assist in the care and rearing of illegitimate and deserted children where other means are unavailing.' It warned of the danger of impulsive adoptions:

> In some cases this desire for a child is a temporary one, prompted by caprice or a flicker of maternal yearning, and the infant is regarded as a plaything of which the possessor ultimately tires. It is then returned in a damaged condition to the mother or charitable care.

Worse than this there are only too many cases in which the infant is desired, so that an unpaid drudge may be available later, or to gratify an instinct for cruelty.

In contrast, a well-looked-after adopted child may be at any time removed by its mother and 'often this claim is only a pretence and is based upon improper motives'.[106] Following on logically from these comments the Council was one of the few organisations supporting the legalisation of adoption which favoured making it compulsory to get a court order when a child was adopted. The system that was introduced under the 1926 Adoption of Children Act still left it up to the individual adopter to decide whether to make the adoption official.

3
Pressure for Government Action

The first conference on adoption

Adoption was not one of the most prominent issues after the First World War, but among those interested in child welfare it became an increasingly important one. The rapid growth of the two new adoption societies and their ability to attract publicity, coupled with the increase in illegitimacy at the end of the War,[1] gave adoption a much higher profile than in the past. A commentator attributed the increase in adoption to a number of reasons: a decrease in the number of cheap foster mothers as working-class women found more opportunities for easier work at higher wages; the shortage of housing accommodation and the preference given to lodgers who could pay higher rents and presented less inconvenience than babies; the 'loss of life during the War seems to have had the effect of accentuating natural love for children, and an increased desire on the part of childless couples of all classes to have children to care for has been noticed'; and also 'a definite desire on the part of unmarried mothers to place their children secretly and safely in ordinary family life'.[2]

Organisations interested in child welfare, and the societies involved in promoting adoption, began to press for adoption to be legalised. The welfare groups wanted what they saw as a growing practice to have some form of regulation imposed upon it, the adoption societies wanted adopting parents to be free from the fear of natural parents reclaiming their children when they became economically useful. An earlier argument for legalising adoption had focused on its potential role in combating baby farming by making it compulsory to sanction permanent fostering through the courts. However, provisions in the 1908 Children Act had already strengthened the regulation of those paid to care for children other than their own and it is not clear how the form of non-compulsory enabling adoption legislation now envisaged would have prevented baby farming. In any event this practice appears to have been in decline. In February 1919 a case was reported in Walton-on-Thames where nine foster children had been starved, two of them to death,[3] but post First World War 'baby farming' cases were often pathetic stories of abuse such as the complex tale, which appeared in September 1919 of a depressed alcoholic woman who wanted to look after babies but ended up neglecting them.[4]

On 12 November 1919 representatives of various organisations interested in adoption came together at a conference 'to discuss the question of the desirability of the Adoption of Infants', organised by the Associated Societies for the Care and Maintenance of Infants. Papers were presented, discussion ensued and a wide range of opinions aired, and it was resolved to set up 'a small chosen Committee' to look into the matter.[5] The Committee included a number of representatives of various child welfare and women's organisations, together with the two main adoption societies, the National Adoption Society and the National Children Adoption Association, and was chaired by Adeline, Duchess of Bedford. The Committee took its brief extremely seriously, holding fourteen sittings, sending welfare groups a questionnaire on adoption to which it received seventy-six replies and receiving evidence from thirteen organisations.[6] Its five terms of reference were centred mainly on the role of the newly active adoption societies:

1. To consider whether Adoption is right in principle, and if so, within what limits.
2. To consider whether the formation of Adoption Societies is desirable.
3. To consider whether the complete separation of the mother from her child, as practised by existing Adoption Societies, is desirable or justifiable, and whether the safeguards adopted by the Societies or individuals are adequate and effective.
4. To consider the dangers that may arise from Societies or individuals arranging for the adoption of children, and receiving money for so doing which is not applicable for the benefit of the children so adopted.
5. To consider how far Adoption should be subject to statutory restrictions or safeguards.[7]

The evidence submitted to this Committee from all the organisations, ranging from the Church Army and the Charity Organisation Society to the National Council for the Unmarried Mother and Her Child and the Diocesan Associations for Rescue and Preventive Work, showed a strong consensus of opinion that adoption was undesirable except in 'exceptional circumstances'. Agencies such as the Church and Salvation Armies often used what would now be termed a kind of 'open adoption' in which a child would be fostered on a long-term basis but the mother would remain in contact with it. They were firmly against complete separation of mother and child, for a variety of reasons: mainly the likelihood of encouraging immoral behaviour in the women and the potential insecurity for the children. Caution about adoption at this time seems to have been a prevalent attitude across the political spectrum, not just in the welfare sector. For example, *The Times'* response to the Associated Societies' report was clear that 'Adoption in fact is a last resort, and the reasons against any extended system of the practice are many and cogent. It is a remedy and not a preventive.'[8] And the following year, in response to the Hopkinson Report (see below) the feminist journal, *Time and Tide,* argued for compulsory registration of adoption when it occurred, but called for 'a fair balance ... between the rights of the real and the adopting parents'. It 'applauded' the Report for its 'emphatic recommendation against severance on merely economic grounds' and suggested the 'corollary would seem to be endowment of parenthood'.[9]

Most witnesses to the Associated Societies' Committee were also not in favour of agencies specifically dedicated to arranging adoptions and felt that 'the existing child-saving societies are ample'.[10] Both the adoption societies insisted that they believed the mother should keep her child if possible. The NCAA said it only dealt 'with exceptions – but there are thousands of exceptions'.[11] The NAS also said it urged mothers to keep their children if they could, although its Chairman initially suggested:

> It is common experience that large families tend to be born to people who are least able by financial position, education and training to bring them up properly. It would in his view be better, therefore, that the excess of these families should be taken by persons who really desire children and have not got them. This distribution of families, or what would be called by some the breaking up of the family, would be good for the child if the child were given a better environment, material and moral, than its own family environment.[12]

The Committee's Report briefly considered both 'adoption' by Poor Law Guardians, and the placement of emigrated children with Canadian farmers which was sometimes called adoption. They decided that neither of these was adoption in the sense that they were considering. And the long-term fostering arrangements made by agencies like Dr Barnardo's they deemed only *limited adoption*. What they defined as *complete adoption*, in terms of a final severance between the child and its natural parent or relative, was only carried out by the adoption societies and a number of individuals. The Report noted the rapid expansion of both societies' work, and the vast number of applications they received from both would-be adopters and would-be relinquishing mothers, but its conclusion was not so much that this showed they fulfilled a vital need, but that it was the 'wide publicity afforded to these new schemes' which led to their inundation:

> It is not unnatural to suppose that relatives of the unmarried mother who have hitherto assisted her to support her child should seek to avail themselves of the proffered relief, or that the girl should be tempted to part with her child, having persuaded herself that she is acting in its interest and her own.[13]

The Report concluded that adoption should only be practised, 'in exceptional cases in which the separation of mother and child is practically inevitable'; that it would not appreciably diminish the number of illegitimate children because many were unsuitable for adoption; that publicising the advantages of adoption inevitably increased the demand; that all adoptions should be regulated by Statute; and that

> the formation of voluntary associations for promoting or effecting adoptions is undesirable, for the reason (amongst others) that their existence tends to encourage young mothers to part lightly with their children before their maternal feelings have been fully developed, and to increase immorality by fostering a sense of irresponsibility in the parents of illegitimate children.[14]

The NAS and NCAA representatives on the Committee agreed to all the other conclusions, but, not surprisingly, disassociated themselves from this one, asserting that 'we are of the opinion that the Societies we represent offer valuable safeguards against unsuitable adoption and foster-mothers.[15] The final conclusion (which they did accept) was that 'if and as long as such voluntary associations continue their activities they should be officially registered, and should be made subject to some form of public control'.[16]

So in many ways the main concern of this first, albeit unofficial, report was about the way in which the adoption societies were run, rather than emphasising the need for legislation around adoption itself. In fact it was over fifteen years before there was any official move to investigate the adoption societies, and regulation was not introduced until 1943. Debate over the next few years also steered firmly away from making it compulsory to record all adoptions; even bringing in enabling legislation was controversial. It is curious that the adoption societies avoided official scrutiny for so long, as there was a low rumble of criticism about their methods from their inception. It may have been because those concerned about adoption had to devote so much energy to the legalisation process but also because the main adoption societies, particularly the NCAA, acquired and maintained powerful and aristocratic supporters; and their energy and talent for publicity (as the Associated Societies' Report admitted) meant that they skated over much of the potential criticism.

The Hopkinson Committee

In March 1920 a deputation from the National Council of Women[17] met with the Coalition Government's Home Secretary, Edward Shortt,[18] and pressed the case for adoption. The NCW had not been represented on the Associated Societies' Committee but had sent in evidence and had arranged its own conference on the subject with a number of interested welfare organisations on the 18 December 1919 which had resolved 'that the principle of adoption be recognised by the Law'.[19] The NCW argued that 'promiscuous adoption was going on which was fraught with danger for the child'. As representatives of a body 'largely composed of the housewives of the country, the mothers and the home-loving and home-making women' they said that 'the women of this country feel very keenly that the interests of children are often subservient in the case of adoption'.[20] They were certainly not proselytizers for adoption and produced stories of callous adopting parents casting their children aside, for example:

> people with a great deal of money … had the child for nearly two years and at the end of that time they changed their mind. They had adopted the child from a workhouse and … they proposed to return the child to the workhouse without making a farthing provision in any monetary sense.[21]

The Home Secretary replied that 'the subject has been raised a good many times, and was not entirely non-contentious', but said he would consider the suggestion of the leader of the deputation, Sir J. G. Butcher, that he set up a committee to investigate it.[22] In May during the debate on the second reading of Neville Chamberlain's Bastardy Bill he said that

> he believed that by a system of carefully guarded and legalised adoption a great deal could be done [for illegitimate children], and that was a matter which at the present moment was taking up a great deal of his time and consideration. He was considering the personnel of a Committee which he hoped shortly to set up to go into the whole question of legalised adoption in this country. It was not an easy matter, but was one of great importance.[23]

In August 1920 Mr Shortt announced the composition of this Committee.[24] It was chaired by Sir Alfred Hopkinson and its members included Neville Chamberlain MP, Lady Priscilla Norman, Miss Lilian Russell, James A. Seddon MP and Frederick Sherwood (see Biographical Notes for information about the Committee members). Their brief was to consider 'whether it is desirable to make legal provision for the adoption of children in this country, and if so, what form such provision should take'.[25] They held twenty-one sittings, heard twenty-six witnesses and received a number of memoranda.

From the evidence presented to the Hopkinson Committee it becomes clear that the debate over adoption was not just about finding homes for unwanted children. It was also about the issues of illegitimacy and unmarried mothers and the attitudes taken by society towards them. There are no official figures for pre-1926 adoptions, and in 1920 there were still war orphans, but the majority of adoptees appear to have been illegitimate (at least 75 per cent of the adoptions arranged by the NCAA, even just after the War, were of illegitimate children).[26] As described in the first chapter the number of illegitimate births had gone up during the First World War both in real numbers and proportionately – and the mortality rate during the first year of life was more than double those of legitimate births. The evidence of Mrs H. A. L. Fisher, Chairman of the National Council for the Unmarried Mother and Her Child was broadly representative of opinion. The Council favoured adoption being put on a proper legal footing because of its experience with difficult cases. Mrs Fisher said they had several cases where 'mothers have arranged for the adoption of their children and have had the children back on their hands under circumstances of great difficulty and trouble',

Figure 3.1 Sir Alfred Hopkinson, 1928 (from the ©National Portrait Gallery, London)

and the Council was 'always having trouble with adopting parents'.²⁷ Conversely, she herself had personal experience of cases where natural parents wanted their child back long after it was adopted either because it was of wage earning age or very pretty.

Mrs Fisher was clear 'that we do not regard [adoption] at all as a solution of the problem of illegitimacy. We think in the interests of the child, the mother and child should be kept together'. She said that the NCUMC believed

> that the attitude in the past has been far too much in favour of saying that the thing to do was to whisk away the child from the mother

and provide the mother with work. Our experience has been that very frequently the result of that course is that there is another child to keep a year or two afterwards, because the psychological moment has been lost for developing a sense of responsibility. Her instincts have been stifled and another illegitimate child is the result.[28]

The only cases where they would sanction adoption were exceptional ones: illegitimate orphans; illegitimate children born in wedlock where the husband would not support another man's child ('although it is astonishing how many men are willing to accept the child'); and cases where the mother was 'definitely either morally or physically ill'. Mrs Fisher said she herself 'should be sorry to adopt such a child, but they have to be provided for'.

Most of the witnesses before the Hopkinson Committee shared the views of the NCUMC to a greater or lesser degree. Mr S. Cohen, the spokesman for the Jewish Association for the Protection of Girls and Women, was also 'opposed to [adoption] on general grounds', but would rather regulate it than prevent it. It was not, he explained, part of Jewish culture for parents to part readily with their children. He described the work of his organisation in trying to keep unmarried mothers with their children by helping them financially, training them and then finding them jobs.[29] Commissioner Adelaide Cox of the Salvation Army explained that they also tried to keep them together, encouraging adoption only where children were orphaned or their mothers quite unable to look after them. She explained that it was now very hard to find foster mothers (a point made by other witnesses): 'No one is going to be troubled to take care of a little baby who can earn treble as much money without so much trouble'. So whereas foster mothers once would have looked after illegitimate children during the day or boarded them for a few months while their mothers worked, the Army now had to look for other solutions. Unmarried mothers could go to one of their homes (six in London) where they could live until they went to the mothers' (maternity) hospital to have the baby. They then returned to the home where they lived and fed their babies for as long as they wished to stay – on average about four months as they usually wished to get back to work as soon as possible.[30]

Some witnesses hoped that legalising adoption would make it more difficult. 'The easy adoption of the first illegitimate child is a definite and distinct temptation to the mother ... tending to make it more easy for her to fall a second time',[31] was the opinion of Dr Menzies, the Principal Medical Officer of Health at the County of London, but he expressed what many others believed, especially those working with unmarried mothers.³² Adoption was also considered too easy for adopters. Lady Henry Somerset (who looked after children in her home for the National Society for the Prevention of Cruelty to Children (NSPCC) and individuals) described a recent incident:

> A man came a little while ago to us and said he and his wife wanted to adopt a child and had we one for adoption? I said No, I had not. The next day he came back and said he had been to a bureau which had forty children, all of whom could have been adopted, and he could have picked out one and taken it away, but there was not one which happened to suit him. That is really putting it on a par with being able to buy a domestic pet of any kind.³³

The National Council of Women, represented by Mrs Edwin Gray and Miss Amelia Scott, also hoped that adoption legislation would lessen the number of adoptions. As Miss Scott said, it 'would not make it so easy for the mother, as she can do now, to hand a child over to be adopted without going into Court or taking any responsibility'.³⁴ Mrs Gray believed that there were far more adoptions going on than was generally thought: 'Anyone who is constantly at an infant welfare centre will know that'.³⁵

The two Clerks to Poor Law Guardians (quoted in Chapter 1) were generally negative about adoption. Tom Percival from the Tynemouth Union listed the children whose parents frequently sought to relinquish them:

- the illegitimate child whose unmarried mother could not keep it while she worked;
- the illegitimate child of a married woman whose husband would 'overlook her moral lapse' but would not have the child in the home;
- the illegitimate child of a soldier's widow who feared losing her pension;
- the illegitimate child whose mother subsequently married a man who at first agreed to take it on but when his own children were born found the position too difficult.

Those who sought to adopt he listed as:

- childless married couples;
- relatives of orphans;
- persons whose pity was aroused by the plight of an infant child of a friend or acquaintance;

- persons of facile emotions whose sympathies have been temporarily aroused by the blue eyes and curly hair of some little one. This class includes a type of impulsive or neurotic woman who is taken with a sudden fancy, which she as suddenly loses;
- persons desiring to adopt children for companionship (such as the wives of seafaring men) or to use them as 'little drudges'(for which reason all applications to adopt children over ten years of age should be viewed with suspicion).[36]

Miss Puxley, representing the Maternal and Child Welfare department at the Ministry of Health, questioned 'whether it is desirable to take a large number of children away from their mothers',[37] even though her department gave an annual grant to the National Children's Adoption Association hostel in Kensington under its Maternity and Child Welfare Act powers and she thought the home was run very well. She said giving the grant 'does not mean that we necessarily approve of the system' and admitted that although Miss Andrew 'has been to see us constantly ... I think she has never been able quite to convince us that sufficient care is taken [with adoption procedures]'.[38] Miss Puxley expressed concern about the adoption societies' focused solely on 'wholesale adoption' when in her view it was clearly preferable to keep the mother and baby together except in special cases, and she said the Ministry's medical officers, including Sir George Newman and Miss Campbell, agreed with her. She saw no reasons other than financial ones why babies could not stay with their mothers if they were illegitimate. She suggested providing working women's hostels for unmarried mothers and said that there had been discussions under the aegis of the late Permanent Secretary of the Ministry of Health, Sir Robert Morant, about some kind of grant to enable mothers to keep their babies but since he died this had lapsed. She concluded: 'It really amounts to mothers' pensions, which is an extraordinarily big question and is rather held now to depend on a reform of the Poor Law.'[39]

The idea of 'mothers' pensions' or some financial help to enable unmarried mothers to keep their children was mentioned in vague terms by several other witnesses. The Principal London MOH, Dr Menzies, suggested subsidising the unmarried mother until she was in a position to earn a livelihood, or perhaps allowing local councils to contribute towards the costs of fostering.[40] The reforming Metropolitan Police Magistrate, W. Clarke Hall, believed that 'almost any individual home is better than the best institution', and was in favour of adoption – but only as long as it was not used as a solution to the question of the unmarried mother and her child for whom he believed the best solution 'would be to have pensions for mothers, whether the children were legitimate or illegitimate'.[41]

In 1918 the manifesto of the National Council for the Unmarried Mother and Her Child had called for schemes to provide accommodation and maintenance for unmarried mothers and their babies to be funded through central government, local authorities and voluntary fund-raising.[42] However as an idea it appears to have remained unformulated, and although some of the early twentieth-century socialists included maternity pensions among their demands and there was some discussion of them in Labour and Trade Union circles in the 1920s, the two ideas do not appear to have been linked. A Liberal introduced a motion in 1923 calling for pensions for widows or mothers with an incapacitated family breadwinner, and the Conservatives brought in the 1925 Widows', Orphans' and Old Age Contributory Act which paid out pensions to some widows and orphans but neither referred to unmarried mothers.[43] The main focus for helping low income families in the 1920s centred on the campaign for family allowances organised by Eleanor Rathbone and the Family Endowment Society and the debate over the 'family wage'.[44] Rathbone rarely mentions unmarried mothers and illegitimate children in her writing on the issue,[45] but in her major book, *The Disinherited Family* (first published in 1924), she did briefly discuss them, albeit in a fairly negative way. She said she shared the view of those 'who fear that if family allowances were freely granted to the mothers of illegitimate children, they would tend to raise the illegitimate birth-rate'. She continued:

> While it is true that society's treatment of the unmarried mother and her child has hitherto been harsh and unjust, there are surely more suitable and effective ways of remedying the injustice than through a scheme expressly devised to improve the quality of the nation's 'child supply' by giving the family a fuller recognition and a more assured and honourable status.
>
> ... it might be better to leave provision for the children of irregular unions as well as for the 'chance child' to the Poor Law, or whatever body, after its promised 'break up', has inherited those of its functions which are concerned with the care of children.[46]

It is not clear how far this viewpoint was shared by others in the family endowment movement and whether this affected the general lack of impetus around the idea of securing an income for unmarried mothers, in spite of the support evinced for it by various individuals and organisations. Clearly the 1920s were not a propitious time to gain widespread backing for such a campaign and on the whole it does not appear that there was any organised attempt to start one.

Another witness to the Hopkinson Committee, Metropolitan Police Magistrate, Cecil Chapman (who later became a vice president of the NCAA), also believed that an illegitimate child should be kept with the mother 'for the mother's sake. It is the only thing which keeps her at all human and straight'. The mothers should be taught skills to enable them to get jobs and support their babies and the putative fathers forced to take more responsibility. However he said he had changed his mind in favour of legalising adoption because now that 'the Societies have started to bring about adoption on a large scale, I feel almost that it is a necessity'. He said that he knew

> so many of the idle rich who have no children and whose lives are really spoilt from having nothing to do with their money or affections. It would do them an infinite amount of good to have children to look after if they felt inclined. I know a certain number who do feel inclined, but who do not do it because they do not understand what the law would be ... they cannot get a child without the feeling that the mother or father might break into their drawing room at any moment and claim the child, to the scandal of their neighbours.[47]

Discussion about illegitimacy with the Committee's witnesses led on to consideration of their attitudes towards secrecy. The adoption agencies established during and just after the War saw secrecy as an essential part of the way they worked. Like other pioneers of new practices, the adoption society leaders like Clara Andrew were utterly convinced of the rightness of what they did and saw secrecy as a vital part of it. The concept of 'secrecy' meant not just that the legal proceedings be secret but also that the natural parent should know nothing about the adopting family – above all that she should not know where her child was going. She could inquire subsequently whether her child was alive and well but would receive no other information. Miss Andrew was adamant that all classes were against people knowing they had adopted their children, even if it was more important for the upper classes:

> Miss Andrew: ... I remember the first adoption I ever did was in Devonshire. Some worthy people took the child. The man had been a small merchant skipper. They were people of very small means, but

very respectable. They said they had a fight all the time to prevent their neighbours knowing how they got the child. They said it was no business of anybody's to know it was not a relation of their own. Of course, all the adopters like to take home a baby and pretend it is a relative of some sort.

Lady Norman [member of Hopkinson Committee]: They call it a niece or something like that, do they not?

Miss Andrew: Yes. The better class the adopters are the more determined they are about that matter.[48]

And when she was asked if it was right 'to help people to enter into contracts which tend to destroy the identity of the child and its origin and to hide it from its mother?', she replied: 'Yes; I think certainly in all illegitimacy and cruelty cases the best thing that can happen is that the child's identity should be hidden'.[49] However, she also believed that the child should be told as soon as possible that it had been adopted and said that 'if it will give it any happiness' it can be told who its parents were.[50] The adoption societies were not so concerned about the adopting family having knowledge of the birth mother. The NCAA allowed them to know the mother's name and let them see papers relating to the child's origins.[51]

The witness after Miss Andrew was Miss Peto, who had adopted seven children herself since 1908 (and arranged adoptions for other people), who told how she had above all a horror of revealing to her children that they were illegitimate. She told them that their parents were dead. She told their schools the same – otherwise, she said, 'they would not have been accepted, or would be expelled'.[52] A few years later, as adoption legislation came closer, an adopting parent, Charles Singer, wrote to a member of the second committee on adoption, pleading for secrecy of proceedings to be included in the bill, as 'no far-seeing adopter, with the interests of his child in mind, would exchange secrecy for legal status'.[53]

W. Clarke Hall agreed with Miss Andrew 'that at the point of adoption the whole past history of the child should be shut down: that is, that when a child is adopted, its life from that time should begin *de novo*'.[54] Otherwise he felt that the fact the child was illegitimate would become known. Indeed he suggested that if no enquiries could be made about a child's birth the parents of illegitimate children could adopt them themselves. The witness brought in to explain American adoption processes, R Newton Crane, was horrified by the idea of telling an adopted child of its origins.

Personally that is abhorrent to me. If it were done under certain circumstances I can imagine it would make a very great disturbance in the mind of the child ... In the majority of cases I should say the child does not know, in fact, that it is not the child of the adoptive parents.

When questioned, he dismissed the likelihood of incestuous marriage: 'In that case I have no doubt whatever there would be a revelation to the child of the impossibility of such a marriage.'[55]

However, not all the Committee witnesses supported this stance. Mrs R. P. Wethered from the Associated Societies for the Care and Maintenance of Infants felt, like many of the other witnesses, that legalised adoption was an unfortunate necessity, but she believed it to be 'a very serious thing to cut anyone off from their blood relations'.[56] Considering the issue from the point of view of the child rather than the relinquishing or adopting parents, she believed that children should be told they were adopted and should later have the right to find out their history: 'I think you will find all experienced workers will say the same ... After all you give a child away in adoption, but when it gets to be a man or a woman, I think you must let them have that information.'[57] Commissioner Cox of the Salvation Army favoured telling children they were adopted from an early age but not encouraging them to contact their natural parents.

In general the witnesses coming from a senior legal or judicial position were far less likely to see a reason for secrecy once legislation was passed. This appeared to be less out of consideration for the psychological needs of children, or birth parents' desire for continuing knowledge of their children, or even a reluctance to end the inalienability of parental rights which was so much a part of English Common Law,[58] but more a brusque inability to understand why, on an emotional level, adopting families might continue to desire secrecy. His Hon. Judge Edward Abbott Parry had experience of sanctioning schemes for the adoption of orphans who received payments under the Workmen's Compensation Act and could see no point in shrouding the procedure in secrecy: 'I do not much like the idea of hiding up things; I am rather against that. There might be some reasons why the adoption should not take place, and it might be that the people locally ought to know of it'. He doubted that it was possible to keep adoption secret. 'The child is going into a new household and going to be taken over by childless people, say. They may say it is a niece or nephew, if you like: but as a matter of fact, the whole street will know all about it very quickly'.[59]

Another witness, H. B. Drysdale Woodcock, a barrister and Recorder, who had retired as chairman of the National Adoption Society due to ill health, took a similar line despite his earlier links with the NAS which was firmly in favour of secrecy. He believed that secrecy was only necessary when new parents could be blackmailed – once adoption was legalised it would cease to be a relevant issue.[60] And an expert on comparative law, Ernest J. Schuster LLD, who discussed European laws, property rights and the rights of unmarried fathers with the Committee, saw no reason why in most cases the natural mother should not know where and with whom her child was; any attempt to 'blackmail' adoptive parents would be contempt of court and could be dealt with as such.[61]

The question of secrecy linked directly into one of the other main issues the Hopkinson Committee discussed with the witnesses. This was a consideration of the mechanism for regulating adoption if it was made a legal entity. Miss Andrew was again at one end of the spectrum of opinion. She wanted a binding legal agreement but not through the County or magistrates' courts because of the need for secrecy; only the High Court, being set apart from local courts, would be acceptable. In an answer to a query from a Committee member as to whether there could be a two-tier system with 'fastidious' people going to London to the High Court and others using the local county court, Miss Andrew was adamant that 'even the working people would rather go to another town'.[62] As for the upper classes, she said:

> I went down to see a child last week which was adopted twelve months ago by some county people – some hunting people. They said to me, 'If we had to go into a court, even a magistrate's room, to have this legalised, we would not do it. We would give up the child rather than that it should be known that she came through a society'.[63]

Other witnesses coming from a 'welfare' background expressed no preference about which courts should be used but the senior judicial and legal witnesses favoured the County Courts. His Hon F. R. Yonge Radcliffe saw no reason why County Courts should not deal with adoption cases as they were already used to dealing with applications under the Workmen's Compensation Act. The two magistrates preferred Courts of Summary Jurisdiction (magistrates' courts) as the legal setting for adoption as these courts had facilities to make enquiries about the cases – in comparison to County Courts where the judge 'was only in town for a few hours'.[64] Other witnesses felt that using magistrates' courts would associate adoption too closely with the criminal system.

Differing views were expressed about the necessity for continuing supervision and about whether adoption orders should be revocable. The NCAA did not inspect families either before or after adoption although Miss Andrew claimed that if she was in the locality of an adopting family she would drop in 'and I have never once had a cold reception'. Although she was content for the Association's hostels to be inspected she was firmly against the idea of state inspection of adopting families which would be seen by people as 'interfering with the sanctity of home life'.[65] A Committee member, Mr Seddon, suggested that working-class people would demand inspections if adoption was legalised: 'The memory of children taken from workhouses in Lancashire particularly, is very bitter and deep from generation to generation,'[66] but Miss Andrew was unconvinced: 'If you call it friendly visiting, I do not mind. If it is inspection, it would ruin our work, because even the poor man is proud,'[67] She was confident that the public, 'especially the working man,' was behind their work. Her philosophy was simple:

> [O]ne point I want to elaborate, and that is that the children do so much better after they are adopted than they do in institutional life. The matron and I have got some statistics. Even the children who have gone into working class homes have made weight faster than they did in our hostel. That seemed to us an incredible thing. It simply shows that the individual love and attention make up for lack of scientific feeding.[68]

Miss Andrew said that when it had been necessary, NSPCC inspectors had visited homes. A Committee member, Mrs Russell, pointed out that the house might be unsuitable without it actually being bad enough to warrant NSPCC action. Miss Andrew briskly dismissed this: 'There are hundreds of homes which are quite unsuitable. I think the adopted child has got to stand a little, like the child who is born to people'.[69] The National Council of Women representative took a similar standpoint against the need for inspections post-adoption. In written evidence she argued that adopted children should not be singled out and could be left to the existing safeguards such as health visitors and local education authorities. There would be no more risk to them than for other children and probably less, as their parents will have been 'carefully selected which is more than can be said of ordinary parents'.[70]

Other witnesses were in favour of continuing inspection. Miss Peto advocated it 'because if you do not do that, the children are so often adopted in order to get unpaid drudgery'.[71] Salvation Army officers inspected the children who were adopted through them but did not wear uniform to make their presence less obvious. In cases where foster parents adopted their charges Barnardo's retained the right to continue inspections. Lady Somerset felt there should be continuing supervision of adopted children as family circumstances might change, for example the wife might die. The two Clerks to Poor Law Guardians argued for a legal compulsion to visit adopted children four times a year 'because if a child is unhappy it is none too frequent to ascertain whether there are any changes going in its treatment'.[72]

In its memorandum to the Committee the NSPCC stated that continuing inspections were essential to prevent abuse and criticised the lax practice of adoption societies who transferred babies to adopting parents at railway stations without making any visit to their homes. The NSPCC's Director, Robert J. Parr, presented a dossier of the 622 cases affecting 764 'adopted' children it had dealt with over the past two years.[73] The Hopkinson Committee presumably took the question of continuing inspection quite seriously (although they did not eventually recommend it), because they interrogated Miss Puxley of the Ministry of Health about the class of those who might carry these out. They asked if health visitors would be 'superior' enough for the well-to-do 'villa class – the class of people who might not wish their neighbours to know too much about the adoption?'[74]

Most of those who were asked about abrogation of an adoption order were against adoptive parents being able to do this, although Lady Somerset considered that the authorities should retain the right to terminate an adoption which was perhaps the logical outcome for those who favoured continuing inspection of adopted children. There was a general feeling that if parents took on a child it was 'for better or worse', although Miss Andrew said the NCAA had taken three children back from the adopters after the probation period when the child had in theory been permanently adopted. She was not asked why this had happened.

The Hopkinson Report

In April 1921, in response to a question from Neville Chamberlain (one of the Hopkinson Committee members) in a debate in the House of Commons, the Home Secretary Mr Shortt affirmed that he had received the Report of the Departmental Committee on Child Adoption and would be publishing it.[75] In June that year the Under Secretary at the Home Office, Sir J. L. Baird, reported that the Report had been published but that he was as yet in no position to make any statement about legislation.[76]

The Committee summed up the evidence it heard as falling into three areas: the current situation in England regarding adoption (with evidence from voluntary workers and government and local authority officials); proposals and comments from the judiciary and the authorities who might deal with a system of legalised adoption; adoption legislation in other countries. In its report the Committee concluded that for children

> for whom their natural parents provide no proper home, it is as a rule very much better to place them in some other home as members of a family ... than that the children should be gathered together in an institution with a number of others. Cases of clearly marked serious physical or moral defects are generally best provided for in institutions, but family life should be the normal condition.[77]

The Committee decided that this desire to place a child in a 'family home' when the only alternative was institutional life was one of the reasons for the growth in adoption; together with the increasing tendency to value 'child life'[78] and desire the companionship of a child; and finally because 'some women are without the mother sense, or for some other reason, such as economic pressure or a desire for greater personal liberty, are unable or unwilling to carry out the obligations they should feel towards their children'.[79] This is an interesting conclusion, but the evidence presented to the Committee does not really give weight to it, unless it refers to unmarried mothers whose impossible financial situation was commented on by many witnesses.

In common with many of the witnesses who appeared before it, the Committee urged caution before rushing to wholesale adoption. It stated as 'principles' that

1. Nothing should be done to impair the sense of parental responsibility or, unless essential to prevent injury to the child, to interfere with rights and duties based on the natural tie between parent and child. This applies not only to legitimate but also to illegitimate children and
2. The mother and her child, whether legitimate or illegitimate, ought not to be severed unless for strong reasons in order to secure the welfare of the child, and all possible encouragement should be given to the efforts of philanthropic persons who seek to avert such severance taking place solely on economic grounds.

This will involve the consideration of the question of assisting necessitous mothers in the bringing up of their children by some form of allowance, where there is no father contributing to their support.
3. Nothing should be done to discourage voluntary efforts made by societies and individuals to help neglected or orphaned children.[80]

These are clear statements and indeed there was considerable consensus among the witnesses. Every witness felt that adoption should be legalised in some form but many, with the obvious exception of the adoption societies, were not especially keen to encourage the practice on a wide scale. Few were particularly concerned about the precise form it should take, although the arguments about the appropriate court would continue, and contribute to the delays in effecting legislation.

The Hopkinson Report was a more detailed document than the later Tomlin report which went over similar ground five years later. In considering evidence from other countries, it dismissed that from 'continental countries' (except for Scandinavia) as 'based on ideas with regard to the family and other social conditions which differ in important matters from those that obtain here', but concluded that the 'adoption of children does receive legal recognition in almost all civilised states'.[81] It attached 'great importance' to legislation in English-speaking countries, especially the USA, where Massachusetts had first passed adoption legislation in 1851 and had been followed by 48 states, and His Majesty's Dominions including Australia (where the state of Western Australia had legislated in 1896), Canada and New Zealand. The Committee discussed the current situation in England and Wales and concluded that adoption was inevitable, had grown extensively and would continue to increase, and that it was better to regulate it than leave it unfettered. On the whole the Committee was fairly positive about adoption, seeing it as preferable to life in an institution, although citing the NSPCC's evidence about cruel and neglectful adoption cases.[82] It also cautioned strongly against economic necessity forcing mothers to give up their children for adoption.

The legal provisions it suggested were relatively simple. Sanction should rest with a 'regular judicial authority' rather than a local authority or administrative department, and it had to be local as many applicants would be people 'of small means'. The main court would be the County Court with its facilities for keeping good records, its Standing Committee for framing rules and its distance from the criminal system. Concurrent jurisdiction would go to the High Court. There were lists of those to be consulted, and those to give consent, including the child itself if over fourteen, and in all cases 'the Judge, or some suitable and responsible person acting on his behalf, should see the child and if it is of sufficient age and intelligence, ascertain its feelings, and consider its inclinations'.[83] Both natural parents of a legitimate child would have to consent but only the mother when the child was illegitimate, although the views of its father should be considered where the parentage was admitted or proved and he contributed to the child's support. There were also instances where consent could be dispensed with; for example where the parent could not be found or had abandoned the child or was incurably insane or guilty of cruelty or neglect of the child.

Those who could adopt were married couples jointly if over 25, a married person with the consent of their spouse if the adopter was over 30 and single men or women over 30. Adopters should not – except with the Judge's discretion – be less than 20 years older than the adopted child. Judges would have to satisfy themselves that all relevant consents were obtained, that the proposed adopter was of good character and was a suitable potential parent and that 'the proposed adoption is likely to promote the true welfare of the child'.[84] They were given a wide discretion in deciding suitability but it was suggested that two references should be provided from responsible people, and a personal interview with the adopting parents should be carried out by an official person, probably female, possibly a public health officer, infant welfare officer or voluntary social worker.[85]

The Report recommended that judges make initial interim orders of three to four months but that when finalised there should be no further need for inspection unless the judge felt there were special grounds for doing so. If the child had property the judge should be able to make allowances from it for the child's maintenance, education and safekeeping. The religion of a child 'as a rule' should be that of the natural parent or that in which the child had been brought up. Once the adoption order was sanctioned the relationship between the adopter and adopted was to be 'the same as those of the natural parent and child'.[86] The adopted person would have the rights of a natural child regarding the property of the adopter (mainly in regards to intestacy) but not in relation to the property of the adopter's relatives. The adopted parents would have similar rights in the case of the child's intestacy but the adopted child would retain the right of succession in the case of the natural parents' intestacy.

The 1920s – an era of legislative reform

As pressure grew for legislative action on adoption it is worth looking at the parliamentary context in which the campaign would operate. The 1920s were not traditionally seen as a great decade of legislative reform but in fact many laws were passed affecting aspects of domestic life and family and personal relationships and the pressure for adoption legislation and its eventual enactment can be seen within this context. Recently there has been renewed debate over the significance of all this legislative activity. Previously industrial relations and foreign policy were seen as the defining features of the 1920s; for example, A. J. P. Taylor's Oxford History of the era mentions housing and education but has virtually no reference to any domestic legislation except for women getting the vote.[87] The reclamation of this side of the 1920s has been part of historiographical rethinking about feminism and the women's movement during these years. Joanne Workman has described the original critique of the women's movement after 1918: 'Once partial enfranchisement was attained feminists are charged with abandoning activism, maintaining only a semblance of a movement until 1928 when, with the attainment of complete suffrage, the movement collapsed'.[88] There was criticism among women activists themselves at the time for what some considered a damaging concentration on domestic issues, encouraging the reinforcement of women's traditional role. For example, Winifred Holtby distinguished herself from the 'new feminists' like Eleanor Rathbone who campaigned for family allowances: 'while the inequality exists, while injustice is done and opportunities denied to the great majority of women, I shall have to be a feminist, and an Old Feminist, with the motto Equality First.'[89]

However, viewed from hindsight it is less clear that this division, 'between old "equal rights" feminists fighting for full gender equality and "new" "welfare" feminists concerned with more limited social improvements in women's lives', was as deep as it was perceived by women like Holtby and by later historians because 'these goals could be held simultaneously and were complementary'.[90] *Time and Tide*, the journal in which Holtby was writing about her beliefs and which was founded and edited by the then still militant suffragist, Lady Rhondda, strongly supported the Six Point Group whose points included 'satisfactory legislation' on child assault, for the widowed mother and for the unmarried mother and her child, and equal rights for guardianship for married parents, as well as equal pay for teachers and equal opportunities for men and women in the civil service. Those who campaigned for these measures included women activists across the political spectrum, and by the end of the 1920s there had been considerable – if not completely 'satisfactory' – legislation on at least the first four points. In fact as Pat Thane pointed out, 'at least twenty-three pieces of legislation were passed between 1918 and 1930 for which women's groups lobbied because they believed that they would promote gender equality'.[91] Thane herself had 'no doubt that more women, from a wider range of backgrounds, were actively campaigning for gender equality in the nineteen-twenties and thirties than before the First World War'.[92]

However, not all historians are convinced that this legislation was more than a reinforcement of women's traditional role. For example, Martin Pugh agreed that the amount of legislation passed in the 1920s was considerable but saw it as more about the move towards domesticity in this period discussed in Chapter 1; 'the bulk of the legislation is linked by a common theme: it bears upon the role of women, in a legal and material sense, as mothers and wives. This was undoubtedly the perspective through which most politicians preferred to view women'.[93]

The legislation included measures to equalise the rights to sue for divorce between men and women, to equalise the property rights of married men and women and guardianship rights over children, the introduction of state pensions for widows and orphans, raising and equalising the age of marriage for both sexes to sixteen and also the age of consent in cases of indecent assault, an increase in the maximum payable by fathers under affiliation separation orders, and the legitimation of children by the subsequent marriage of their parents (when both were free to marry at the time of their child's birth). Improvements were also legislated for in midwifery and nurse training and the care available to women and babies before, during and after childbirth. The Sex Disqualification (Removal) Act of 1919 at least theoretically outlawed discrimination in gender and marital status for entry to the professions and universities. It has been dismissed by some commentators for its failure to prevent discrimination over women's employment in occupations like teaching. However its enactment led to women being allowed into the professions which had previously refused to admit them – in particular both branches of the law – and also gave them the right to be magistrates and jurors. Other reforms included a more sympathetic treatment of infanticide and restrictions on young people buying alcohol. And in 1928, in an act 'promoted by the government for no particular reason'[94] and passed with relative ease, women were finally given the vote on the same basis as men.

The 1926 Adoption Act fits into this body of legislation. As we have seen, many agencies involved with women and children who were campaigning for the other reform measures supported it. For *Time and Tide*, the feminist journal mentioned above, adoption legislation was not a priority but it commented favourably upon it from time to time. It wrote of the Hopkinson report that 'The proposal that the whole matter [of adoption] should be brought under a regular judicial authority is ... eminently sane'.[95] Later it said of the Tomlin Committee's draft adoption bill that 'There is a strong feeling in a large section of the community that something ought to be done quickly to legalise the position of adoption in England, and the Bill suggested by the departmental committee is a sound one'.[96]

The legislation of the 1920s obviously owes much to the civil servants who had to draft the measures and steer them through Parliament. Supporters of adoption legislation were frequently critical of what they perceived as conservative obstructiveness in the civil service but the officials usually had considered reasons for taking things more slowly than the campaigners wanted. As will be shown in the next chapter, their notes and letters make it clear that they were often motivated by concern for the interests of vulnerable people, and reluctant to rush into far-reaching legislation without consideration of the consequences for all parties.

The years after the Hopkinson Report

The Hopkinson Committee also produced an Interim Report proposing legitimation of illegitimate children where their parents subsequently married. In February 1922 Mr Shortt, the Home Secretary, suggested that legislation to this effect would be brought in (although in fact the Legitimacy Act was not passed until 1926, the same year as the first Adoption of Children Act). However he felt that 'there appear to be very great difficulties in the way of carrying out the proposals for the legislation of adoption' and when – not unreasonably – he was asked by committee member Neville Chamberlain what these difficulties were, he replied that they were of 'a very complicated nature and they can hardly be given in reply to a supplementary question'.[97]

In his history of family law Stephen Cretney suggested that 'the Hopkinson Committee's Report was not well received within the Home Office or the Lord Chancellor's Office (LCO). But that did not make it any easier to resist demands from inside Parliament and outside for something to be done'.[98] Before it was published an official wrote: 'The report is not a very good one',[99] and behind the scenes the civil servants were unimpressed by the stated urgency for legislation. The Home Office reported that the Report had 'been very favourably received and several resolutions have been sent to the Home Office approving the Committee's findings' (from Boards of Guardians, the NSPCC and women's organisations),[100] but its officials were dubious from the beginning. In July 1921 S. W. Harris, then Assistant Secretary of the Children's Branch,[101] said:

> [t]he Committee do not appear to have taken any evidence as regards the administrative questions involved for the Lord Chancellor's Department or from the Home Office or Ministry of Health and I am not at all sure that their proposals are in any case sound from the administrative point of view.[102]

He admitted that 'there is a good deal of demand for legislation on this question' and suggested an interdepartmental conference to decide whether a Bill should be introduced and what form it should take.[103]

This conference was held in November 1921 with representatives from departments including the Home Office, the Lord Chancellor's Department, the Ministries of Pensions and Health and the Board of Education. It was called, said Sir Ernley Blackwell, Legal Under-Secretary at the Home Office,[104] 'to advise the Home Secretary whether the Government should introduce a Bill to legalise adoption, or in the event of a Private member putting forward a Bill, what the Government's attitude should be'.[105] It followed a deputation to the Home Office of adoption campaigners arguing for legislation, after which S.W. Harris circulated a memo about them:

> Although they talk a great deal of 'the legalisation of adoption' for the purpose of securing the position of the adopters and the rights of adopted children what they really have in mind is the satisfactory disposition of illegitimate infants and the prevention of mischief in connection therewith.[106]

At the start of the conference Sir Ernley Blackwell briefly summed up the Hopkinson Committee's recommendations but was dismissive of their arguments – he felt the proposals would 'do little or nothing to check the evils attendant upon the disposal of illegitimate children' and 'pointed out that the Committee regarded the legalisation of adoption as an urgent matter, but gave little or no information in support of their recommendation'.[107] Another high-ranking and powerful civil servant – Sir Claud Schuster,[108] the Principal Secretary to the Lord Chancellor – 'strongly opposed' the proposal to place adoption procedures within the County Courts saying that 'The County Court judge was as a rule neither qualified to form an opinion on the merits of these applications, nor had he any staff at his disposal for making necessary enquiries'.

Mr Kenneth Milne from the Ministry of Pensions explained that his ministry wished the foster parents of children whose fathers had been killed in the war to be exempt from any adoption legislation because the Ministry was responsible for these children and was 'anxious that the foster parents should not be able to obtain a legal right over the children which might deprive [the Ministry] of some of its powers'.[109] Mr Stutchbury, representing the Ministry of Health, did not want the powers of the Boards of Guardians disturbed – 'they worked fairly well at present'.[110]

Sir Ernley Blackwell concluded from these opinions that 'as far as can be judged from the matter in the Committee's report there is no real necessity for any measures legalising adoption'. The conference recommended legislation, as proposed by the Hopkinson Committee, to legitimate children born out of wedlock whose parents subsequently married, and said that there was a case for tightening up provisions of the Children Act 1908 regarding unauthorised adoptions which was already being looked at by the Ministry of Health.

So over the next three years the private members' bills on adoption which followed the Hopkinson Report were all blocked behind the scenes or failed in Parliament through lack of support. The first Bill was introduced in May 1922 by Reginald Nicholson, a Coalition Liberal MP.[111] The Bill was judged by an anonymous Home Office official to be 'delightfully simple but it ignores all the difficulties and it would be disastrous to let it pass.'[112] The Bill was amended in Standing Committee but fell at the dissolution of Parliament in October 1922.

During the following year two bills were introduced along similar lines – presented by Conservatives Sir Leonard Brassey[113] and Gerald Hurst.[114] The latter was seen as by a Home Office official as 'so far the best Bill … provides most of the safeguards recommended by the Committee',[115] but was criticised for its lack of guidance about religious persuasion and the name a child should take – and for its proposed use of the County Courts. The Lord Chancellor's Department refused to accept the duties it would have imposed.[116] The NSPCC also criticised these bills. Its Director, Robert Parr, wrote that they both dealt 'with the subject of adoption from the point of view of the person adopting'. He continued:

> Our anxiety centres round the child and our desire is that no adoption shall be sanctioned until the parties adopting have satisfied the

Court as to personal fitness and suitable home conditions. We desire further that reports at regular intervals should be submitted to the Court so that if any unsuitable person succeeded in obtaining a child the chances of its retention would be reduced.[117]

In the two years ending 30 April 1923 the NSPCC had dealt with 738 cases involving adopted children which resulted in 14 prosecutions.[118]

By now the Conservative Government was making it clear that it was not prepared to countenance legislation on the issue for the foreseeable future. The spokesman for the Home Secretary was adamant: 'I am afraid the Government cannot undertake to introduce legislation on this subject at the present time, and the pressure of Parliamentary business makes it impossible to give special facilities to a private Member's Bill.'[119] Later in the year when asked if the evidence and memoranda submitted to the Hopkinson Committee would be printed and published, he was definite that he did not feel the expense would be justified.[120]

In March 1924 two more Bills were introduced in the Commons. The Ulster Unionist MP Sir Malcolm Macnaghten's, was similar to Mr Hurst's, and Sir Thomas Inskip's was 'merely a bald provision for legalising adoption without any statutory safeguards or any of the necessary provisions as to property rights', according to Home Office notes.[121] Meanwhile the Duke of Atholl[122] was introducing a Bill in the House of Lords which the Home Office briefing said 'provides wholly illusory safeguards ... and many of its detailed provisions are open to serious criticism'.[123] All the private members' bills were deemed unacceptable because they proposed using the County Courts which did not have the resources to carry out proper enquiries.

Eight bills to legalise adoption were presented between the publication of the Hopkinson Committee Report in 1921 and the introduction of the bill which was finally passed in 1926. Of those presenting them, Reginald Nicholson was the executive chairman of the National Children Adoption Association when he introduced his bill, Sir Thomas Inskip was Hon. Counsel to the Association when he presented his. Gerald Hurst (later Sir Gerald) spoke at a major public meeting on adoption organised by the National Adoption Society in 1923 and later chaired the 1954 Parliamentary committee on adoption. He expressed strong support for adoption in his 1942 autobiography and called the 1926 Adoption Act 'a peculiarly blessed statute';[124] Sir Leonard Brassey's wife, Lady Violet, was a member of the Governing Body of the NCAA, and the Duke of Atholl's wife was, like him, an advocate for adoption, and hosted a fund raising charity ball for the NCAA shortly before he introduced his bill.[125] The adoption societies – particularly the NCAA – were very effective at lobbying and maintaining Parliamentary support despite the lack of enthusiasm from the civil service.

The civil servants, particularly those in the Home Office, the Ministry of Health and the Lord Chancellor's Office, appear to have accepted that adoption legislation was inevitable but felt that the proposals put forward were inadequate and likely to make for poor legislation. The officials were probably correct in seeing County Courts as a less satisfactory place for jurisdiction than the magistrates' courts which had more facilities for checking potential adopters. Certainly when both lower courts were given the right to carry out adoptions the public overwhelmingly chose to use magistrates' courts. The officials' concerns about altering intestacy rules and property rights were very cautious but adoption legislation was a very new departure. Above all, as will be discussed in the next chapter, it was the issue of secrecy which came to give rise to particular concern among the civil servants most involved with the adoption legislation.

As we saw in the evidence presented to the Hopkinson Committee, there was a consensus among the voluntary and statutory organisations that adoption should be legalised but there was little enthusiasm among them – apart from the adoption societies – for adoption as a concept. The feeling was rather that as adoption was happening on a wide scale it should be regulated, but the real priority was to find a way of enabling unmarried mothers to keep their babies and live respectable lives. It was above all the adoption societies who, with the help of their powerful supporters, ensured that the impetus around adoption legislation continued.

In this context the flurry of bills proposing legislation about adoption at the beginning of 1924 makes sense. The first Labour Government came into office on 22 January 1924 and adoption supporters would have felt it was worthwhile putting pressure on the new Government to include adoption legislation in its reforms. In fact, throughout the Coalition Government which ended in 1922, the Conservative Government 1922–4, the Labour Government of 1924 and indeed the Conservative Government which followed on at the end of that year, the governmental approach to legislation on child adoption was very consistent, probably because it was always directed behind the scenes by civil servants, particularly those in the Home Office and the Lord Chancellor's Department. The new Government's official response to these bills was to set up another committee to look into the issue of legalising child adoption.

4
Legislation Takes Shape

By March 1924 the civil servants obviously had their plans for another Committee well under way. As early as 8 March, Home Office notes were definite that all adoption bills were to be blocked 'in view of the decision of the Secretary of State to set up a Committee to enquire into this subject'.[1] (Although behind the scenes correspondence[2] between Sir John Anderson, the Permanent Secretary at the Home Office,[3] and Sir Claud Schuster at the Lord Chancellor's Department leaves it unclear whether the Home Secretary even knew about the decision.)

The decision to set up another Committee was precipitated by the Duke of Atholl's Bill in the House of Lords which was taken more seriously by the civil servants than the earlier bills even though they severely criticised it. Accompanying Home Office notes on this Bill conclude that

> [w]hile [the Government] are in favour of the principle of legalising adoption and would like to see a simple and effective means of securing that object, they do not see how a satisfactory Bill can be framed without further investigation. They propose, therefore at an early date to appoint a competent committee to take this work in hand. It is not proposed that the enquiry should be a lengthy one nor that the Committee should take a great deal of evidence as much of the ground has already been covered by the recent Committee and the Committee will have before it the various Bills that have been framed.[4]

Even the chief civil servant at the Home Office, Sir John Anderson, took an interest. Despite being 'always to some degree remote from the internal concerns of the (Home) Office', according to the official history of the department,[5] he was involved both in writing letters about the issue and, according to Home Office notes, took a personal role in choosing the members of the new Departmental Committee.[6]

The speedy announcement of the new Committee suggests that the civil servants felt something urgent must be done to take control of the issue if they were not to end up with confused and ill thought-out legislation. Lord Gorell asked specifically why the Government had set up another committee to inquire into child adoption. The briefing notes for this question suggest that the Government's policy did 'call for a little explanation' and admitted that 'as the appointment of a committee of enquiry has sometimes been used as a method of shelving an unattractive proposition the suspicion of those who are anxious to see some form of adoption legalised may have been aroused'.[7] It explained that no 'practicable legislation' had come out of the Hopkinson Report and detailed the failings of the private members' bills as described in the previous chapter. It was firmly asserted that

> the Government are in favour of the principle of legal adoption, but ... it is necessary to devise machinery which will enable adoption to be legalised by simple effective means and will at the same time secure the protection of the child from exploitation and safeguard its legal rights.[8]

The Tomlin Committee's report

The new Committee was officially appointed on 4 April 1924 by the Home Secretary, Arthur Henderson, with the brief 'to examine the problem of child adoption from the point of view of possible legislation and to report upon the main provisions which in their view should be included in any Bill on the subject'.[9] Its Chairman was Mr Justice Tomlin, recently appointed to the Chancery Division of the High Court and whose 'judgments and opinions are marked by learning, clear thinking, and lucidity of statement. The point at issue is always made clear and the right solution is sometimes made to appear obvious'.[10] Presumably it was hoped that this quality would be brought to the issue of adoption legislation.

Three of the other six Committee members were civil servants and the Secretary was Miss Enid Rosser from the Lord Chancellor's Office. S. W. Harris was the Home Office representative. He had been considerably involved with the issue of adoption over the previous few years and was the Head of the Children Department. M. L. Gwyer represented the Ministry of Health where he was Solicitor and Legal

Adviser, and W. R. Barker was from the Board of Education. One of the other members was the Duchess of Atholl MP, whose interest in the subject was demonstrated by her recent introduction of a Bill similar to her husband's to legalise adoption in Scotland,[11] although she was replaced by Mrs Eleanor Wilson-Fox when she became Parliamentary Secretary for education in the Conservative Government elected in November 1924. The last members were Miss Dorothy Jewson, a Labour MP concerned with women's issues, and Geoffrey W. Russell, a solicitor (see Biographical Notes for more details of the members). Although it had been suggested that the Tomlin Committee would not need to collect a great deal of evidence as this had been done by the earlier Committee, in fact it held more sittings and interviewed more witnesses than its predecessor. Witnesses from the major adoption societies and welfare organisations appeared before both committees, and judges, lawyers and magistrates were interrogated by both.

Reporting seven years after the end of the First World War, the Tomlin Committee was less convinced than its predecessor that there was a great popular demand for legislation on adoption. It published three reports and opened the First (and most substantial one) by explaining that

> we have been unable to satisfy ourselves as to the extent of the effective demand for a legal system of adoption by persons who themselves have adopted children or who desire to do so. It may be doubted whether any of such persons have been or would be deterred from adopting children by the absence of any recognition by the law of the status of adoption. The war led to an increase in the number of 'de facto' adoptions but that increase has not been wholly maintained. The people wishing to get rid of children are far more numerous than those wishing to receive them and partly on this account the activities in recent years of societies arranging systematically for the adoption of children would appear to have given to adoption a prominence which is somewhat artificial and may not be in all respects wholesome. The problem of the unwanted child is a serious one; it may well be a question whether a legal system of adoption will do much to assist the solution of it.[12]

It was dubious about the claims of the two groups agitating for adoption legislation. It was not convinced that natural parents were likely to interfere with adopters and seek to regain their children when they reached an age to earn and in any case 'the Courts have long recognised that any application by the natural parent to recover custody of his child will be determined by reference to a child's welfare and by that consideration alone'.[13] However it did accept that for reasons of sentiment there was a case 'for alteration in the law whereby it should be possible under proper safeguards for a parent to transfer to another his parental rights and duties, or some of them'.[14]

The other group of adoption supporters were 'those whose eyes were fixed upon the evils which result from traffic in children and who believe that the establishment of some form of legal adoption would diminish those evils'.[15] The Tomlin Committee was dismissive of these ideas. 'It is obvious that if there be a legal system of adoption it will not be resorted to by those persons whose transactions give rise to the greatest evils.'[16] They suggested this issue was best dealt with by improving statutes concerned with child protection such as the 1908 Children Act. In fact, in March 1925 the Committee's terms of reference were extended 'further to enquire into the working of the Children Act 1908, which deals with the protection of infant life and the visitation of voluntary homes and to report what changes, if any, in the law or its administration are required'.[17]

So with muted support for the idea of legislation, the Committee discussed the form it should take. It supported judicial sanction rather than alternatives such as a registration process through local authorities. Its stated reason for this was protection of vulnerable mothers:

> Inasmuch as many cases of adoption in fact have their origin in the social or economic pressure exercised by circumstances upon the mother of an illegitimate child, it is desirable that there should be some safeguard against the use of a legal system of adoption as an instrument by which advantage may be taken of the mother's situation to compel her to make a surrender of her child final in character though she may herself, if a free agent, desire nothing more than a temporary provision for it.[18]

This argument was expanded in the last paragraph of the Committee's draft Report which was eventually omitted from the final version. It considered the work of the adoption societies and signalled concerns about their activities. The omitted paragraph stated:

> [O]ur attention has been directed to the work of Adoption Societies. Many of these societies are operated by persons of integrity and good intentions, but we are not satisfied that their activities are entirely beneficial. Their work lies mainly in attempting to find permanent

homes for illegitimate children, and there is a substantial body of opinion which holds that efforts to facilitate the separation of mother and child are prima facie misdirected, or at any rate are not so worthy of support as efforts to assist the mother to a position in which she can retain and maintain the child.[19]

This is quite a strong criticism of the societies and it went on to query the societies' level of resources to organise inquiries about potential adopters and ensure the welfare of the children whose adoptions they arranged. It concluded that 'we think that the work and methods of these Societies are matters requiring closer examination and consideration than we have hitherto been able to give them'.[20]

A note from M. L. Gwyer (the Ministry of Health committee member) to S. W. Harris of the Home Office (also on the Committee) explained that the paragraph had been omitted as 'it is not easy to think of any effective remedy at all'. He said that he would like to prohibit payments or even contributions for adoption and would also like to see a registration process for adoption societies but that Judge Tomlin was against these suggestions.[21] A paragraph in an unpublished memorandum prepared by Gwyer on behalf of the committee spoke in strong terms about the more unscrupulous adoption societies:

> In some cases substantial sums of money are asked for and received, and the transaction often assumes the character of what we can call no less than the sale of the child. The possibilities of abuse which exist in any system of this kind are so manifest that we are convinced that they require the attention of Parliament.[22]

In this memorandum he wrote strongly that 'we feel bound to criticise certain of the methods followed, which seem to us open to grave objection and to involve risks not lightly to be incurred by any body of private individuals.'[23] Fundamental to the Committee's underlying concern about the role of the adoption societies was the societies' espousal of secrecy. Gwyer again expressed anxiety that although the welfare of the child is paramount to the societies, 'in many cases the welfare and interests of the mother are not sufficiently taken into account', and it might be better to spend time and energy reviving and encouraging 'the maternal instinct' and assisting her 'to maintain the child by her own efforts'.[24] The memorandum then described how the adoption societies' representatives 'laid great stress upon the necessity for securing an absolute and irrevocable break between the adopted child's past and future, and maintained as an essential part of their methods that the mother must never know the ultimate destination of her child'.[25]

The Committee did not agree with this practice. It described the way that the adopting parents were told of the child's antecedents, but that the mother 'is never brought face to face with the adopting parent and knows nothing of him or her'. It accepted that the societies were making every effort to satisfy themselves that the adopting parents were suitable:

> But we are unable to agree that any body of private persons, however well-intentioned, ought to ... be involved in the permanent and irrevocable separation of mother and child. The existence of the mother who parts unwillingly from her child under pressure of circumstances was fully admitted by the witnesses who appeared before us, and they did not deny the mental anguish and distress which is necessarily caused in such cases by the strict rule of secrecy.[26]

The adoption societies justified this policy by arguing that the child's interests were paramount and this was most likely to secure their best future interests 'even if this involves the sacrifice of the mother'. The memorandum was clear:

> We profoundly disagree; and we are not prepared to admit that the future of the child and the wish of the adopting parent for its companionship and society are to outweigh altogether the claims of a mother's natural love and affection for her offspring.[27]

Further, as the memorandum sensibly pointed out, 'there is the further risk of the loss of all evidence as to the child's real identity'. Even if, as the societies assured the Committee, they carefully preserved all their records, these would remain 'in private custody ... without any real guarantee or safeguard against destruction. This, again, is a responsibility which a private body of individuals ought not to be allowed to assume'.[28] This was a foresighted comment. A glance through a guide to adoption records quickly reveals that most of the societies' records of adoptions from the interwar period are untraceable – either destroyed in fires, damaged during the War, or simply missing.[29] As early as 1920, H. B. Drysdale Woodcock had warned of the danger of inadequate record keeping by the societies in his evidence to the Hopkinson Committee.[30] As a former chairman of the National Adoption Society (NAS) he presumably had first hand experience of the inadequacies of the society's administration.

In its published report the Tomlin Committee devoted a relatively long paragraph to the question of secrecy. Its emphasis was slightly different from the way it raised the issue in the unpublished memorandum: it was still very critical of the practice but not quite so bluntly against it. It described the way in which some of the adoption societies 'deliberately seek to fix a gulf between the child's past and future', and saw this policy as originating

> partly in a fear (which a legalised system of adoption should go far to dispel) that the natural parent will seek to interfere with the adopter, and partly in the belief that if the eyes can be closed to facts the facts themselves will cease to exist so that it will be an advantage to an illegitimate child who has been adopted if in fact his origin cannot be traced. Apart from the question whether it is desirable or even admissible deliberately to eliminate or obscure the traces of a child's origin so that it shall be difficult or impossible thereafter for such origin to be ascertained, we think that this system of secrecy would be wholly unnecessary and objectionable in connection with a legalised system of adoption and we should deprecate any attempt to introduce it.[31]

However, they accepted that it might be appropriate for adoption cases to be dealt with in legal settings where the public and press were not admitted and that there should be a limit on the rights of the public to have access to the Adoption Register which they proposed be set up.

Other proposals of the Tomlin Committee included an age difference between adopters and adopted of at least twenty years and a prohibition on anyone under twenty-five adopting. Married couples might adopt jointly or separately but in the latter case the other spouse must give consent. Joint adoption was only permitted for married couples. Unmarried women might adopt children of either sex, unmarried men could adopt male children but only female children in what a court deemed special circumstances. As for the age of the adopted child, most would be 'of tender years', but they saw no reason not to extend the right of adoption to all unmarried minors (i.e. under 21). It rejected the idea of enshrining a right of revocation which they saw as inconsistent with the idea of adoption as an irrevocable transfer of parental rights although it saw no reason why an adopted child might not be adopted by another family. It also recommended that a probationary period of up to two years should be fixed by the tribunal dealing with the adoption case. And the consent of the natural parents (or guardians) should always be obtained unless the tribunal specifically dispensed with this in an individual case. Adopted children should be allowed to marry adoptive relatives even in cases where if they had been blood relations they would not have been allowed to do so.

As far as the disputed issues were concerned, in discussing the appropriate tribunal the Committee considered the High Court particularly suitable but not sufficiently accessible to the majority of people. It decided to propose the Magistrates' Court as the usual tribunal for adoption cases but made it clear that the most important issue was that

> whichever be the tribunal selected it is important that the judicial sanction, which will necessarily carry great weight, should be a real adjudication and should not become a mere method of registering the will of the parties respectively seeking to part with and take over the child.[32]

It recommended appointing someone to act as 'guardian *ad litem*' (literally 'guardian at law'), who would be appointed by the court to protect the best interests of the child during legal proceedings.

As for legal and inheritance rights, the Committee tried to be as non-contentious as possible. It proposed that adopting parents have the same rights as natural parents vis-à-vis the Poor Law and any other public authorities but felt it better to proceed with 'a measure of caution' as far as the law of succession was concerned and not interfere with it at all. It suggested that the sanctioning tribunal should have the power 'to require that some provision be made by the adopting parent for the child'.[33] In testamentary documents 'children' and 'issue' would continue to mean 'lawful natural' children. It would be up to adopting parents to make plain their intentions towards their adoptive children.

The Committee's Second Report was a draft Bill, 'embodying the recommendations made in our First Report'. One clause stresses that 'the order if made will be for the welfare of the infant' and 'due consideration being for this purpose given to the wishes of the infant, having regard to the age and understanding of the infant'.[34] It also 'shall not be lawful for any adopter except with the sanction of the Court to receive any payment or other reward in connexion with the adoption of any infant under this Act or for any person to make or give or agree to make or give to the adopter any such payment or reward'.[35] Children who had been brought up by persons other than their parents as their own children for at least two years when the Bill became law were to be allowed to be the subject of an adoption order without consent of parent and guardian, 'if it is just and equitable for the welfare of the infant'.[36] The Registrar-General would be made responsible for keeping an index of the Adopted Children Register which people would be entitled to search and then receive a copy of an entry in the same way as with births and deaths; but the public would not be able see the linkage with the births register.[37] All these clauses became part of the eventual Act although (see below) some amendments were made to other suggested clauses.

On the whole the Tomlin Committee's First Report was cautious and conservative. It agreed to legislation but proposed the minimum necessary to get a system under way. Adopted children would not be legally like natural children in all the ways adoption societies would have liked – for example, they would not have the same rights or prohibitions in the areas of intestacy and marriage of near relatives. The Hopkinson Committee had been more enthused by the passion of the adoption societies and had reported relatively soon after the First World War, with accompanying reports of needy war orphans and bereaved parents, and the immediate post-war optimism. The Tomlin Committee clearly did not believe that legalising adoption was really going to solve many problems, and on the whole it was suspicious and discouraging of current adoption practice, especially as carried out by the adoption societies. However caution led it to avoid proposing registration or regulations which might have curbed their excesses. The Government was aiming for the initial adoption legislation to be enabling and non-controversial. And although the civil servants in particular were concerned about the way the adoption societies operated, the societies were a powerful and well-organised lobby and this was not seen as an appropriate time to engage in conflict with them. Only after the enabling legislation had taken root, and generally been judged successful, did the concerns about the societies begin to be addressed, a decade later when the Horsbrugh Committee was established to look into their operation.

The Committee's Third and Final Report was the result of the extra duty imposed on the Committee to look at the working of the Children Act 1908 Part 1 dealing with the protection of infant life and visitation of voluntary homes. From comments in the paragraph in the draft First Report omitted in the final version[38] it appears that at one point the Committee did consider including a critique of adoption societies in its Third Report but eventually settled for a fairly brief report with no direct comments on adoption or adoption societies. The Committee was satisfied that the existing child protection legislation 'has proved an efficient instrument for combating [baby farming] and has, in fact, largely eradicated the mischief against which it was directed'.[39] It proposed a few administrative amendments, the most important of which was that the Guardians of the Poor Law should cease to be the 'local authority' for the purpose of Part 1 of the Children Act (apart from the City and County of London) and the borough and county councils should take over this role[40] (which happened under the 1930 Poor Law Act).

The second part of the Committee's extended brief was to consider the efficacy of the inspection system of voluntary homes for children. This came under Section 25 of the Children Act and the Committee did not consider the legislation provided adequate cover. There was no machinery for obtaining necessary information and its operation needed to be extended. Local authorities usually, but not invariably, carried out the inspections and the Committee recommended that they should always do them rather than other bodies or societies. Lastly, they advocated the introduction of powers to remove children from homes in which their safety or welfare was being endangered.

Parliamentary debates on adoption

Even while the Tomlin Committee was deliberating the Parliamentary supporters of adoption remained active. In April 1925 Sir Geoffrey Butler[41] introduced the Adoption of Children Bill 1925, the seventh adoption bill since 1921. An annoyed Home Office note says that it was the same as the Bill introduced by Sir Thomas Inskip the previous year and had been given to Sir Geoffrey by the Whips after he secured a good place in the ballot for private members' bills. 'We have explained to him and Mr Harris of the Whips Office that apart from the merits or demerits of the Bill we could not support it pending the Report of the Adoption Committee.'[42]

At the Bill's relatively lengthy Second Reading there was an amendment: 'That this house refuses a Second Reading to a Bill which would encourage the breaking up of families and the shirking of the duties of parenthood'.[43] This was put down by the Liberal, Lieut.-Commander Kenworthy, and some Conservatives and a Labour member, the Rev. Herbert Dunnico. The Bill was proposed by a Conservative and seconded by a Labour MP, Sir Henry Slesser, the Solicitor-General in the previous administration. Adoption was never really a party issue; it attracted supporters and detractors on all sides, although there were moments during this parliamentary debate when it was portrayed as a class issue by some speakers. The Bill's proposer made the usual points about unwanted children benefiting from family life rather than institutional care and the need to ensure that the adopting parents would have a secure right to their children. The supporters of the amendment painted the picture in a different way:

> In some cases, you have people who are too selfish to have children themselves. Very often, when young, they will not have children for extraordinarily selfish reasons, and they leave the matter too late and cannot have children. Then in their later years, they feel a want or gap in their lives. There is a starved feeling of parenthood that requires satisfaction. They go to poor people with large families, and they probably induce the parents to part with a child. I know of actual cases which have arisen. Then perhaps the family from which that child has been taken improves its position in the world, becomes more comfortable, and the parents wish to regain possession of the child. Under this Bill that is impossible.[44]

The Labour MP, Arthur Hayday, spoke passionately about the issue:

> If the wage conditions were good enough, and if mothers' pensions were instituted that would wipe away the care and fear from the mother's mind as to the possible infliction of suffering upon her child, there would not be the need for half the present extent of adoption ... Why should the offspring of the poorest people be bartered as a piece of merchandise to people who may or may not have a family; to people who may think the encumbrance and risk of child-birth is too much for them?[45]

On the other hand another Labour MP, John Rhys Davies, supported legislation 'for the sake of the children and not merely of the parents or the foster-parents', and suggested adoption should be available for older children and that children themselves 'ought to have a "say" in these matters'.[46]

Sir Geoffrey Butler was persuaded to withdraw his bill and the debate was adjourned after the Home Office Under-Secretary, Godfrey Locker-Lampson, promised that the Government would do its best to expedite the new Committee's report, would ask it to report on child adoption without waiting to complete its work under its extended references and would bring in a Bill on the subject during the life of the present Parliament. A note in the Home Office files, handwritten after the debate, says 'it was clear that the House of Commons was overwhelmingly in favour of the legalisation of adoption'.[47] Another Bill, the Adoption of Children (No. 2)

Bill 1925, the second introduced by the Ulster Unionist MP, Sir Malcolm Macnaghten, also came up at this time but was dropped in anticipation of the Committee's report and the Home Secretary's assurances.

The Tomlin Committee's First Report was forwarded to Sir William Joynson-Hicks[48] on 8 April 1925, almost exactly a year after the Committee was appointed. Sir William was Secretary of State for the Home Office in the Conservative Government which had regained power in November 1924. Three months later their Second Report, the draft Bill, was sent to him. It was accompanied by a handwritten note from S. W. Harris, the senior Home Office official who was a member of the Tomlin Committee:

> [I]t is unusual for a Committee to indicate so exactly the precise way in which its proposals could be carried out but in this instance the course adopted seemed to have advantages as so many private members' Bills have been introduced without success.[49]

The Second Report was presented to Parliament on 21 July 1925 and published soon afterwards. The issue remained in abeyance for a few months with the occasional question raised in Parliament. Finally there was activity at the beginning of 1926. Sir Henry Slesser raised the omission of any mention of adoption from the King's Speech,[50] and a couple of days later it was announced that the Conservative MP Mr James Galbraith, who had been successful in the Private Members' Ballot, was going to introduce a Bill based on the Committee's draft.[51] It was pointed out behind the scenes at the Home Office that the Prime Minister had promised legislation in his autumn 1924 Election Address so something would have to be done.[52] Officials asked the Lord Chancellor's Office for comments and it was suggested that the legislation was best dealt with as a Private Member's Bill.

The Adoption of Children Bill received its Second Reading on 26 February 1926. This was the occasion for a long debate on the issue. In his proposing speech Mr Galbraith declared that the National Children Adoption Association had arranged 2050 cases of adoption since September 1917 and was currently carrying out at least twelve a week. He went through the Bill clause by clause and pointed out the ways in which the two Committees had differed in their conclusions: in particular the possibility of revoking an adoption order which was recommended by the Hopkinson Committee but rejected by Tomlin, although it suggested making orders provisional for two years. And also in relation to rights to property where Hopkinson, unlike Tomlin, had recommended adopted children have the same rights as natural children of the adopting parent – although not in regard to other relatives – and that adopting parents have similar rights to the property of the child, that is, mainly in cases of intestacy.

Another contested issue was the question of which court would make adoption orders. Both Committees agreed the Chancery Division was most appropriate as for many years it had dealt with matters relating to children and guardianship, but for the majority of cases which would be decided locally the Hopkinson Report had favoured the County Court as it was a similar kind of court to Chancery, already dealt with maintenance of orphans under the Workmen's Compensation Act, and had no tinge of criminal casework. The Tomlin Committee had recommended the Magistrates' Court because it already dealt with a great deal of civil jurisdiction and had the experience of running the juvenile courts. Surprisingly, although his Bill (drafted by the Tomlin Committee) specified magistrates' courts, Mr Galbraith said that 'quite frankly ... in my view the County Court is the better of the two as an alternative', and commended the matter to debate in the House and deliberation at the Committee stage.[53]

Secrecy was the other crucial issue on which the two Committees came to different conclusions. The Hopkinson Report recommended that although the Registrar-General would be notified when an adoption order was made, no information would be passed on to him that would allow the adopting parents to be identified. The Tomlin Report, however (with which Mr Galbraith agreed), concluded that 'the necessity of secrecy is done away with once legal effect and force is given to adoption', and proposed a mechanism so that details of a child's origins could in special circumstances be retrieved. The seconder of the motion for the Second Reading, Mr (later Sir) Gervais Rentoul, the Parliamentary Private Secretary to the Attorney General, pointed out the underlying desire for secrecy, 'over 75 per cent of the children adopted are illegitimate and it has been thought that if you are giving them a start in life, as it were, it is better to veil from them the facts of their origin', but agreed that 'these points may be largely obviated if we have a definite, legal definition of adoption.'[54]

Mr Rentoul, like the main proposer, felt the County Court to be the most suitable tribunal for dealing with adoption cases. He candidly admitted that it might well not be possible 'at one blow to hammer out a perfect scheme [of adoption legislation]' but trusted 'that that will not be used, as I fear it has on many occasions in the past, as an excuse for not passing this Bill into law at the earliest possible moment, dealing as it does with a very much needed reform of our legal system and one that in justice and equity is long overdue'.⁵⁵

In some ways more positive about the Bill than its proposers were Major Clement Attlee (the future Labour Prime Minister) and the Home Secretary, Sir William Joynson-Hicks. Attlee was enthusiastic about adoption:

> I was amazed, when I first went down to East London, to find the extent to which adoption existed ... what we find [there] is that, where some misfortune befalls a family, there is nothing so common as the adoption of the children by neighbours – adoption frequently by a couple who already, one would think, had quite a heavy enough burden in looking after their own children.

He argued that adoption procedures must be cheap 'to be brought within the reach of people who are not only on the poverty line but under it'.⁵⁶ The Home Secretary offered his and the Government's full support to the Bill and to adoption: 'I believe that if a suitable home can be found, the best interests of the child are served by adoption in that home rather than in the very best institution in the world.'⁵⁷ He made a vigorous defence of the magistrates' courts as the appropriate courts for adoption cases. They were less formal than county courts and

> in the children's courts and magistrates' courts outside London, you get local knowledge, you get magistrates of all classes now sitting on the bench, you get a magistrates' clerk who lives in the town, and they know and are pretty well likely to know the people whose children are going to be adopted, and the people who are going to adopt the children, and it really will be a kind of parental jurisdiction which the courts will exercise rather than any purely legal one.⁵⁸

Ironically this defence of magistrates' courts reveals many of the reasons why adoption agencies and some adopters were so against them. They did not want a 'parental' jurisdiction which would have intimate knowledge of their lives. They wanted a legal process which would give them legal title to their children, no more, no less. Sir William did concede that the Government would 'not stand out against anything approaching a unanimous decision of the Committee upstairs in favour of the county court', but this was not what he would be recommending.⁵⁹ Like previous speakers he believed that legislation would remove the need for secrecy as it would end the possibility of blackmail or taking back the child when it reached an age of maturity. Sir William ended his points on a note of regret that legislation had not been passed before; it was an experiment which might need amending in a year or two 'when we find out how it works', but one 'well worth making ... giving a new form to legislation, which might well have been made, I think, many years before in this country. However, it is not too late to mend'.[60]

J. H. Palin, a Labour MP, spoke of the detrimental effect of institutional life: 'It saps the independence of character. It tends to make men, at any rate, with less moral fibre than we associate with the average Britisher.' It was all too easy to move from one institution (an orphanage) to another (prison). He welcomed the Bill but urged caution and the necessity for safeguards:

> People do not always adopt children because they love children, and the older a child becomes before adoption takes place, the greater care someone has got to take to see that these children are not adopted in order to become slaves, because members of boards of guardians who have had any experience well know that very great care has had to be taken in the past ... in order to prevent their being exploited in this way. Particularly is this the case with girls.[61]

Lieut.-Colonel Cuthbert Headlam, a Conservative MP, revealed that he was an adopting parent, and argued strongly for the importance of secrecy: 'In many cases a child will never be legally adopted unless there is a large measure of secrecy.' He spoke of the mother 'who will not wish it to be known that she is the mother of the particular child ... It is for children of this class [presumably middle and upper class] that secrecy is so absolutely essential, for these are the children who are most in need of adoption'.[62] The Labour MP, Mr Frederick Pethick-Lawrence, raised the possibility of an adopted child unbeknownst marrying a family member in later years 'if the complete identity of the child is lost', and urged a means of checking for this.[63]

Ellen Wilkinson, the Labour MP, refused to join in 'the chorus of praise' with which the Bill had been received, although she gave it 'qualified support'. She began her speech with a damning description of potential adopters:

> There are certain dangers which ought to be pointed out. There are, for example, cases in which rather empty-headed women, without children of their own, but feeling they would like a child, and being casually attracted by some fluffy-haired, blue-eyed little thing, will

adopt that child while it is young and pretty in the rather casual and haphazard way that they do. When the child grows older, gets to the gawky stage of childhood, needs a good deal more attention, and is not a pet to play with, then the woman wants to get rid of her responsibility, and the child is probably finally sent to the workhouse, or got rid of in some other way, perhaps by being boarded out.[64]

However she felt that 'any action ... which will bring home to that woman her responsibility, and make her responsible for the child beyond the stages of its childhood, would be all to the good'. Miss Wilkinson was concerned that people in desperate circumstances, giving up their children for adoption, might later come to regret their action, especially if their circumstances changed but by then it would be too late to alter the situation. She urged what would be now seen as counselling: 'the people who give over a child for adoption ought to have explained to them how completely irrevocable is the step they are taking.'[65]

Like many of the speakers, she disputed the need for secrecy:

> I have doubts as to how far it is wise to cut away from a child all memory and knowledge of its natural parents and their surroundings. Even if those surroundings were bad, even if the people were immoral, even if it were an illegitimate child, nothing but trouble would ensure [sic] from an attempt to keep the facts from the child when it is old enough to understand. A great deal of misery might be avoided if the child were told the truth and knew the whole circumstances of its case. If we are to have legal adoption it ought to be made as open as possible; it should be an honourable act and not something which the child should be made to feel had cast a stigma upon it.[66]

The Conservative MP, Herbert Williams, had sympathy with her suggestion of ending secrecy although he recognised it was unlikely to happen:

> But if there is to be secrecy it obviously cannot be complete secrecy. We are not entitled to deprive a child of any rights that may accrue to it and of which it might be deprived by information never reaching it ... If there is to be secrecy, no general publication, there must be some means of communication between the natural parents and the adopting parents ... we cannot erect a Chinese wall between the natural parents and the adopters.[67]

In general, Labour MPs supported the Bill but expressed anxiety about the possibility of poor children being taken from their families, either by force, on the grounds that 'the physical and moral conditions of the home were such as to justify the waiving of the parental consent',[68] or by moral blackmail, that this would provide the child with a better chance in life.

The question of intestacy and rights to property was raised several times. Some MPs felt that it was up to an adopting parent to make specific provision for an adopted child, others that the adopted child must have the same rights as natural children. Others urged continuing inspection of families after they had adopted their child and raised the possibility of revoking an adoption. The issue of matching the religious persuasion of child and adopting parents was only raised briefly, at the end of the debate.

Having received its Second Reading, the Bill then went through to the Standing Committee stage. The Standing Committee came up with various amendments to the Bill.[69] The most controversial of these related to the question of inheritance rights and adopted children, in particular the case of intestacy. The Committee amended the Bill to give the adopted child some rights on the intestacy of the adopter to inherit part of his or her property. The Solicitor-General, Sir Thomas Inskip, in the subsequent House of Commons debate, called this an 'inconvenient' middle path and following considerable discussion behind the scenes the Home Secretary, Sir William Joynson-Hicks, decided that the Bill must revert to its original form.[70]

The major change to the Bill was made not in Standing Committee but at the Third Reading and could be seen as a considerable success for the 'will' of the House. This was an amendment adding County Courts to the courts with jurisdiction over adoption. It was moved by Sir Alfred Hopkinson, who had chaired the initial committee on adoption which had recommended using County Courts rather than magistrates' courts, and was now an MP. The Tomlin Committee had come up with the officially preferred proposal of magistrates' courts but the supporters of County Courts remained vocal and determined in their conviction that the use of magistrates' courts would add a stigma to adoption which would deter people from using the legislation.

For the *Times Educational Supplement*, looking at the issue in a major article on adoption, the desire for an alternative to the magistrates' courts came back to the crucial issue of secrecy:

> [It] is induced by a fear on the part of the experienced and careful societies arranging adoptions ... that the arrangements made for

children's courts, both in London and in the country, under their present constitution do not ensure the necessary secrecy. They fear that unless scrupulous care is taken to avoid all publicity and all meetings between the parents of the child and the adopters the whole aim of the Bill will be defeated, and people will resort to private agreements.[71]

During the Commons Third Reading Sir Alfred Hopkinson argued that

> For well-to-do people there could not be a better tribunal than the High Court but it is perfectly ridiculous to imagine that to poor people in Newcastle or Carlisle the High Court is a possible tribunal. The only tribunal there is the County Court sitting at their own doors. They do not want the associations of the Police Court in dealing with a civil matter.[72]

Despite the concerns of the civil service, the Government decided that it was not worth holding out on this issue.

An amendment that was agreed allowed courts the discretionary right to make an adoption order where the age gap between adoptee and adopter was less than twenty-one years in cases where they were related (technically 'within the prohibited degrees of consanguinity'[73]). The proposers particularly had in mind siblings who adopted younger brothers or sisters or aunts or uncles. However an amendment to remove the clause prohibiting sole male applicants from adopting female infants met with little support and was withdrawn. Its proposer, Sir Robert Newman,[74] expressed outrage about the Bill's assumption

> that the ordinary man who wants to adopt a child must necessarily do so for improper reasons ... Why a man, because he happens to be a bachelor or a widower, should be assumed to be an unfit person or not to have a proper reason for wishing to adopt a female child, I cannot understand.[75]

Mr Galbraith pointed out that both Committees had come to the same conclusion about males adopting female children, and that in any case the court could make an order in such cases when it was satisfied that there were 'special circumstances' justifying 'an exceptional measure'.[76]

Other attempted amendments included giving relatives the right to adopt a child (if judged 'fit and proper' people) in preference to an outside person. It failed but provoked considerable discussion. For its supporters such as Lieut.-Commander Kenworthy, the idea of strangers adopting a child when there might be available grandparents symbolised the nation's decline:

> one of the things that is being undermined ... to the detriment of the whole country at the present time is family life, the unity of the family, on the one hand by poverty and bad housing and on the other by the modern, mad desire for pleasure and luxury at all cost.[77]

There were also suggestions for extending the legislation in limited ways to Northern Ireland and Scotland or even to other parts of 'His Majesty's Dominions' in special circumstances. These were withdrawn or rejected because of the impracticality of dealing with the different legal systems and introducing complicated extensions to the legislation at so late a stage. Lord Crichton-Stuart then moved an amendment stating that where a Roman Catholic child was in the care of a state authority an adoption order should only be made for them where the applicant was Roman Catholic. The following speaker suggested this right be extended to Protestant children which the Lord agreed with. However Captain Hacking, speaking for the Government, was dismissive of the idea, saying that the Home Secretary had invited representations on this issue at an earlier stage but had received none.[78] He said that as the Court's duty was to take the interests of the child into account it would inevitably consider religion – which the next speaker argued did not 'quite meet the point'. It was left to the Bill's proposer, Mr Galbraith, to conclude the debate on the amendment with a moderate but determined rejection of religious zealotry:

> I am not for a moment suggesting that the question of religious belief is not a most important thing, but it is not the only thing, and if we put in the Clause words which make it peremptory that the only person who can adopt a child must be of the same religious faith we may be doing something which in certain cases may be against the interests of the child.[79]

There was discussion about whether adoption hearings would have to be held with all the parties involved present together. Mr Hurst felt that 'the effect of requiring their physical presence is to bring the adopting parent and the natural parent face to face, and that is something which I am sure both sides would desire to avoid'.[80] He was reassured by Captain Hacking that there was considerable flexibility in this matter.

Sir Robert Newman brought up the issue of children consenting to adoption, proposing an amendment which would make twelve years the age at which a child's consent must be given before the order could go ahead. He compared adoption to apprenticeship – a less drastic step in a child's life – which children could not be bound to unless they agreed, and suggested that 'as the Bill stands, a young man or woman might be handed over to another family without his or her consent'.[81] However, other MPs felt the existing wording of the Bill (and subsequent Act) gave sufficient weight to children's feelings and offered them protection from undue pressure or influence. It said the Court must be satisfied 'that the order if made will be for the welfare of the infant, due consideration being for this purpose given to the wishes of the infant, having regard to the age and understanding of the infant'.[82]

A month later the Bill received its Second Reading in the House of Lords, moved by Lord Desborough. The Labour peer, Lord Muir Mackenzie, praised the Commons for the way it had dealt with the Bill 'with an amount of general agreement which is not often secured, and at the same time with very full consideration and debate'. Whereas some Bills were rushed through with the minimum of debate, 'in this case there is no doubt that the other House did at every stage give the most complete consideration to the Bill'.[83]

The following week the House of Lords considered the Bill in Committee. Most of the debate was on amendments which had already been discussed in the Commons and were now brought to the Lords in what the Government and civil servants hoped was to be their final polished form. Some of the Lords tried to bring in amendments which had already been rejected or withdrawn in the Commons but few changes were actually made.

The Adoption of Children Act 1926

Finally the Bill came back to the Commons. Last minute amendments included a measure giving the Court discretion to dispense with the consent to an adoption of a 'person liable to contribute' – shorthand for a putative father who might have handed over small amounts to support his child and then might, it was suggested, seek to prevent an adoption 'on grounds, perhaps, merely of spite against the mother; or even attempt to level blackmail by refusing his consent except for a consideration'.[84] The Courts were also given discretion to dispense with the consent of a separated spouse to an adoption if they were satisfied that the separation was likely to be permanent. The last amendment passed was at the instigation of insurance companies who wanted clarification about what happened, if a child was adopted, to the funeral insurance policy taken out for it by a natural parent. The answer now included in the Bill was that the policy (and its liabilities) would automatically be transferred from the natural to the adopting parents.

Next day, 4 August 1926, the Bill received Royal Assent, and on 1 January 1927, it came into operation. Its Parliamentary supporters had high hopes for the legislation. Sir Alfred Hopkinson said, 'I feel quite certain, (it) will have the effect of bringing great happiness into a number of young lives and into a number of older ones as well ... I feel certain ... it will prove to be one of the most useful pieces of work we could have done in this House'.[85] Others, like Susan Musson of the National Council for the Unmarried Mother and Her Child, were unsure what effect the legislation would have:

> She thought it would have the effect of reducing adoptions, inasmuch as when mothers found that they had to give up their child for ever, and not be able to get it back again just when they wanted, they would not be so willing to part with the baby. The one drawback to the Act was the fact that it was voluntary not compulsory. It would not prevent all the irregular adoptions which were entered into at the present time.[86]

In fact, there had been no discussion during the debates around the Bill about making it compulsory to register adoptions. The idea was mentioned in the Tomlin Report but quickly dismissed:

> It is true that some of those who have given evidence before us have suggested that a legal system of adoption should be supplemented by a prohibition of all transactions involving the bringing up of other people's children unless they are legalised by the forms prescribed by the Adoption Law. This is a proposal the mere statement of which is sufficient to disclose its impracticability.[87]

The legislation appears to have been seen, certainly by the civil servants, as a first attempt. Even before the Bill was passed, Sir Claud Schuster at the Lord Chancellor's Department stated firmly that amending legislation would have to be brought in 'comparatively soon'. The Act was a way of introducing the practice gently to English society. The civil servants involved in the discussions about adoption legislation during the 1920s were obviously keen to approach adoption legislation cautiously and prevent the passing of hasty laws. The adoption societies' supporters interpreted the civil servants' motives as stemming from an innate conservatism and mistrust of change. During the debate on Sir Geoffrey Butler's Adoption Bill in 1925 Gerald Hurst MP said:

> I have every reason to be exasperated with the obstructive tactics of the Home Office, which defeated the adoption Bill of two years ago [the one he introduced] and which may be employed again to hamper the Bill today. I hope the leaders of the Conservative party will show themselves able to withstand the wiles and the obstinacy and the tactics of the bureaucracy.[88]

Adoption supporters saw themselves as part of a modern, rational movement, removing children from unsuitable, immoral or deprived situations and placing them, as Mr Hurst explained, with the 'enormous number of men and women living in this country who are eminently fitted to bring up children and to give them every care and attention'.[89] For them it was logical that the children should make a new start in a new home and there should be no messy links or even knowledge of their previous situations. Their illegitimacy was at a stroke removed, the relinquishing mother could start again and the new parents need have no fear of unpleasant reminders of the past disturbing their respectable lives. They wanted the County Court or the High Court swiftly to expedite the adoption process, away from the prying eyes of neighbours or nosy officials.

Yet viewed from another angle, the civil servants were extremely sensitive to the potential pitfalls of adoption legislation, and sought to approach it with caution so that effective and fair law was passed. They were suspicious of the societies' desire to rush through an enabling law which would enshrine as much secrecy and little compulsory inspection as they could persuade Parliament to accept. They were concerned about the methods of the adoption societies – the casual approach to references and inspections that even the most reputable societies employed – and their concerns would be borne out by the findings of Miss Horsbrugh's Committee ten years later.

The civil servants were also uneasy about the importance placed on secrecy by the societies, which arose from the much-stated fear that the natural parent would seek to interfere with the adopting family if she could trace them.[90] Their uneasiness may have been partly an inability on the part of highly educated and confident upper-middle-class males to empathise with the passion for respectability felt by aspiring couples from the lower classes and to understand how deeply they feared the stigma of illegitimacy. They were certainly very removed from these people. Gail Savage compared the educational background of higher civil servants with the education of the general population, quoting figures to show that 63.6 per cent of high-ranking civil servants in 1929 had attended the twenty best-known schools in the country (all independent) and over half had attended Oxford, at a time (prior to the First World War) when only two per cent of manual workers' sons obtained a secondary education at a grammar or independent school.[91] Both S. W. Harris and M. L. Gwyer came from exactly that elite background.[92]

However these civil servants articulated a genuine concern and disquiet about the consequences of secrecy which meant a child losing all knowledge of its identity and the natural mother being completely cut off from her child. And in fact they were not necessarily so removed from the realities of life. The most senior official at the Ministry of Health dealing directly with adoption issues, Mr Stutchbury,[93] was one of the original executive committee members of the NCUMC, so was presumably well aware of the difficulties facing unmarried mothers and their children. And the legal historian, Stephen Cretney, has written of S. W. Harris, the senior civil servant at the Home Office most closely involved with adoption (and a member of the Tomlin Committee), that 'the modern observer must note with admiration the effectiveness of his concern for securing the public good in general and the welfare of children in particular.'[94]

As we have seen throughout the previous chapters, during this period the desire for complete secrecy in adoption was not shared by all the interested parties in the adoption debate – in general only the adoption societies and their supporters. Many of the witnesses to the Hopkinson Committee were uneasy about cutting off all links between natural parents and their children, as were many of the speakers in the Parliamentary debates on adoption. Nor was there wholesale enthusiasm for the process of adoption, particularly among the voluntary welfare groups. The highly effective publicity and lobbying techniques of the adoption societies and the social and political prominence of their supporters obscured the mixed feelings about encouraging adoption felt by many other organisations. So the civil servants' mistrust of the rush to legislation and need for secrecy in adoption procedures may have been more in tune with opinion in the early 1920s than the adoption societies and their supporters were prepared to accept.

5
The First Years of Legally Sanctioned Adoption

Initial reactions

The Tomlin Committee had suggested that the report produced by Sir Alfred Hopkinson and his Committee overestimated the potential demand for legal adoption, ascribing the demand in the early 1920s to the aftermath of war and suggesting that when the backlog of cases were dealt with the numbers would fall.[1] This prediction proved unfounded. Adoption orders were made for over three thousand children in the year after the Adoption of Children Act came into force (1 January 1927).[2] This figure was in a sense inflated, as the Tomlin Committee had predicted, because some of these children had been informally adopted prior to the Act and their adopting parents were keen to make their position legal. The *Daily Express* reported an instant reaction:

> Foster-parents are quickly taking advantage of the Adoption of Children Act which came into operation on Saturday, and gives them the rights of parents.
>
> A woman waited for the court to open at Tottenham on Saturday to ask that a child she had adopted should be registered as her own. Another woman, of Loudoun Road, St John's Wood, made a similar application at Marylebone. They were told that the applications would be heard at the children's court.[3]

However, apart from a very slight drop in the early 1930s, the annual number of registered adoptions rose steadily in the decade following legislation. By 1936 it was over five thousand per annum.[4] The legislation appears to have worked relatively well. The National Archives' files have a number of queries from magistrates and solicitors, and there was the occasional controversial case, but overall the legal process which dealt with over forty-two thousand adoptions in the Act's first ten years seems to have worked quite smoothly. In 1933, the proposer of the Adoption Act, James Galbraith MP, told Parliament proudly: 'I think I am entitled to say that that Act has proved a complete success and has been made use of by an increasing number of persons in all ranks and walks of life in the population.'[5]

Not all commentators were so positive. The National Children's Home and Orphanage ran an extremely negative article in its journal not long after the Act came into force. It raised concerns about identifying children who had been abandoned and authenticating written consents in court, although its main criticism was the lack of secrecy in the adoption process which would mean adopted children being made aware of their antecedents. Its conclusion was: 'the legal recognition of adoption is the one great and practically the only substantial benefit and advantage of the Act, the difficulties in the way of those seeking to gain this benefit are, at present, very great and may in many cases seem to outweigh this benefit.'[6] On the other hand the National Union of Societies for Equal Citizenship[7] tried to persuade the civil service to include in the Act's accompanying regulations the right of an adopted person to ascertain their identity when they came of age. The Home Office notes say that this 'does not seem to be a matter which can be dealt with by rule'.[8] Subsequently A. E. A. Napier (Assistant Secretary in the Lord Chancellor's Office (LCO)), wrote to Eva Hubback, NUSEC's Parliamentary Secretary, setting out very clearly the civil service opinion on the question of secrecy as far as it affected the relinquishing parent, albeit not the relinquished child:

> It is not intended ... that the name and address of the proposed adopter should be concealed from the natural parent. You will remember that the effect of an Adoption Order when made is to deprive the natural parent of his parental rights ... It is essential that before legal adoption takes place, the natural parent should have sufficient knowledge with regard to the proposed adopter to give a real consent.[9]

The adoption societies were not at all convinced about this and at the beginning they were critical of the legal procedures. A few weeks after the Act came in, the National Children Adoption Association (NCAA) complained:

> Many hundreds of adopters seem to have lost their enthusiasm for legal adoption because of the unreadiness of the Courts when they

> applied early in January ... Many have already relinquished the attempt to get their adopted children registered.
>
> This is a matter of extreme regret to us as we have worked very hard for many years past to press for legislation and we feel that a few concessions might make a great difference to the number of people willing to go to Court.
>
> The adopters have in many cases felt a little humiliated and as if they were suspect in the Court.[10]

They felt the lack of privacy was mortifying; the High Court would be preferable but was too expensive. 'The adopters naturally feel there is one law for the rich and one law for the poor.'[11] A couple of months later the National Adoption Society also wrote, welcoming the Act, but asking how people can adopt their child legally

> without the parent (who is so often an unmarried mother) being informed of their identity so that the child can never be confronted possibly by its own mother and told of its illegitimacy ...
>
> All adopters feel that if a mother knows she would at some time be prompted for varying reasons – curiosity, affection, emotional stress, jealousy, blackmail etc – to see the child and wreck the natural tie of parent and child which all the adopters hope will, and it is the Society's experience, does develop.[12]

On the other hand the NSPCC was pleasantly surprised at the numbers presenting in court to take advantage of the Act as they had regretted the lack of any compulsion in the process.[13] They continued to campaign for this throughout the 1930s. Their 1930–1 Annual Report included case histories of informally adopted children:

> A couple in Yorkshire apparently made a practice of adopting children. One had died in their care, another had been tired of and sent elsewhere, and the third was the object of enquiry by the Society. This lad, who was ten years old, was a domestic drudge and was systematically ill-treated.

> A woman who had four illegitimate children advertised for someone to adopt one or more of them. As a result she got into touch with a man who was a bachelor living in a single room, and he took one of them – a boy eight years old. The Society came to hear of the case when the man committed a savage assault on the lad, as a result of which he had to spend a month in hospital. No bench of Justices

would, for a moment, have consented to such an arrangement as the boy being placed in the man's sole care.[14]

Court procedures

The court procedure was regulated by various guidelines which were issued after the Act was passed. The Adoption of Children (Summary Jurisdiction) Rules 1926 were sent out to all the relevant agencies with suitable explanatory letters. The Home Office wrote specifically to local authorities to draw their attention to the role of the guardian *ad litem* which was given more prominence than perhaps might have been inferred from the original legislation, 'in view of the paramount importance of ensuring that the interests of the infant in any case are adequately safeguarded'.[15] The letter pointed out that the Act, which says the Court must make such an appointment in all cases, 'contemplates' the appointment of a local authority in suitable cases – subject to their consent – and gives the Court power to authorise the authority to incur the necessary expenditure. It points out that the Rules make provision for the payment of certain costs incurred.

As far as the Magistrates were concerned, the Summary Jurisdiction Rules laid down that all the applications to the Court of Summary Jurisdiction would be made to the Juvenile Court. Privacy was stressed. Every application must be dealt with *in camera* – public and press were banned from the hearing – and all information obtained in the case 'must be treated as confidential'.[16] Under Rule 9 the Courts were given the power to see the parties separately if they saw fit. It was made clear that there must be no 'rubber-stamping' of decisions:

> It is important ... that the Court should not come to a decision until it is satisfied that the conditions required by the Statute are complied with, and in particular that the proposed adoption will be for the welfare of the infant concerned. Due consideration must be given to the wishes of the infant having regard to the age and understanding of the infant.[17]

Although there had been virtually no debate about the role of local authorities in adoption before the legislation had been passed, the letter to the local authorities clearly envisaged that they would have a major involvement in adoption cases:

> [The Secretary of State] is of opinion that in respect of applications coming before the Juvenile Court or County Court the duties can

best be undertaken by a responsible public authority with adequate facilities for making the necessary enquiries.[18]

The role of guardian *ad litem* was emphasised; in all cases the Court must appoint one, including those of *de facto* adoptions which had already existed at least two years. The Court was allowed to appoint anyone but 'generally speaking it is desirable that the guardian *ad litem* should be a responsible person who is independent of the parties to the application'.[19] It was recommended they use the Local Authorities for Elementary Education or they could approach the Local Authorities for Higher Education or for Maternity and Child Welfare.

It is interesting, in view of the long argument about which court was most appropriate for the adoption process, to see that the Juvenile Courts were overwhelmingly the court of choice for the majority of people. Out of the 41,914 adoption orders made between 1927 and 1936, 38,408 were through Juvenile Courts, 2765 through the County Courts and a mere 741 through the High Court.[20] It does appear that the civil servants and others who had argued that the Courts of Summary Jurisdiction would offer accessibility and expertise were justified in their beliefs. Sir Stafford Cripps' answer to a parliamentary question in 1931 about the costs of obtaining an unopposed adoption order gave some information about relative costs; fees in the High Court were nearly £3, in the County Courts £1, and 'a few shillings in a Court of Summary Jurisdiction'. The guardian *ad litem* inquiry cost about £11 in the High Court but in the County Courts and Courts of Summary Jurisdiction the costs of the guardian *ad litem* were seldom charged to the applicant and the Solicitor General did not know what they were.[21]

Confidentiality rules make it hard to find out much detail about how the courts' decision-making processes. A Minute Book giving notes about the working of the Adoption of Children Act 1926 between 1927 and 1933 in Bath gives fairly perfunctory notes about the cases heard in the Juvenile Court. Each case has the details of the relinquishing mother, and the father's name if known, and whether the mother's attendance was dispensed with. There is usually a line saying that the Town Clerk's Office or Guardian Ad Litem report concluded 'that the result of enquiries was quite satisfactory', and whether the child was seen.[22]

Most orders were passed, apparently with little controversy, but a number were turned down during the six years. Usually these gave only brief statements saying that following reports from a doctor, and sometimes the police, it had been decided it was not 'in the child's interest' that an order be made. One such was a family where there were both financial and emotional question marks – the father had had to provide for his children 'on a small amount of money' but there were eight daughters of whom four were now earning and although 'the husband not in good financial circumstances last few years [sic]' he was considered 'better now'. The real problem appeared to be that the parents had two boys who died and they 'want child as it is a boy'.[23] This must have been a common reason for wanting to adopt a child, so one can only presume that there was something that made the guardian uneasy or which was not written in the minutes.

The Bath Juvenile Court also occasionally used interim orders. In another case a child's father refused consent to an adoption application. Her mother had died eight months previously and the NSPCC had warned about the child's condition since then, although it is not clear how she had become a candidate for adoption. The magistrates made a two-year interim order with the condition that the natural father would be allowed to see the child every three months on giving written notice to the adopting parents.[24] They also made an interim order where the father of an illegitimate child had just resumed living with his wife and they were jointly applying to adopt the illegitimate child.[25]

The High Court was favoured by those who could afford it because of its assurance of complete confidentiality. Although ironically, while access to the lower courts' adoption records is now invariably restricted across the country until well into the twenty-first century, it is possible to see some individual case records from the High Court at the National Archive. These show the use of the High Court by middle- and upper-class people who were not just straightforwardly adopting a child from an adoption society; they were using adoption as a tool to formalise or legitimise existing family relationships.

For example:

> Couple A's children were born to them while Mrs A's first husband refused to give her a divorce. He finally agreed and the As are married and now want to adopt their own children to legitimise them.
>
> Mr and Mrs B want to adopt Mrs B's legitimate children from her first marriage. Mrs B is considerably older than her new husband but has been interviewed by the Official Solicitor who 'was favourably impressed by her' and despite the age difference 'there should be no reason why it should not be a happy and successful marriage'.
>
> Couple C are now married but had a child while Mr C was still married to his first wife. The child, by now four and a half, has been

living in a 'private home for infants' and then with a friend of theirs. They now wish to adopt him.

Child E is the illegitimate child of Mrs D who married Mr D when E was seven and they are applying to adopt him together. Because he is now fifteen the Official Solicitor interviewed him to ensure he understands the effect of an Adoption Order and that he wishes to be adopted.

F, a retired royal courtier, applies to adopt his 19 year old great nephew. The boy's widowed mother has agreed to renounce parental rights. 'The Official Solicitor has not thought it necessary in this case to submit the usual schedule of questions or ask for references'.[26]

On a more general level there is some information about the operation of the Adoption Act in the Home Office's Fourth Report on the work of its Children's Branch which came out in 1928. These reports did not come out on a regular basis and varied in the amount of information offered but in 1928 the officers decided that 'it would be interesting to include ... some account of the working of the Act', and wrote to the courts of summary jurisdiction, the County Courts and the High Court to ask about their experience.[27]

There were 1041 Juvenile Courts (based in the courts of summary jurisdiction) which were available to deal with adoption applications, 1022 responded to the Home Office's survey, of which 528 had received no applications for adoptions. So in the first 15 months of the Act's operation 494 Juvenile Courts dealt with 3841 applications and made 3548 adoption orders and 102 interim orders, refused 80 cases and 190 were withdrawn or pending. Of these 494 courts, 360 only dealt with between one and five applications during the fifteen months; 30 dealt with 21 or more. The highest figures are given – the Juvenile Courts at Shoreditch Town Hall dealt with 214 applications, Lambeth Town Hall 176, Liverpool 175 and Manchester 166.

About half of the children adopted had been in their adopters' care for two years or more before 1 January 1927; so their orders could be expedited without the consent of their natural parents. About 30 per cent of the children adopted were under two years, and about 5 per cent were aged between 14 and 21 years. The vast majority of adopters (about 85 per cent) were married couples adopting jointly but 'about 450 men and about 150 women' adopted singly. About two-thirds of the children were illegitimate and 'among these were a small number of whom one or both of their parents sought to adopt',[28] which would become an increasingly popular practice.

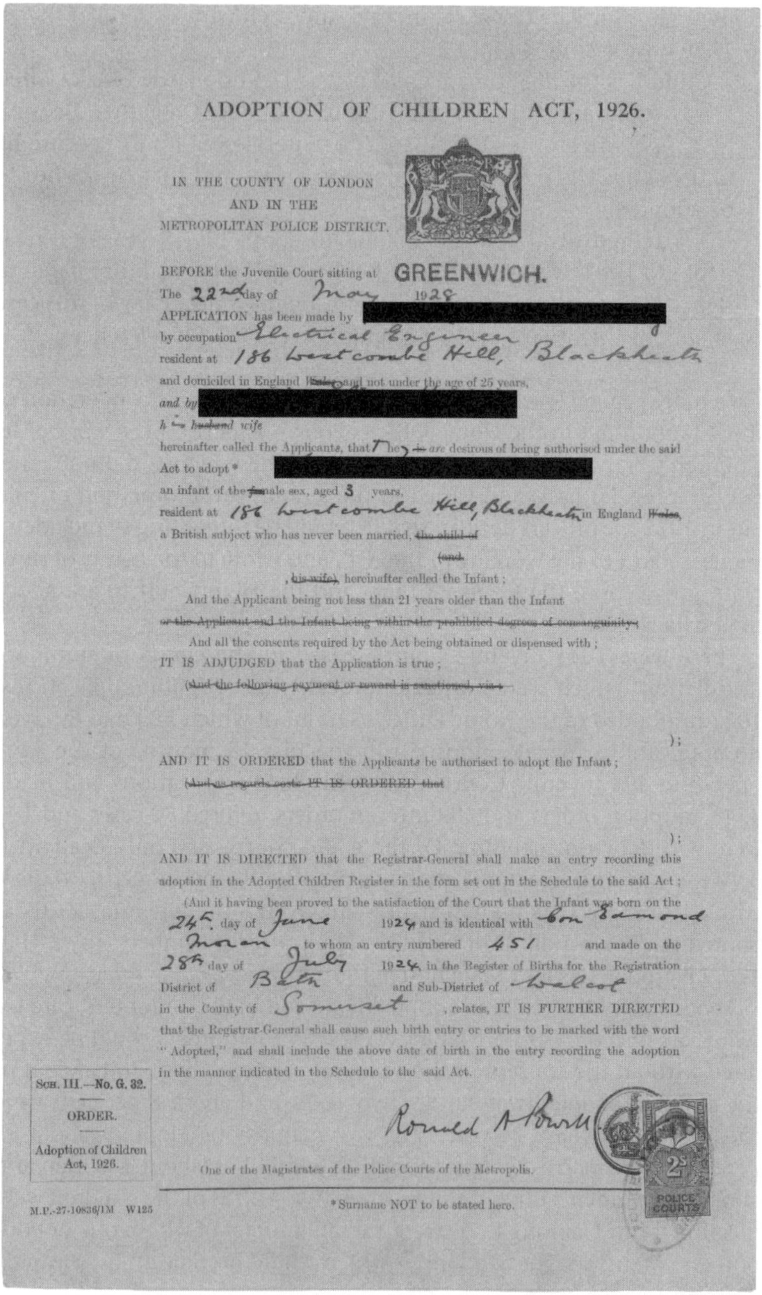

Figure 5.1 Adoption order, 1928 (from a private collection)

Reports were obtained from 453 County Courts of whom 331 had received no applications. The remaining 122 Courts dealt with 311 applications during the first fifteen months and made 281 orders, 18 interim orders and refused only one. Of the adopted children 71 were under two, 107 were aged between two and seven, 88 were aged between seven and 14, and 15 were aged between 14 and 21. No other details about the County Courts are given.

The High Court dealt with 234 applications during this period and made 210 orders with no interim orders or refusals. Of those adopted 36 were under two, 66 were aged between two and seven, 88 were aged between seven and 14, and 20 were between 14 and 21 years. Of those adopted 138 were illegitimate and 17 were the illegitimate children of the adopters. Over two-thirds (147) of the orders were for *de facto* adoptions, that is, children who had lived with their adopters for two years or more by 1 January 1927. More than a third of the High Court adoptions were by people adopting singly: 21 were men and 51 were women. There were 138 married couples who adopted jointly.

The Report considered the practice of the guardian *ad litem*. In the High Court this role is taken by the Official Solicitor. In most of the other courts, 'the Local Education Authorities readily complied with the invitation sent to them, and the Courts appointed their officers', and in several instances paid 'a tribute to the value of the help' they gave.[29] Occasionally the Child Welfare authority or the Poor Law Guardians took on the role and in some other cases Probation Officers or even clergymen, solicitors, NSPCC officers, social workers and private individuals. The Report queried the occasional use of Clerks to the Justices and their assistants, and police officers, raising 'the question whether, having regard to the circumstances, such appointments are desirable'.[30] It mentioned a few minor legal points which are discussed later in this chapter and concluded: 'Generally speaking, the replies of the Courts indicate that the Adoption of Children Act is working well and smoothly and that considerable benefit results both to adopting parents and to adopted children.'[31] A couple of Juvenile Court Clerks were quoted in praise of the Act. One said: 'I have been much struck by the fact that in all cases before us, the children adopted appear to be getting much better homes than the large majority of the children in the homes of the working classes, where there are a number of children.'[32]

A journalist, J. W. Drawbell, who adopted a child in the mid-1930s, described attending the formal adoption process in the County Court, and his feelings that day. He went with his wife, adopted child and solicitor; all were shown into the Judge's private room before the regular Court business began:

> The proceedings took less than a minute. The papers were placed before the Judge on his table, the circumstances were explained. He looked over them, glanced benignly at us, murmured questioningly, 'You have another little girl of your own?', picked up a pen and said: 'I sanction the adoption'.

One had the feeling for a moment that it was all too easy. It was too easy to take this child, the offspring of someone else, and make it your own. But the Judge was only giving his consent to something that had started a long time before, something that there had been many arrangements concerning. And there were now obligations in law where formerly there had only been humanitarian instincts and inclinations.[33]

In re Carroll

The main legal case arising out of the new adoption legislation in the years after the Act was passed was *In re Carroll*, decided in December 1930. An unmarried Roman Catholic mother gave birth to her second illegitimate child in the workhouse and

> [t]he Catholic authorities were proposing to find a Catholic home for the child, but according to their set policy, which was not to make things too easy for the mothers of illegitimate children, lest such mothers should be encouraged to rely on an illegitimate child's being provided for as soon as born, they were not hurrying the matter.[34]

The mother, needing to leave the workhouse and find work as a domestic servant, became impatient. Hearing of Mr Beesley at the Homeless Children's Aid and Adoption Society and F. B. Meyer Children's Home, a Protestant rescue society, she wrote to him to ask for help to get her daughter adopted. She eventually signed a form which she was told was a permanent surrender of her maternal rights. She told them the child had been baptised but not whether it was Protestant or Roman Catholic. The child was handed over to adopting parents who did not meet with the mother and who signed an agreement that the child would be brought up in the Protestant Evangelical faith.

When the Catholic Rescue Society made clear to the mother the implications of what had happened she went to court asking for a writ of *habeas corpus* for her daughter. Her proposal (backed by the Catholic Rescue Society) was that the child be placed with a foster mother selected by the Society till she was of school age when she would be transferred to schools managed by the Catholic Sisters of Mercy and then emigrated or found a position in England. Her mother would continue to have access to her. The Protestant society's proposal would leave her with the adopting family with whom she was now living, but otherwise there was no information about where she would be schooled or even in which Protestant denomination she would be brought up. Her mother would have no contact or knowledge of her.

In the lower courts the decision had been made upon consideration of the child's welfare – it being deemed 'that it was better for the child to remain under the kindly care which it has found'.[35] However, Lord Justice Scrutton, delivering the Court of Appeal judgement, said that

> it was not universally accepted that a 'home' with no external education was the best thing for a child. Many home-brought-up children were spoilt and deprived of independent initiative … It was argued that the advantage of a home instead of an institutional training outweighed the disadvantage of the departure from the religion desired by the mother. It was said that an institution was 'detrimental' to the child so that the parent's wishes might be disregarded. He could not regard the difference between home training and training in a respectable institution as sufficiently important to entitle the Court to disregard the parent's wishes with regard to religion in the case of a child so young as to have no wishes of its own.[36]

The third Appeal judge, Lord Justice Greer, dissented from the majority ruling. He said: 'To justify an order interfering with the *prima facie* right of the mother to determine the custody of her child the Court must find "that it is clearly right for the welfare of the child in some serious and important respect that the parent's right should be suspended or superseded"'. In his opinion that was clearly the case here:

> [H]e was judicially satisfied … that the welfare of the child required that, if possible, it should be brought up in the atmosphere of a respectable home, and under the control of respectable and kindly people who were willing to undertake the responsibility of parents to her, rather than that she should be brought up for a few years by a paid foster-mother … and afterwards brought up in an institution.[37]

There appears to have been remarkably little legal argument in this case. It was about conflicting opinions: about whether a mother's rights or a child's welfare were paramount, and what constituted a suitable upbringing for a child. It touched on the changing views of the value of children and family life which were discussed in Chapter 1. Indeed, the two contrasting judicial views presented different sides of the debate over the importance of domestic life and the value of the child.

The Kings Counsel acting for the adoption societies was Sir Thomas Inskip, who, as shown in earlier chapters, had been involved with adoption for some years, as well as holding governmental office. He was currently out of office (and Parliament) for the duration of the Labour Administration of 1929–31. The Appeal Judge who concurred with Lord Justice Scrutton in allowing the appeal, was Lord Justice Slesser who as Sir Henry Slesser had been Solicitor-General in the 1924 Labour Government and had seconded Sir Geoffrey Butler's Adoption Bill in 1925.

Other legal issues

Various issues and queries arose from the new adoption legislation.[38] For example, there was the situation where the mother of an illegitimate child subsequently married a man who was not the father of the child but who wished to adopt the child jointly with her. If he was less than twenty-one years older than the child this would never be possible (unless there was consanguinity, i.e. they were closely enough related to be forbidden to marry).

Another question was raised over the effect of adoption orders on existing affiliation orders. Some lawyers argued that if an illegitimate child was adopted and thus provided with parents, it ceased to have the status of an illegitimate child and those who had been liable for maintaining it were no longer liable. Others argued that an affiliation order remained until terminated by a court and that the payments should be paid to the adopters. The Home Secretary, Sir W. Joynson-Hicks, alluded in Parliament to such a case in Manchester where a stipendiary magistrate held that a bastardy order was not dissolved by an adoption order.[39]

The Home Office received many letters requesting clarification of legal points. The National Adoption Society asked what happened when the parent of a child who had been adopted informally for some years cannot be traced. The Home Office wrote back (with a copy to the Highgate Juvenile Court who raised the issue) confirming that the necessary notices should be served or sent to the last known address of the respondent and if they could not be found the Court was empowered to dispense with their attendance.[40] Solicitors from Ashton-under-Lyne wrote to ask if the names of the natural parents could be omitted from an adoption order where illegitimacy was concerned. This was a persistent query but the Home Office maintained its opposition to this kind of secrecy. It would 'be quite improper for an Adoption Order to contain no reference to the parents (or parent) of the child. Where no birth certificate is produced, for instance, it could mean that the identity of the child could not be established at all'.[41]

Another query came from the Chairman of Colchester Juvenile Court Panel. A four-year-old had recently been adopted by 'very respectable working people' but he had then developed a severe case of venereal disease and was in hospital: 'It is not impossible that he will become imbecile [sic]'. He asked if adopters 'can free themselves from such an unlooked for burden – I fear not'. He also wondered if justices should insist on blood tests which could provide an almost completely reliable guarantee of the absence of syphilis. S. W. Harris of the Home Office said he doubted that was necessary but did feel that careful medical examinations before adoption were 'certainly desirable' and understood that adoption societies such as the National Children Adoption Association organised these for children in their care. He confirmed that there was no way in which an adoption order could be rescinded.[42] A similar query came from a couple who had adopted a child with a cleft palate who turned out to have other problems – fits, discoloured face, sickliness. It was reported that 'it has caused them so much trouble and anxiety that the husband has threatened that he will not live at home if the child remains there'. The comment on the Home Office file says, 'They must now abide by their bad bargain.'[43] Six months later the child died.

A minor piece of legislation affecting adoption was passed in 1934. This was the Adoption of Children (Workmen's Compensation) Act which brought adopted children in line with natural children as far as entitlement to the benefit of the Workmen's Compensation Act 1926 was concerned. A decision of the Court of Appeal had laid down that an adopted child was not a child within the meaning of that legislation. A Bill to reverse the effect of this decision was introduced by Mr Galbraith who had also introduced the 1926 Adoption of Children Act. The Bill met with no opposition and was given Royal Assent in July 1934.

Adoption of Children (Scotland) Act 1930

The 1926 Adoption of Children Act had only applied to England and Wales but in 1930 the Labour MP, George Mathers, brought in a Bill to extend the legislation to Scotland. The Bill, he explained, was 'identical with the English Act of 1926, except, of course, that, where necessary, provision has had to be made for the difference in legal machinery and practice in Scotland'.[44] He regretted the need to bring in the Bill 'because it indicates that Scotland has lost the lead that she had over England at the beginning of the 18th century in respect of beneficent legislation'.[45] The Bill passed smoothly through both Houses and received Royal Assent on 1 August 1930. Although both Mr Mathers and the Earl of Lucan who presented the Bill on behalf of the Duke of Atholl in the Lords assured their audiences of the similarities with the English legislation there was in fact one major difference: from the age of seventeen adopted persons had the right to be given the information which would link the Adopted Children's Register with their original entry in the Birth Register, without recourse to a court order, as was the case in England and Wales.

After the Second World War this difference became more significant as the debate about secrecy intensified, and at one point there was discussion of removing this right from Scottish adoptees. No action was taken, and finally in 1975 a similar entitlement was extended to English adoptees over eighteen. Quite why there was this original difference between the two countries remains unclear. The social work academic John Triseliotis, who extensively researched the issue of adopted people tracing their origins, pointed out that there are no minutes of the debates of the Standing Committee on Scottish Bills during which Mr Mathers successfully inserted this section into the 1930 Act.[46] He speculated that it might have related to the right that adoptees had to inherit from their natural parents and not their adoptive parents. Without information about their origins this would be impossible and it was not until 1964 that the position for Scottish adoptees was reversed (i.e. they could inherit from their adoptive parents but not from their natural ones). However the English 1926 Adoption Act had the same provisions about inheritance as in Scotland; the position was reversed earlier but still not until 1949.[47] Writing in the early 1970s before the 1975 Children Act, Triseliotis said that as far as he knew, Scotland and Finland were the only countries in the Western world where an adopted person could obtain information from official sources that could lead to them tracing their birth parents.[48]

The London County Council

Local authorities were involved in legal adoption from the start but most limited their involvement to providing guardians *ad litem*. The London County Council (LCC) was probably the largest organisation involved with adoption in the interwar years and it gradually took a pioneering role in arranging adoptions. Immediately after the Adoption of Children Act came into force, the Education Officer was approached by magistrates from Bow Street, Clerkenwell and Westminster, as well as Mr Clarke Hall at Old Street, asking the Council to act as guardian *ad litem* in adoption cases. The Education Officer said they would consider it and reported to the Special Services Subcommittee:

> It would appear ... that no other person or body is so well able to obtain the requisite information or has had so much experience in dealing with similar circumstances as the Council acting through the Cases Section of the Special Services Subcommittee. Effective machinery also exists for supervision if the Court wishes to defer making a final decision, but to grant an interim order.[49]

In early February the LCC's General Purposes Committee recommended that the task of acting as guardian *ad litem* be shared by the Education and Public Health Committees. The Medical Officer of Health would be responsible for cases where a child came under Part 1 of the Children Act 1908, and the Education Officer for all others. A Joint Committee of the two departments was established and it was agreed that they would deal with cases for an experimental period of one year.[50] By the middle of December 1927, the Council had acted in 426 cases; 88 under the Children Act, of which 83 were given full adoption orders, three interim orders, one withdrawn and one adjourned. Of the 338 other cases (those dealt with by the Education Department), 298 were given full orders, ten interim ones, nine were refused, fourteen withdrawn and seven adjourned. The Council's recommendations were accepted in all but six cases.[51] In a report of a conference in June 1927 an LCC officer is quoted as saying that

> 'the applicants for adoption orders were, for the most part, people in rather poor circumstances'. He had evidently been greatly impressed by the kindness of the applicants, and quoted some striking instances, eg applications to adopt a child whose parents were both deaf and dumb, another whose father was in prison and the mother in an asylum, several mentally deficient children, and one whose father had murdered its mother.[52]

Over the next few years the LCC acted as guardian *ad litem* in about 500 cases a year.[53]

In July 1932 the LCC decided to take on a much greater role in adoption. Under the Poor Law Act 1930 it was maintaining about 8500 children up to the age of sixteen and was responsible for placing them in employment and for their after-care up to the age of eighteen. The Council had parental rights and powers for about three thousand of these children under Section 52(1) of the 1930 Poor Law Act, five hundred of them under rights and powers assumed in respect of them by resolution of the Public Assistance Committee since April 1930: the rest had been transferred to the Council from former Boards of Guardian by the Local Government Act 1929. These three thousand children were commonly spoken of as 'adopted' by the Council (although not in terms of the 1926 Act) and were mainly orphaned, deserted or from 'parents [who were] deemed unfit or incapable for some prescribed reason to have control of them'. The rights and powers had in fact 'frequently been assumed by the authority for the protection of the child from known parents'.[54] Of the other five and a half thousand children maintained by the LCC, many were orphans or deserted but in the absence of special reasons it was not judged necessary to assume parental powers over them.

Apart from about two hundred boarded out with foster parents, the rest of the eight and a half thousand children lived in the Council's own residential homes or institutions or homes run by voluntary organisations. Under the 1930 Poor Law Act – and earlier Poor Law Acts – there was a provision allowing the Council to let a child be adopted by a private person and, as was discussed in Chapter 1, some of the now disbanded Boards of Guardians had availed themselves of this provision and transferred the custody of individual children to people who applied to adopt them. Adoption was now a much more widely publicised activity and as growing numbers of requests were made to adopt the children in its care the LCC realised it must decide on an adoption policy for them.

It considered first whether it should agree in principle to the adoption of children in its guardianship. The most important issues were whether it was in the interests of the child and of the community in general. On the first aspect it was felt that although individual circumstances of the child, the residential home, the adopter and the adopter's home obviously affect this question enormously.

> In general ... it will probably be agreed that an ordinary child has a better chance of happiness and social adjustment by being brought up in a reasonably good family home than in any public or charitable

institution ... In the child's interests, which should be paramount, adoption by private persons would seem to be preferable in most cases to institutional maintenance under the poor law.[55]

As far as the question of the community's interests was concerned the Council felt that 'it may be said that what is good generally for the children's welfare should in the long run be good for the community'. It considered that 'every successful adoption, besides causing gratification to the adopters, would mark the absorption into the ordinary domestic structure of society of one odd member.'[56] It also pointed out that the financial effect of the Council's proposals for adoption would be a saving of at least £25 a year for each child adopted.

The Council considered the possibility of children being adopted, as in the past, under the Poor Law legislation but, having looked at the way this operated, it concluded that the lack of 'an absolute or permanent arrangement' would leave the child in an unsatisfactory position. The legislation stipulated twice-yearly visits by the authorities to the child and its adopting family for three years and the authority's right to revoke their consent and recall the child at any time during this period. Then after this long probationary period there was a lack of clarity as to the child's status and security within the adopting family. The Council discussed the alternative, effecting the adoption of children under the Adoption of Children Act 1926, and concluded that, 'on social grounds, and particularly in the children's interest', it was a much better system.[57]

It was envisaged that the departments currently dealing with guardian *ad litem* work – Education and Public Health – would be able to use their officers and processes to extend this work to dealing with the Council's maintained children who became the subjects of adoption. The Council accepted that it would be improbable that the courts would allow them to act in the dual roles of respondent and guardian *ad litem* but felt that they could speed up the adoption process by providing the guardians *ad litem* with as much information as possible. In a letter to the Chief Clerk at Bow Street Juvenile Court, the LCC's Education Officer described the Council's procedure in its first few months of arranging adoptions and suggested that the court's guardian *ad litem* might have access to their information:

> Before handing any child over to prospective applicants under the Act, the Council interviews them, investigates the references which they give and arranges for their home to be visited. In some cases

a further visit or visits will be made whilst the child is with the prospective adopters on probation. By the time, therefore, that the period of probation has ended and an application for permanent adoption is made the Council will have much information about the applications which will be required by the guardian *ad litem*.[58]

The visits mentioned above do not sound particularly gruelling. The Education Officer told his divisional officers that in dealing with the adoption of children from LCC establishments:

> [F]rom time to time, you will be asked to arrange for a suitable member of your staff (usually a special attendance officer) to call on applicants and to report to me the general impression gained of their home. It should be particularly noted that it will be unnecessary for applicants to be interrogated on any matters other than the question of living accommodation for the child or whether there are persons other than the applicant residing in their house (or apartment). Applicants should of course be told that the results of enquiries will be treated as strictly private and confidential.[59]

Applicants who were approved were then invited to visit particular institutions and pick out a child for adoption.

By November 1932, a few months after the new procedure was introduced, the Council had received 105 inquiries about adoption, including fifty written applications. Seven applicants had been interviewed and another 31 were awaiting an interview. A few had been declined following their interview or just on the basis of their written information. An internal LCC memorandum says: 'The first interviews have confirmed the anticipation of the conference on this scheme ... that each case requires individual consideration as to the manner in which the character and circumstances of the applicant shall be vouchsafed or inquired into.'[60] The memo goes on to list some of the applicants, emphasising the need for flexibility in dealing with them:

- a most eligible couple in comfortable circumstances at Wandsworth Common;
- a postman and his wife at Catford;
- an airforce corporal and his wife on Salisbury Plain (man's commanding officer being asked for confidential report);
- an invalid woman of means in North London who wanted to come to County Hall by car and be interviewed on the ground

floor [a note says two ladies – possibly voluntary workers – were invited to visit her but they declined so a letter has been sent to her to put her in touch with places where girls of eighteen can be found];
- a clergyman in Devonshire who will be visited, if he proceeds with his application, by the Exeter LEA;
- a couple of the artisan class who live at Ashford, Middlesex, close to our own residential school. The Superintendent or matron of the school will be invited to visit in this case, and the child offered (if any) will probably be from Ashford School.[61]

The issue of appropriate age for adoption soon arose. The Education Department sought advice from the Medical Officer although his reply is not in the file. They were arranging for applicants seeking children under three years old to be referred to the Medical Officer once they had been interviewed and their references taken up:

> The point arises, however, as to what is the lowest age at which it is desirable to allow children to be taken by prospective adopters. In the majority of cases ... children from two to three years are required but an applicant who was recently interviewed wants to obtain a child of only six months old. She was informed that there might be difficulties in the way and was asked to consider as to taking a child of one or two years old.[62]

Presumably part of the problem for the LCC was that it would have had relatively few very young babies in its care because it was seeking adopters for children who had been deserted, orphaned or removed from their parents for reasons such as abuse or neglect, and by the time the necessary legal procedures were completed the children were inevitably older. In contrast, the adoption societies dealt with children whose parents had voluntarily relinquished them, usually at a very early stage, so they were used to dealing with babies, and do not seem to have been concerned that they were too young to be adopted. The age of potential adopters does not appear to have been discussed – possibly the LCC simply followed the minimum ages and age differentials laid down in the Adoption Act.

At the end of 1932 the superintendents and matrons of children's homes and residential institutions were asked to draw up a list of children, preferably under ten, who might be suitable candidates for adoption, and a month later the Education Officer sent it to the Managing

Committee on Adoption which was coordinating the different departments.[63] He pointed out that the children would still have to have medicals and must be 'of satisfactory physical and medical condition'. He explained that 'in ordinary circumstances' it was not proposed to offer a child who had brothers or sisters for private adoption.[64] For most cases there was a six-month probationary period before the adopting parent could apply for an adoption order, and a boarding-out visitor, already experienced in visiting families, would visit at the end of five months.

The London County Council did not rush wholesale into adoption. By 1936 when it gave evidence to the Departmental Committee on Adoption Societies and Agencies it had been responsible for seventy-two completed adoptions and thirty children were with prospective adopters on probation.[65] Even so, the Council had 'arranged considerably more adoptions than any other authority',[66] and the Departmental Committee commended it for its procedure 'which seems to us admirable'. By then the policies had been firmed up. Applicants had to give two references, one of them preferably a minister of religion or medical practitioner. Those who passed the initial stage of an application form were interviewed by two officials of the Education Department, one of whom was a woman, and if they were approved at this stage they were visited by a Boarding-Out Inspector. In these first four years 259 applicants reached the interview stage. Of these, thirty-seven were then turned down at the interview, six on unfavourable home reports and two because of unsatisfactory references.[67]

The probationary period was by now usually three to six months. The applicants would be visited again 'but the main object of the period of probation is to enable the adopters to satisfy themselves that the adoption is likely to be successful, and it is found that a considerable number of children are returned as unsatisfactory.'[68] No figures or details were given about these 'unsatisfactory' children. Other points which emerged were that the Council had decided on a policy that no children be adopted under one year, very few people wanted children over five, and ninety-five per cent of applications were for girls.[69]

The LCC adoption programme has more in common with contemporary adoption practice through local authority social services departments than that of the adoption societies, in that it was placing children who had become the Council's responsibility because of problems in their family background. It is not clear whether parents whose children had been removed from them for reasons of abuse or neglect ever contested these adoptions.

Who were the adopters, the adopted, and the relinquishing parents in the early years?

This is not a question that can be easily answered. There were no surveys or samples of adopted children or parents or relinquishing parents during the period to 1950 and very few official statistics were kept about adoption then. In 1920 Miss Andrew of the NCAA had described the adopters coming to her society as being a quarter working class, 15–20% upper class and the rest middle class. This sounds like a quick guess but is quite feasible. The evidence is all anecdotal: earlier in this chapter I quoted a Juvenile Court Clerk saying that most adopting homes were better off than those the children came from, but later I cited an LCC official suggesting that most of those adopting were 'in rather poor circumstances'. The Home Office report discussed earlier makes no mention of class but says two-thirds of adoption orders were for illegitimate children. It does not say whether the rest were orphans, relatives or unwanted children from large families. The Official Solicitor, who acted as guardian *ad litem* in adoption cases in the High Court, said in 1928: 'The Act has ... revealed the keen desire which appears to be very prevalent amongst well to do and childless people to adopt a child or children.'[70]

Opinions are widely divergent on this. The social work academic John Triseliotis said that until the 1940s adoption 'was mainly confined to the working classes and it is only since then that adoption as a custom has been fully accepted into the ethos of middle-class society'.[71] He appears to have based this assertion on court records in Scotland in 1935 showing that only 7% of families adopting were middle class. Nothing I have found in any of the, admittedly sparse, information for England suggests that the situation was similar. Indeed in her second survey of mainly working-class family life in North West England [1940–70], the oral historian Elizabeth Roberts said to an interviewee who had adopted two children that, although she had come across families bringing up relatives' children in her earlier survey, 'I don't think in my other survey [1890–1940] that anybody adopted anybody, it seems to be something that has happened ... in the 50s and 60s'.[72] This is an anecdotal comment based on a small number of interviewees but shows how difficult it is to make generalisations about who was adopting pre-war.

There have been a few retrospective surveys of adoptive outcomes which have included people adopted during this period. In 1955 the National Association for Mental Health (later MIND) carried out a survey based on case records of five unnamed adoption societies of which a third dated from the mid 1930s and the rest from the 1940s.[73] Unfortunately, although a great deal of material was apparently gathered about the work status and class of natural parents and adoptive parents, none of this was revealed in its report. This was concerned with whether adoptions were problematic or satisfactory and only looked at the different status of natural and adoptive parents to see if there was any link between the status of the adoptive parents as opposed to the natural parents, and the success of the adoption.[74]

Of the 163 records looked at, 151 adopters were married couples adopting, 12 were single women and 55 of the adoptive mothers were over 40 years old. The survey also looked at individual case records from adopted children attending two child guidance clinic records. These are summarised in some detail but obviously cannot be seen as a representative sample and do not give any consistently useful information apart from the fact that in the first clinic three of the 17 children had been adopted by single women and one by a widow, three by relatives and one by its natural mother and her husband; the rest were married couples, their ages usually not given. At the second clinic, of 12 cases, all had been adopted by married couples, the only particularly noticeable factor being that at the time of adoption three of the 12 adoptive mothers were over 40, two over 50.

In the mid-1950s a social worker, Alexina McWhinnie, interviewed 58 adopted adults (including six who had been long-term fostered) aged 18–60 years who were living in South East Scotland and all but five of whom had been brought up there. She contacted them through GPs and found they 'followed fairly closely the pattern of distribution by social class of live legitimate births in Scotland for the year 1955'.[75] McWhinnie provides detailed and interesting case studies for many of them but it is difficult to make useful historical generalisations from them as her focus is that of a social worker assessing their 'adjustment' to their adoption. Of the 52 adopted she judged 15 to have 'good', 10 'poor', 21 'intermediate' and six 'fairly good' adjustment. About two-thirds of the adoptees were born in the interwar period, most were women, brought up by two parents and as only children. Two of the sample were brought up by widows, one by a single woman. The vast majority were illegitimate and their age at placement varied from a few days to four years.

In 1988–90 NCH (formerly known as the National Children's Home and Orphanage[76]) conducted a survey of adoptees who returned to the agency for birth record counselling but the majority were adopted after the Second World War. They describe a couple of cases from 1927 which presumably they saw as representative examples. One of these was

> [i]n her mid-30s, from a poor country family and badly educated ... in the domestic service of an elderly Methodist couple in London.
>
> Lonely and vulnerable she eventually met an older man with whom she had a brief affair. When she became pregnant the man confessed to being married with a family. She never saw him again. Distraught, knowing her family would not welcome her back, she turned to her elderly employers.
>
> They had heard of the new 1926 Adoption Act and advised her to go to NCH for help. They were also willing to employ her, but would not allow a baby in their home.
>
> [She] gave birth to [her son] in Fulham and immediately handed him to a foster mother. After six weeks [she] took [him] to the NCH Highbury Nursery and handed him over, along with a layette, a birth certificate and a rattle. [She] never saw [him] again.[77]

The majority of those adopting were married couples, presumably wishing in the main to adopt because one or other or both were infertile. Infertility does not seem to have been discussed very much in this period. Medical treatment for the ten per cent or more of couples who had trouble conceiving was relatively primitive or even non-existent.[78] Many more suffered from ignorance and embarrassment about sexual problems for which advice and information was not easily available even if they could have conquered their feelings of shame to ask for it.[79] Discussing the 'sterile couples' in their survey of married couples' attitudes during and just after the Second World War, Slater and Woodside stated:

> In a few there was an assignable cause ... but in others it was entirely unknown. Most of these couples were resigned and fatalistic. Ignorant that a remedy might exist, shy of making a complaint of something that was hardly an illness, afraid of doctors and hospitals, few but the younger ones had taken any steps.[80]

Naomi Pfeffer has described the development of infertility treatments during the twentieth century and argued that not until the mid-late 1930s did sterility become any kind of a political and public issue. The falling birth rate had been long debated but only then did attention turn to sterility as an issue (at least as it affected women). Women began to seek help for infertility and commentators became aware that the numbers not having children were growing. Of those born during 1881–90 (who would have completed their childbearing by the 1930s), 20.9% of upper- and middle-class, and 14.2% of working-class, women were childless. As Pfeffer pointed out: 'Unfortunately, the data cannot tell us how many of these women were childless by choice, nor how many were married to sterile men, nor whether their numbers were increasing.'[81] This was also a time when over 14 per cent of women never married, which presumably affected these statistics. However even if sterility, as Pfeffer suggested, 'began to be considered an urgent public health problem which the state should tackle,'[82] it had not become a subject of everyday discussion, and one of the reasons for some adopters' desire for secrecy may have been the embarrassment and shame they felt about revealing their infertility. In this era adoption was the only way that those with fertility problems could create a family for themselves. They did not even need to adopt more than one child as small families became quite normal. Michael Anderson showed that a quarter of the marriage cohort of 1925 had only one child (almost as many as had two),[83] and Ross McKibbin suggested that 'the "only child", something hardly known before 1914, was becoming an interwar phenomenon and nowhere more so than in the new suburbs'.[84] Fewer married women were in paid employment in 1931 than in 1901,[85] so with more than 95 per cent based at home there was inevitably social and emotional pressure on them to have a child to look after.

Of course not all adopters were married couples adopting non-related children. Official figures from the 1950s, when detailed statistics start, show that close to a third of the illegitimate children who were adopted were adopted by either their mother or father on their own, or by their parents jointly or by their mother or father jointly with a partner (mothers with a partner being by far the biggest group – for example in 1955, of the 10,341 illegitimate children adopted, 111 were adopted by their parents jointly, 19 by their father with a partner, 3000 by their mother with a partner, 18 by their father on his own and 87 by their mother on her own). The figures are similar through the 1950s.[86] The MP introducing the Adoption of Children Bill in 1949, Basil Nield, said that he had been told that a third of the illegitimate children subject to adoption orders were adopted by their own mothers,[87] which suggests the figures were similar before the 1950s.

Writers Dorothy L. Sayers and Rebecca West are examples of unmarried mothers who adopted their own illegitimate sons to make them legitimate. Sayers' biographers disagree as to whether she officially adopted her son or not and I can find no listing of a legal adoption in the official records. Initially the son thought Sayers was his cousin; from about seven he thought she was his mother and when he was eleven she told him that she and her husband had adopted him.[88] West adopted her son Anthony during an emotional battle with his father, H. G. Wells. In 1929 she wrote: 'I put down £60 of my hard-earned money to adopt Anthony so that he could show an adoption instead of a birth certificate and need not pay strangers' death duties on my estate'. As the contributing father Wells had the right to be consulted and he opposed the adoption. It was granted but with conditions about Wells' access to Anthony.[89]

Single childless people also adopted children during the interwar years. Single men were allowed to adopt boys under twenty one, and girls with the permission of the court, and single women could adopt girls or boys. Other than the Home Office figures for 1927–8, there are no official figures about how many took advantage of this until 1950 (when 28 single males and 155 single women adopted non-related children out of 8259 adoptions of non-related children[90]). In those first 15 months of the legislation described by the Home Office more than a third of the High Court adoptions were by people adopting singly – 21 men and 51 women – and in the County Court, 450 single men and 150 women obtained adoption orders during that period. Some of these would have been legalising long-standing informal adoptions but it does indicate that adoption by single people in the early years may have been more common then than after the Second World War.[91]

The men who adopted remain in the shadows but a number of quite visible single women adopted. The doctor, Alice Corthorn, was one such example. Born in 1859, she supported herself while training as a doctor and for some years had a wide circle of friends including Havelock Ellis and Eleanor Marx. Aged 54 and working as a GP, she adopted a baby from the mother and baby home where she was medical officer, whom she named Olive after her friend and early mentor, Olive Schreiner. After she retired at 60, she and her adopted daughter lived in considerable poverty and isolation for many years until Olive was old enough to support them both. When Olive was eight, before the 1926 Adoption Act, her natural mother tried to reclaim her, but appears to have been deflected by a solicitor friend of Alice's. Olive Renier, as she became, was positive about her adoption despite the difficulties: 'I am still quite convinced that no natural mother-child relationship could be closer than that which subsisted between my adoptive mother and myself as a child.'[92]

Other single women who adopted included the suffragette, Mary Richardson,[93] and the journalist, Martha Gellhorn.[94] Middle-class professional women appear to have carried off single adoptive motherhood relatively confidently but a couple of the women Katherine Holden interviewed who came from poorer backgrounds found it more difficult to deal with the potential embarrassment of being viewed as an unmarried mother and made their adopted children call them 'aunty' rather than mother.[95] In contrast, Mary Abbott quotes a story from the autobiography of Rosamund Essex who as a single lady working for the *Church Times* adopted a son. Although she was determined there be a clean break between her son and his birth mother he always knew he was adopted and took it for granted. In his teens while away for a few days he met a bishop at a church function and said: '"I think you know my mother, Miss Essex". The bishop was aghast. But he kept his cool and managed to stammer out, Yes, yes he did, and then disappeared into the crowd to think it over.'[96]

By the early 1950s the tide was turning against single adopters. In 1956 a 'spinster adopter' of two girls wrote to *Child Adoption*, the journal of the Standing Conference of Societies Registered for Adoption, to defend the practice:

> I understand that since the war it has become increasingly difficult for spinsters to adopt children and I think this is a pity. If a spinster has health and intelligence, more money than she needs for herself, time on her hands and the desire to adopt children, I fail to see why she should not be allowed to do so, with all the same safeguards and provisos as apply to married women.[97]

A few years later another single adopter, this time a widow, wrote about her experiences in the same journal. She also made a plea for single women and widows to be allowed to adopt although the journal introduced her article somewhat ambiguously, saying it expressed 'a viewpoint on adoption that was perhaps more frequent a few years ago than now, but in any event reflects an attitude that continues to affect present adoption thinking'. It is not clear if this refers to her single state or her rather choosy attitude about picking out a 'neat pretty little baby'.[98] The NCAA, which had accepted single adopters pre-war, declared in 1953: 'Unmarried or widowed applicants are not considered, as it is desired above all things to give a child a normal balanced home life, and with so many suitable couples waiting to adopt, it is always possible to provide a child with two parents.'[99] McWhinnie considered that in her sample of adopted adults, 'adoption by one parent was never associated with good adjustment'. She expanded on the reasons given by the NCAA:

> This is not really surprising when related to theories of child development, all of which stress the need for two parent-figures for the child to identify with at different stages of development, so that, when they come later to make relationships in the adult world, they have the experience to equip them for making discriminating relationships with people of both sexes.[100]

Apart from rare and exceptional circumstances, such as adoption of orphans by single relatives, it was not until the 1990s when adoption for children in local authority care was expanding that adoption by single people would again be considered as a serious possibility.

6
Action on the Adoption Societies

Concern about the role of adoption societies

There had been concern about the way adoption societies operated since they began their work during the First World War. In Chapter 4 it was shown that members of the Tomlin Committee had considerable unpublished reservations about the societies' obsessive desire for secrecy and their attitude to relinquishing mothers. As the Adoption of Children Act 1926 became an established and widely used piece of legislation the emphasis of those who were interested in the issue of adoption began to concentrate on the operation of the adoption societies themselves. Criticism centred on certain societies; on the whole the two main ones, the NCAA and NAS, were exempted. The Official Solicitor, who admittedly dealt only with cases involving wealthier families in the High Court, wrote glowingly of these societies:

> I am decidedly impressed by the care exercised by them in placing children and by the substantial and in many cases immense benefits conferred by their help on children whose lot in life in most cases, would otherwise be far from enviable. I have had not occasion to criticise any of their methods.[1]

However in 1930 the petition from the NCAA for a Royal Charter was turned down, despite its many worthy supporters and a list of well-connected signatories who included, besides Princess Alice and Clara Andrew, Lucy Baldwin, wife of the Leader of the Opposition; Dame Margaret Lloyd George, the wife of a former Prime Minister; Mrs Ethel Snowden, wife of the current Chancellor of the Exchequer; and

Sir Thomas Inskip, then out of office but either attorney-general or solicitor-general for most of the period 1922–36. The petition was turned down on the recommendation of the Home Office, partly because the NCAA had only started in 1917 and its activities were 'subject to no supervision by any local or public authority'. But surprisingly the main reason was the NCAA's practice of 'maintaining secrecy in all their transactions' (like the other adoption societies). The Home Office said that in this respect 'the policy of this Association is not entirely consistent with the principles which Parliament laid down as antecedent to legal adoption'.[2] The NCAA took issue with this through their solicitors, protesting that judicial proceedings under the 1926 Act were held *in camera* and the Adoption Register was not made public but the Home Office refuted such arguments, saying 'the policy of secrecy followed by the Association in seeking to break off all connection between the child and its past is quite a different matter', citing the Tomlin Report on the inadvisability of secrecy.[3]

There were attempts to use the Children and Young Persons Bill (see below for more details), which was introduced in 1931, to include some regulation of societies. In April 1931, the Labour MP, Mr James Lovat-Fraser, asked if the forthcoming Bill would include provision for the banning of advertisements dealing with 'taking children for reward'. The newly elected Conservative MP for West Willesden, Mrs Tate,[4] took a considerable interest in the issue and in her maiden speech during the Second Reading of the Bill she suggested: 'There are societies in this country at present into which it would be of very great advantage to have exhaustive inquiries made into how they look after homeless and illegitimate children.' She praised what she called the National Children Adoption Society but called for 'Clauses which would protect those unhappy little children from other societies which are much less particular and much less disinterested'.[5] The previous day she had asked the Home Secretary if he would consider introducing legislation requiring a society or individual acting as an agent for the adoption of children to hold a licence granted by him. Sir Herbert Samuel replied that he had 'so far seen no evidence that such legislation is necessary'.[6]

A couple of weeks later Mrs Tate had a meeting with the Parliamentary Secretary for Health, Ernest Brown, a Liberal National MP in the 1931–5 National Government, and the Principal Assistant Secretary at the Ministry of Health, A. B. Maclachlan.[7] She was much more forthcoming about specific problems than in her parliamentary debut. In particular she cited 'the Rev W F Buttle's Church of England Adoption Society and Mr E. T. Beesley's Homeless Children's Aid and Adoption Society – who took unwanted babies for considerable sums of money and within a few hours sold them for much larger sums to people who did want them, including Americans'. She said

> that Mr Buttle ... and Mr Beesley had both repeatedly been shown up in Truth, but the police had never been able to get a conviction against them. Their method was to induce a child's mother to sign a worthless agreement which she could not understand, and, if she subsequently asked for the child back, to bluff her with the 'agreement' into believing that she had no longer any legal claim to the child. Mr Buttle advertised in America where British babies command fancy prices; what happened to the babies when they got there was unknown. Mr Beesley's activities were similar to those of Mr Buttle. There were also some very unsatisfactory children's homes eg the Mission of Hope, South Croydon. Mrs Tate said that these abuses had increased during the last year or two and had now reached such dimensions that genuine adoption societies (such as the National Children Adoption Association and the National Adoption Society) found it very difficult to obtain babies for bona fide adoption.[8]

Mrs Tate also brought up the issue of advertisements offering places for unwanted children which were often found in provincial newspapers under box numbers. Brown and Maclachlan suggested it might be possible to introduce amendments to deal with these issues and possibly make compulsory the notification of the person from whom it was received when a baby was handed on to a third party for reward. However 'it did not seem possible to deal in the Bill with the abuses of the baby export trade'.[9]

The Magistrates' Association also lobbied for change. As described in the previous chapter, magistrates presided over the vast majority of adoption cases so they were presumably talking from considerable experience. Women had been appointed as magistrates from 1920, and by 1923 there were already about nine hundred of them. From the beginning they were accustomed 'to meet in smaller or larger groups in order to compare notes as to their work, and to study its problems',[10] so they would have presented a formidable addition to the Association. Magistrates specifically asked for Part V of the Bill which dealt with

Infant Life Protection to include provision for some governmental control over adoption societies. They wanted societies licensed and they called for every association, society and individual involved with adoption of children

> to keep records giving full particulars of children adopted through their agency and of the adopters concerned. Such records shall also supply details of any financial payment whether in respect of expenses or otherwise, made by the parents or adopters, and shall at any time be open to inspection by persons appointed by the Secretary of State.[11]

They also called for a ban on children being taken out of the United Kingdom to be adopted or being adopted by 'aliens' whether resident in the country or not.

The Children and Young Persons Act 1932[12] did attempt to deal with the minor points raised by Mrs Tate and Mr Lovat-Fraser. Section 68(1) said that no advertisement indicating that a person or society will undertake or arrange the nursing and maintenance of an infant under the age of nine may be published unless the person's name and address or society's name and office address are truly stated in the advertisement. An amendment (Section 65 (2)) to the original 1908 Act added the duty of anyone receiving an infant 'for reward' to notify not just the authority in the case of its death or removal to another party but also 'the person from whom the infant was received'. However it made no mention of registering or licensing adoption societies and did not attempt to deal with the issue of taking children overseas for adoption which was an issue that provoked much popular indignation whenever a case was publicised in the popular press.

In fact the Home Office was considering the issue of regulating societies, as is evidenced by a paper prepared for S. W. Harris, the Assistant Under Secretary of State, which mainly used quotes from an earlier (highly critical) unpublished memorandum about the adoption societies prepared for the Tomlin Committee by M. L. Gwyer of the Ministry of Health (see Chapter 4), and concluded: 'It would appear that the only form of licensing which would be any effective check upon the methods of these adoption societies would be licensing by the Secretary of State, such as is suggested by the Magistrates' Association.'[13]

The popular papers often ran articles about the horrors of adoption. The Home Office files have many cuttings of them. The weekly paper

John Bull ran an article headed 'Stamp Out our Baby Sellers!' in June 1932. It began:

> An appalling traffic in unwanted babies is going on to-day, and as the law now stands nothing can be done to end it.
>
> There are, incredible as it may seem, unscrupulous people all over the country who make a substantial living by dealing in babies as casually as if they were bales of merchandise and as heartlessly as if they were slaves.
>
> Some operate individually in a modest way, others form themselves into societies with pretentious aims and objects.
>
> ... in London alone there are countless bogus baby-adoption offices. There is, in fact, nothing to prevent anyone from taking a room and advertising for children or adopters, and charging fees which are often as high as £150.
>
> ... the latest aspect of this inhuman bartering of babies is that many aliens are now seeking British children for adoption.
>
> Large numbers of little ones have gone to America in this way, and though many of the purchasers may be actuated by the best intentions, it cannot be too strongly stressed that there can be no guarantee regarding the children's future welfare once they have left our shores.[14]

The paper gave scant evidence for all these statements – a couple of cases of people prosecuted for relatively minor offences when babies died in their care, and a number of unattributed statements. Similarly, the *Sunday Dispatch* wrote:

> Investigations by the authorities have brought to light a scandalous traffic in British children. It has been discovered that 'adoption societies' exist in this country, with their agents abroad, for adopting children and selling them on the Continent. The dealers in this nefarious traffic are making vast sums yearly.[15]

This article also provided no facts to back up its claims. An earlier story in the *News Chronicle*, describing the work of 'touts' who traded in children, at least offered a quote from W. J. Elliott of the NSPCC: 'The "tout" would take a child away for £50 and dispose of it to another person for £25.'[16]

The NSPCC was increasingly concerned about the operation of some of the adoption societies. It had always been dubious about adoption, which it saw as an extension of 'baby farming', and it had been disappointed at the lack of compulsion in the 1926 Act. In 1933, its director, William J. Elliott, wrote a letter (also signed by J. C. Pringle, the Secretary of the Charity Organisation Society, and Cecil M. Chapman, a vice-president of the NCAA and retired police magistrate) to the Home Secretary, Sir John Gilmour, calling for 'a full enquiry into the conduct of all adoption societies, in order that something may be done to minimise or remove the dangers that result from the present condition of the law'.[17]

Mr Elliott appended a number of detailed case studies to illustrate the kinds of concerns they had in mind. Apart from the report of a foster mother who was convicted of failure to notify the coroner of the death of a child (having been twice before convicted for similar offences) who came from an adoption society, these were not so much cases revealing deliberate cruelty as examples of inadequate and troubled families being allowed to take vulnerable children into their homes on a permanent basis without initial checks or further inspections.

Several of the children were from the Homeless Children's Aid and Adoption Society run by Mr Beesley, who has already been mentioned. A child adopted through them had been 'found to be verminous, her body poorly nourished and dirty and she appeared weak and was rickety'; the NSPCC had also investigated various children admitted to hospital from the HCAAS' hostel who were 'found to be emaciated and in a neglected condition'.[18] A boy adopted through the Society was well nourished and clean but both the police and the NSPCC had been called in after complaints that the couple who had adopted him had been fighting while the man held the baby in his arms, and on another occasion the woman had threatened the child. The couple, who were unemployed, had received the boy from Mr Beesley's son and the Society had merely taken a completed form and references from them; no enquiries had been made. The couple had applied for an adoption order but five witnesses had objected to it.

The HCAAS appears incompetent and disorganised in these cases: the Home Office had for years known of the concerns about it but was unable to find anything concrete to charge it with. In 1931 it sent its own inspectors to inspect, without notice, the home the society ran in Leytonstone for children awaiting adoption (the Borough of Leyton had judged the home to be exempt from inspection as an institution conducted for charitable purposes). In fact a new matron had just been appointed and the inspectors felt that 'there has been a considerable rise in standards over the past few weeks, and that provided the present matron is given a reasonably free hand, there should be little cause for anxiety as to conditions at the Home so long as she remains'.[19]

The HCAAS also had dubious methods of raising finance. Mr Beesley freely admitted in his evidence to the Tomlin Committee in 1924 that while a child was awaiting adoption in the home the society got the mother to sign a relinquishing contract and then charged her 10 shillings a week if they could. After the child was adopted they charged her 5 shillings a week for three or four years ('and then her liability ceases altogether') and occasionally asked the adopters to contribute as well.[20] According to B. E. Astbury of the Charity Organisation Society, who investigated the HCAAS in depth, the mother was charged until her total contribution reached £60 but although this was meant to be for the child's 'maintenance' none of it went to the adopter.[21] In a case that was sent to the Director of Public Prosecutions in 1937 Mr Beesley's letters to the representative of a child's natural parents 'look as if they were calculated to deceive him in to thinking that the child was still being an expense to the Society' although it had already been placed with an adopter who received no payments. However there was not enough detailed evidence for the DPP to take any action.[22] The Mission of Hope in South Croydon, where Mr Beesley had earlier worked, employed similar financial methods. The NSPCC quoted from its letter to a relinquishing mother:

> Of course, you understand it would be necessary for you to pay something towards the expenses of same [the child being adopted]. It is usual for ten shillings per week to be paid while waiting in the Home and five shillings per week for six months after adoption, and one pound per year until the child reaches the age of fourteen years. This goes towards the adoption expenses.[23]

A memorandum from A. B. Maclachlan at the Ministry of Health a month later was clear that he was 'of opinion that there are very good grounds for Departmental enquiry into the methods of the various adoption societies'. He had

> recently heard of the case of a child of three being passed on to an elderly widower of morose character who it was thought might be livened up by such a course. This is said to have been done by the Baker Street people [National Adoption Society].

Mr Beesley was singled out for a critical aside ('Beesley, of course, has been under suspicion for years'). Maclachlan also mentioned that he had 'known a case where a woman has handed over her illegitimate children to a woman whose name and address she stated she did not know, the exchange being made in the market place of a country town'.[24]

One of the problems was the lack of trained social workers. The social work profession was in its infancy in the UK, and even the relatively organised London County Council used officers in the education and medical departments to carry out its adoptions rather than social workers. In the voluntary sector there were relatively few trained people apart from some residential workers who received in-house training from their organisations and some of the moral welfare workers employed by voluntary agencies who had done courses at the Josephine Butler House in Liverpool. It is easy to see that with so few trained social workers in the field, and almost none with any appropriate training, it would be unlikely that small under-funded adoption societies would appoint any in this period. The position did not change for a long time. In 1947 Eileen Younghusband stated that 'one of the best known [adoption] societies regards a clerical training as the only one necessary for its staff. Its care committee of voluntary members checks applications and helps with interviewing.'[25] Writing four years later she said that still 'the societies which exist solely for adoption purposes do not ... usually employ trained social workers'. She continued: 'in few cases, whoever makes the arrangements, is adequate consideration given to the question of whether it is in the best interest of the child that it shall not be brought up by its own mother if suitable arrangements could be made'.[26]

The National Children Adoption Association became alarmed about the bad publicity being generated about adoption. Its President, Princess Alice, wrote to Cecil M. Chapman, urging him to ask the Home Secretary to receive a deputation advocating the establishment of a Royal Commission to look at the whole question of adoption in England and Wales, which he did in May 1935.[27] At the NCAA's annual general meeting in 1935 the Princess took the opportunity to publicise this request. She drew a firm line between her association and others:

> It would be quite easy to show more spectacular numbers were they to accept a less high standard and were the Case Committee and the physicians less scrupulous in their investigations, and were they less stringent in their rules for the protection not only of the children but of the adopters.
>
> Recently they had regretfully to turn down a baby suffering from congenital heart disease as unfit for adoption. A few weeks later an adopter arrived at their office with a baby she had adopted through

another agency and about whose health she was not satisfied. It turned out to be the baby they had had to turn down which had been presented to her for adoption as a normal baby.[28]

W. J. Elliott of the NSPCC also spoke and said 'it was a sad reflection on our corporate life that it was easier for a person, however ill-suited to have the care of a little child, to secure one by adoption, than it was to purchase a prize canary or a bulldog'. He quoted a couple of cases:

> [A] boy of eight who was adopted by a man who was separated from his wife on the grounds of cruelty to her and her children. There was no Act of Parliament to prevent that kind of thing. It was eight weeks before his society heard of the case, and when they examined the boy they found he had 47 wounds on his body. A little girl of 12, who died recently, was the fifth or sixth child adopted in the past few years by a man and his wife, both aged over 80, who were evidently adopting children to obtain cheap domestic labour.[29]

In late October 1935 the Home Secretary, Sir John Simon, received a deputation from organisations involved with the practice of adoption and child welfare. It was introduced by Lord Mamhead of Exeter and included representatives from the National Children Adoption Association, the Charity Organisation Society, the NSPCC, the National Council for the Unmarried Mother and Her Child and the National Council of Women. It presented evidence of abuses in the adoption system and proposed a number of solutions. It urged on him the necessity of appointing a committee to inquire into the whole situation. 'The Home Secretary promised, in reply, to give careful consideration to the representations submitted by the deputation.'[30]

By November 1935 the decision had been taken to set up a departmental committee to look into the abuses in the adoption system. There was some adverse correspondence from the Lord Chancellor's Office. Its Permanent Secretary, Sir Claud Schuster, wrote to S. W. Harris at the Home Office that

> [The Lord Chancellor] wishes me to say that he thinks it a strange proceeding to appoint a Departmental Committee to inquire into matters with which this Department has been closely concerned without any consultation with him, and that he will not necessarily consider himself bound by any of its findings.[31]

Mr Harris was conciliatory, explaining that the enquiry would deal only with the activities of the societies who negotiate adoption, not with legal questions or the working of the Act. The Home Office was confident that the inquiry would be directed solely at the activities of the adoption societies and specifically rejected the possibility that its Chairman might be 'a person of legal eminence',[32] as both Sir Alfred Hopkinson and Mr Justice (now Lord) Tomlin who chaired the earlier Adoption Committees had been.

The Horsbrugh Committee

The committee was announced in the House of Commons on 13 February 1936, in response to a question from a Conservative MP, Mr Temple Morris, by the Home Secretary Sir John Simon, who said that, following 'representations made to him in regard to the alleged existence of abuse in connection with the adoption of children', he had decided to appoint a committee to inquire into the matter.[33] It would

> inquire into the methods pursued by adoption societies or other agencies engaged in arranging for the adoption of children and to report whether any, and if so what, measures should be taken in the public interest to supervise or control their activities.[34]

The Committee was chaired by Miss Florence Horsbrugh, the senior of the two MPs for Dundee (who became in 1953 the first woman to hold a Cabinet post in a Conservative government[35]). The other members were Mr Benjamin Edward Astbury, Assistant Secretary of the Charity Organisation Society; Mr John Henry Harris, a Metropolitan Police Magistrate; Mr J. J. Mallon, Warden of Toynbee Hall; Mr Brian Manning, a chartered accountant; Mrs (later Lady) Priscilla Montagu Norman (not to be confused with Lady Priscilla Norman who was a member of the Hopkinson Committee), a former member of the London County Council and wife of the Governor of the Bank of England; Mr Geoffrey W. Russell, a solicitor; and Mr J. A. R. Pimlott of the Home Office, as Secretary of the Committee. See Biographical Notes for more information about the Committee members.

Unfortunately the records of evidence to the Committee are not available, but the list of those giving evidence to it shows that all the main adoption agencies and organisations involved with children were represented, including those seen as being of dubious reputation. The Committee met twenty-one times and examined sixty-five

154 A Child for Keeps

Figure 6.1 Miss Florence Horsbrugh, 1931 (from the ©National Portrait Gallery, London)

witnesses, and another seven sent in written statements. Adoption societies included The Adoption Society (sometimes known as the Church of England Adoption Society or as 'Mr Buttle's society'), the Church of England Homes for Waifs and Strays, the Crusade of Rescue, the Homeless Children's Aid and Adoption Society ('Mr Beesley's society'), the Mission of Hope, the National Adoption Society, the National Children Adoption Association and the National Children's Home and Orphanage. Other witnesses came from the Charity Organisation Society, Dr Barnardo's, the London County Council, the National Council for the Unmarried Mother and Her Child, the NSPCC, the Salvation Army, and a number of other smaller organisations and individuals.

Report of the Departmental Committee on Adoption Societies and Agencies

At the beginning of its Report, the Committee announced that it was including *de facto* as well as legal adoption, that is, adoptions that had not been made official as well as those that had. As some of the adoption societies, especially the more questionable ones, did not encourage adopters to go to court this was sensible, as it meant all their activities could be considered, together with the adoptions arranged through professionals such as GPs and nurses which sometimes remained informal. The Committee decided to define adoption as 'the creation of "an artificial family relationship analogous to that of parent and child" ... which is accepted by all parties as permanent'.[36]

From the information it gathered, the Committee calculated that more than 1200 children were placed with adopters every year by groups describing themselves as adoption societies and probably several hundred by other agencies.[37] The latter included children's homes, nursing homes, occasionally welfare organisations such as the Jewish Association for the Protection of Women and Children, and the Salvation Army, and also local authorities, and in a few instances officers of public authorities such as health visitors and probation officers. Some adoptions were also arranged by private individuals.

The Committee set out its basic attitudes to adoption in the early pages of the report. They rejected the idea

> represented to us by some witnesses, mainly because of the risks which are inherent in any system of adoption, that it is usually better for an orphan or an illegitimate child to be placed in an institution or with a foster-parent than that it should be adopted ... We consider that for the child a good family life is to be preferred to life in an institution, however excellent, and adoption has the additional advantage that a child brought up a member of the adopter's own family enjoys a sense of security which otherwise it might not acquire.[38]

However the Committee was adamant that it was 'beyond question that the first duty of the adoption society is to the child'.[39] This might nowadays seem uncontroversial, and even then most societies would probably have said that this was their philosophy, but the whole thrust of this report was that for some of the societies the interests of the child were in practice far from being paramount. The Committee declared that 'An adoption society should therefore make full inquiries not only into the economic and social circumstances of applicants for children, but also into their suitability on other grounds to receive the care of a child',[40] and it stated categorically that

> it should be a first principle that no applicant has a right to a child, and any suspicion that the adoption may not be successful should be sufficient justification for rejecting an application even if this may involve apparent hardship to the applicants. The child and not the would-be adopters should be given the benefit of any doubt.[41]

The Committee looked at procedures for vetting adopters. Some societies made thorough inquiries: an initial detailed form for applicants to complete; references to be taken up; a personal interview; and a home visit. 'If inquiries prove satisfactory, the applicants are allowed to select a child, which is then handed over for a probationary period, during which the home is again visited, before consent is given to permanent retention.'[42] The Committee considered all these stages – application form, taking up of references, personal interview, home visit and probationary period with a further visit to the home – to be essential. They said they were 'disturbed' to find that, by their own admission, even those societies which normally went through all these procedures would dispense 'in special circumstances' with one or more of them. The other concern about the societies which normally had an organised procedure was 'whether in practice they are always sufficiently thorough or whether the persons who carry them out possess the qualifications to perform what should be a very thorough social investigation ... none of the chief adoption societies appears to possess on its staff trained social workers'.[43] And these were the efficient societies. Other societies were less thorough and admitted to the Committee that they accepted applications without a home visit and, in some cases where applicants lived a long way from London, even the personal interview was dispensed with. The application form of one society did not even ask about the available accommodation or the precise ages of the applicants.

The Report gives a number of examples of poor practice where children had been adopted without proper investigations into the adopters' circumstances. They include examples from five unnamed societies. The first example is more detailed than the others but illustrates the Committee's points. The secretary of the society involved admitted that this is what had happened:

> A child was placed with adopters without either an interview or a home visit and was handed over to the adoptive mother at a railway station. Her husband had described himself as a baker earning £150 per annum, and he gave a clergyman's reference which was duly obtained and regarded as satisfactory. In consequence of complaints as to the treatment of the child, inquiries were made and it was found that the man's statement was false, and that he had been unemployed for some years. His character was unsatisfactory, and he is said to have taken the child around with him whilst he hawked produce stolen from allotments. The society's representative admitted in evidence that the man had adopted the child for the

purpose of exploiting it as an object of sympathy by taking it round with his barrow. In these circumstances it was necessary to remove the child.[44]

Another example was:

> A girl of three, who had been adopted by a labourer and his wife, was found to be ill-treated. The adoption society removed her and its secretary admitted in evidence that she should never have been placed with the adopters. Yet the same society had previously placed three other children in this home, all of which has been taken back by the society.[45]

The Committee also felt that adoption societies had a responsibility to adopters to provide them with a healthy child.

> To place for adoption a child which is congenitally defective or otherwise unsuitable for adoption is to do an ill service both to the child and to the adopters, unless the latter take it with full knowledge of its deficiencies and are able to make proper provision accordingly for its special needs.[46]

The societies must therefore ensure that 'a thorough medical examination covering both physical and mental condition' was carried out on each child before it was placed for adoption. The Committee felt that, in view of 'the origin of many of the children which are offered for adoption', this should include a Wasserman test (a blood test for syphilis) on the child, or the mother if the child was too young. Inquiries should also be made into the social and medical history of the child's parents, and the adopters made aware of any pertinent circumstances.

The Committee was ruthless in its approach to possible defect:

> There should be no hesitation in rejecting a child about whose suitability for adoption there is any doubt. This may cause apparent hardship, but the possibilities of suffering if a mistake is made are so great that only very exceptional circumstances should justify any departure from the rule. It is safer that a child about which there is doubt should be placed in an institution or provided for in some other way.[47]

It was 'disturbed' by the society which admitted that it dispensed with a medical certificate in about one case in ten 'and the fitness of the child is judged on sight by the officials of the society'; and it wrote approvingly of the society which 'informed us that it refuses many babies for reasons including bad health, mental defect in the mother, dubious parentage, and lack of information concerning the father'.[48] The context for the Committee's approach was the general attitudes of the time towards disability and the stigma of illegitimacy, and in particular the continuing influence in the mid-1930s of the eugenics movement which still had many followers among the educated and progressive classes and had not yet acquired sinister connotations. The Committee member, Mrs Montagu Norman, and her husband, the Governor of the Bank of England, were known to be interested and supportive of the movement.

In terms which foreshadow modern social work practice, the Committee stated that

> [a]n attempt should be made as far as possible to place the right child in the right home, and it follows that no child should be placed without the fullest consideration of the question whether it is suitable for adoption by the particular applicants.[49]

The idea of matching individual child with particular adopting parents had not really been articulated before, except in very basic terms of class or background or letting adopters choose a child who looked like them. However it appears that, certainly ten years later, even reputable agencies were still not implementing the Report's recommendations. A study of adoption outcomes looked at children born between 1948 and 1951 and adopted through the Thomas Coram Foundation and the National Adoption Society (NAS). Describing the way they first met their child some parents were very critical:

> An adoptive mother spoke of having to make a decision 'when you walk into the room under pressure not to say "No" or you go to the end of the queue'. Several criticised being offered a choice of two or three children in a residential nursery ...
>
> A father who had accompanied his wife to a residential nursery to see the baby the agency was offering them for fostering with a view to adoption said he felt he was in a showroom being shown around by a saleswoman (the matron). He said 'Choosing a second-hand car is bad enough, but going into a Home and choosing a baby is a hundred times worse – imagine looking at babies and saying, "I don't

want that one, I don't want that one"; it's a horrible situation and something I wouldn't want to do again.'[50]

The couple refused two babies and picked a third as its hair was like that of the man's relatives when they were young. As the report commented dryly: 'Unfortunately, the hair did not prove a very sound indicator of affinity, as the parents tended to emphasise the boy's difference from them when the adoption did not go well.'[51]

The Report recommended a probationary period of at least three months as 'the best time to judge whether an adoption is likely to be happy is after the child is in the home', and adopters might find looking after a child too difficult, or the child might not settle in the home. It praised one society's policy of arranging for a home visit during the four-month probationary period which was then reported to its Case Committee. The Committee pointed out that with such a system the society must have adequate provision for children who are returned. If it did not have its own hostels it must make arrangements with a suitable voluntary home. The Committee emphasised the need for good standards in these hostels, quoting the case cited by the NSPCC of children from the hostel of one society (the Homeless Children's Aid and Adoption Society) who were admitted in a poor condition to a hospital where one died of enteritis.[52]

As far as personnel were concerned, the Committee were adamant that each society should have a 'Case Committee' made up of

> persons with experience of different branches of social work and acquainted with the various public and voluntary social services for children, and in view of the nature of an adoption society's work, we regard it as important that married women with children of their own should be among its members.[53]

The Case Committee's functions would include not just giving final approval or supervising the work of the officials but also providing advice and assistance from their 'wider and different points of view'.

Although the Horsbrugh Committee included *de facto* adoptions in its remit, it was keen that adoptions be legalised, for the security provided to both adopters and children, and also the safeguards it provided through the inquiries made by the guardian *ad litem* and the court. They recommended that adoption societies insist that adopters apply for an adoption order and ensure that the child was returned to them if no application was made within a stipulated period. The report said that several witnesses had mentioned the anxiety felt by many adopters that in the adoption proceedings their name and address might be disclosed to the child's parents:

> Despite the security which is given to them by an adoption order, they are afraid that the parent may disturb the child, or may even attempt a mild form of blackmail. It is said that adopters sometimes move to a different part of the country in order to avoid the possibility of being embarrassed by the parent. We understand and sympathise with this desire for secrecy, though no case has been mentioned to us by the adoption societies where adopters have had cause to complain of such interference.[54]

They later mentioned that they asked every witness about this issue as the adoption societies were so insistent about it, and the Chief Education Officer of Birmingham told them that in three of 1200 adoptions in Birmingham 'the mother subsequently made a nuisance of herself to the adopters'.[55] Despite this low figure the adoption societies remained adamant that secrecy was vital. 'Witnesses representing the societies engaged in arranging adoptions have been unanimous in the view that if the identity were disclosed many of the best adopters would be unwilling to take children.'[56]

The Committee noted that to avoid the relinquishing parent becoming aware of the adopters' details most societies admitted they sometimes arranged for the parent to sign the consent form before the adopters' details had been inserted (or these were covered up). In theory, except in certain specified circumstances, the parent (or other person with custody of the infant or liable to contribute to its support) had to consent to their child's adoption (not just give a general agreement to it being adopted). The Committee quoted Lord Justice Scrutton's comment in the case of *In re Carroll* (see previous chapter) that signing a blank consent form was 'a very unsatisfactory form of procedure'. It was aimed, as the Report made clear, at ensuring that the society had a free hand in the choice of adopters, and could guarantee secrecy for the adopters.

The Report did not go far in considering the mother's rights – it suggested that

> societies should always be ready to answer, from properly kept records, any reasonable inquiries by the mother as to the character, position, etc. of the people with whom her child has been placed or

as to the child's progress – at any rate up to the time of legal adoption, while impressing upon her the importance of avoiding any sort of interference and making it clear to her also that her rights over the child will cease entirely once an order is made.[57] [my italics]

However it did say that 'we are not ... satisfied that all the adoption societies are sufficiently concerned to keep in touch with the mother once the child has been handed over to them'. Then, after it had gone into more detail about the way in which some societies deliberately excluded the mother from the court hearing, it said that '[these practices] suggest that the societies who resort to them regard themselves as owing no duty to the mother in the choice of adopters, but only to the child and those who wish to adopt it'.[58] The Committee proposed that when they first applied to an adoption society all relinquishing parents should be given a 'memorandum in a prescribed form explaining in simple language the effect of adoption and their rights and duties in connection with an application for an adoption order'.[59] They would have to sign that they had read and understood it.

The Committee looked at the issue of finance in some detail as this had given rise to controversy over the previous years. The adoption societies were funded, as far as the Committee could see, from four main sources – the charity-giving public, the relinquishing mothers, putative fathers and the adopters. The Committee saw no problem with appeals to the public and other traditional fund-raising measures. Nor did it sympathise with the blanket criticism of asking the mothers for payments – either in the form of a 'voluntary' gift or as a compulsory charge. After all, it reasoned, the mother was being relieved by the society of heavy financial responsibilities and

> it may also be desirable that she should be reminded of her responsibilities, and that the impression should not be cultivated that adoption societies exist for the cheap and expeditious disposal of illegitimate children.[60]

However it did criticise some of the methods used to obtain payments – weekly and annual amounts to cover non-existent 'inspections', and heavy threats to initiate legal proceedings when the amounts were not paid, even when there was no formal agreement to pay. The Committee felt that the widespread feeling that there should be no payments at all involved in adoption was because of the long association of adoption with 'baby farming', and it agreed that there must be strict safeguards against abuse. As far as adopters were concerned, the Committee thought it 'natural and proper' that they be invited to contribute to the society from which they had received assistance, but only after the adoption. 'For we view with grave concern anything resembling the sale of children to adopters, or prices being placed on children according to their desirability.'[61]

The Committee singled out one particular agency (although not named in the Report it was The Adoption Society, otherwise known as the Church of England Adoption Society) for criticism over the running of its affairs. Its Chairman, the Rev. Buttle, had founded the NAS (see Chapter 2), one of the two main interwar adoption societies, but had fallen out with his committee, divided the assets and set this society up in 1931. He had worked over the years to build up a very large endowment fund, mainly sourced from 'returnable donations' – monies lent to the agency with no interest paid and only returnable if requested by the donor. The agency's Rules provided for the usual full range of officials, committees, trustees, annual meetings and audits of accounts. However most of these Rules, on the Mr Buttle's own admission, were ignored. The only officers were himself and a paid Secretary. The two trustees were the Chairman (himself) and a corporation of which he was the sole director. For two successive years there was no annual meeting and in 1935 the accounts were prepared and audited for the first time in five years. In explanation the Chairman said 'he wished to retain unfettered control over the fund which he is building up and for which he is personally responsible'.[62] A very small proportion of the society's income was spent on adoption work, although that was its stated purpose. Staffing was inadequate, so home visits could not usually be arranged even though the Chairman agreed they were desirable. The Committee was unhappy that there was no safeguard against the mixing of the society's funds with the Chairman's personal finances, and they were particularly critical of the misleading impression given to the public of the society having a well-regulated staffing and committee structure and a viable constitution when almost none of this was accurate.

In 1943, after the regulatory Adoption Act came into force, this Society was again in trouble. The London County Council, the relevant regulating authority, initially refused to register it because it had so many concerns about its inadequate staffing levels ('there appears to be no qualified person on the staff available to visit the homes before children are handed over and during the probationary period'[63]), its unorthodox financial arrangements and lack of accountability. Mr Buttle was forced to resign as Chairman and 'ceased to arrange his own adoptions' which he had been doing, although he remained on the Society's Committee.[64]

After much correspondence and promises of change, the Society was approved for regulation in May 1944. It also had to rename itself to be incorporated under the 1929 Companies Act as a not-for-profit society because there was opposition to 'The Adoption Society' as this made it 'sound pre-eminent'. Lambeth Palace objected to the 'Church of England Adoption Society' as it had no responsibility for it, so 'Church Adoption Society' was agreed upon, and it was re-registered under that name in July 1945.[65] The Rev. Buttle continued to be fascinated by financial investment and management and eventually raised a large sum of money (£920,000) to help individual disadvantaged children, which was used after his death in 1953 to establish the Buttle Trust.[66]

The next controversial issue considered by the Horsbrugh Committee was 'Adoption Abroad' – the practice of taking British children overseas for adoption, which had aroused much ire in the popular press. It judged this to fall into three areas: adoptions by British officials and others domiciled in the United Kingdom but resident abroad; adoptions by British subjects in the Dominions and Colonies; adoptions by aliens in foreign countries. The Committee emphasised that the overall numbers involved were extremely low compared to the total number of adoptions in the United Kingdom but nevertheless expressed their concern in particular about the last category. Children were being sent overseas at an age when they were too young to be consulted, 'very often without the knowledge or consent of their parents, and they grow up as members of a foreign community'.[67] It was not possible to make effective inquiries about the adopting family or to enforce a proper system of probation and supervision. The Committee gave several examples of disturbing cases. For example:

> The illegitimate son of an Englishwoman of superior social status was placed with adopters of similar social status in Holland, the father agreeing to pay a sum sufficient to cover the cost of the boy's education until he reached the age of 16. When the boy reached 17 the payments ceased, whereupon the adopters brought him back to England. He knew no English and had been unaware that he was a British subject.[68]

A surprising number of children were going to Holland for adoption and to find out why this was so the Committee interviewed Dr Sark from the Dutch Home Office and the National Federation of Institutions for the Unmarried Mother and Her Child, Holland. He explained that in countries such as Holland there was no provision for formalising adoption and it was in general opposed by the Dutch authorities, which left the children in a precarious legal position. A few children were fostered but the mother might always apply for the child to be returned to her, so many Dutch people seeking to adopt turned to the adoption societies in England.

The Committee discussed prohibiting all adoption societies and other agencies from sending children abroad for adoption in any circumstances, but concluded this 'would be too sweeping', as it would prevent British people temporarily resident overseas from adopting British children. It considered that this was not transplanting them 'into an alien community', and it would be possible to make full inquiries about them. And even though 'greater dangers' were involved, British people resident in the Dominions and Colonies should also be allowed to adopt British children. In both these categories the adopters would have to obtain a licence from a court granting them permission to take the child out of the country. However,

> with these exceptions, we think the disadvantages of adoptions abroad greatly outweigh any possible advantages, and we recommend that adoption societies and other adoption agencies should be entirely prohibited from arranging adoptions in which the child will be taken abroad except where the adopters are British subjects.[69]

There were a couple of dissenting voices. Mr Russell and Mr Manning considered a similar licensing process should apply for foreign adopters as that which the Committee was recommending for British adopters resident overseas.

When the Committee came to look at 'private agents', it was 'glad to be able to state that the evidence which we have received gives no support for the view that there is a widespread traffic in children or that 'baby-farming' is prevalent'. However it continued that it had been 'informed of a number of adoptions in which nursing homes or private persons have acted as intermediaries, and some of these cases give very serious cause for concern'.[70] The report describes several such cases. For example:

> In one case (1935) the wife of an unemployed labourer applied to a midwife and 'booked' for adoption the unborn child of an unmarried woman who was anxious to conceal its birth, and the adopter was asked for and paid £4-6s-7d, ostensibly for expenses. The inquiries of the guardian ad litem when an application was made for an adoption

order showed that both the labourer and his wife were persons of low intelligence, their home was neglected, and their only source of income was unemployment insurance benefit of 26s weekly. The court made an interim order of six months, but there was no improvement during this period. On a further visit by the guardian *ad litem*, the child was found in dirty and unsatisfactory conditions, and when these facts were placed before the court on the renewal of the application it adjourned the hearing *sine die*.[71]

The Committee considered that 'it is dangerous to permit private persons to receive payments for negotiating adoptions' and recommended 'that it should be made an offence for a private person to receive any such payment without the leave of the court upon an application for an adoption order'.[72] Some of the more dubious intermediaries had used advertisements to find children for adoption (and sometimes to offer them). The Children and Young Persons Act 1932 (Section 68) and the Public Health Act 1936 (Section 215) partly dealt with this but the Committee recommended 'the prohibition of all advertisements, offering or seeking children for adoption, except by adoption societies and agencies as defined in our recommendations later'.[73]

As far as local authorities and adoption were concerned the Committee singled out the procedure of the London County Council as 'admirable' (see Chapter 5 for details) and gave details of other local authorities who had adoption programmes including Glamorganshire County Council (36 adoptions since 1927), Huddersfield Town Council (17 between 1933 and 1936), Lancashire County Council (14 between 1930 and 1936) and Essex County Council (14 between 1931 and 1935).[74] It also looked briefly at the adoption work of voluntary agencies other than adoption societies, such as the Salvation Army which arranged 16 adoptions in 1935, and the Crusade of Rescue which was 'ordinarily opposed to adoption as a solution for the difficulties of the unmarried mother' but had been responsible for 47 adoptions since 1924. The Committee said that all its recommendations for adoption societies would apply equally to these agencies carrying out adoption work. Indeed, the lack of experience common to these agencies meant they should be especially careful in arranging adoptions.

The Committee rejected suggestions that arranging adoptions should be restricted to public authorities – or conversely to societies specialising in adoption work. However it regarded certain improvements in the societies' practice as essential, and after 'careful consideration' as to whether these could be introduced without some form of regulation of the adoption societies, it concluded 'that it would be altogether too sanguine to hope that certain of them at any rate would put their houses in order without compulsion'.[75] After some discussion of the alternatives the Report recommended a system of licensing adoption agencies through the larger local authorities (i.e. county councils and county boroughs) which already administered similar systems for employment agencies, nursing homes etc. The local authority would have the right, under certain circumstances, to refuse or withdraw a licence, but there would be a right of appeal by the agency to the High Court.

Turning to the question of private agencies the Committee 'carefully considered' prohibiting all private persons from arranging adoptions, 'but came to the conclusion that such a prohibition would be unreasonable'.[76] It felt that its earlier recommendations about banning payments in connection with adoption except by permission of a court, and imposing strict guidelines on adoptions abroad, would deal with 'the main dangers' of adoptions arranged by private agents. It admitted that there remained

> the risk that even where there is no payment to any of the parties concerned serious mistakes may result from carelessness or ignorance on the part of the agent. This danger is perhaps greatest in cases where the adoption is arranged by the parent or other relatives of the child, or by doctors or midwives who have rendered professional services to the mother.[77]

The Committee recommended that the infant life protection provisions be used.[78] Under these any person receiving a child under the age of nine for reward had to notify this within forty-eight hours to the relevant infant life protection authority which was empowered to visit the home and if necessary remove the child. If the child was not subsequently adopted under the Adoption of Children Act 1926 the implication was that the local authority would have a duty of supervision for three years. The Committee recommended that the notifiable age limit in cases of adoption be raised from nine to sixteen in view of the risk of adolescents being adopted 'as a means of securing cheap labour or for other undesirable reasons'.[79] Without the defining element of 'reward' it was not clear how notification would work or what incentive there would be for private people (i.e. not professional foster parents) to notify the authority. The Committee recognised this and suggested that there be a duty of notification on both the agent and the person receiving the child.

The Report concluded with three pages of dissent from Mr Russell. He considered that despite problems with the operation of some of the societies the situation was not serious enough to warrant engaging 'the responsibility of the State' and setting up 'some new form of statutory control'. He argued that the work of the Horsbrugh Committee had been widely publicised and

> although it has sought information in every direction open to it, it has not in my opinion received much evidence of any vital mischief which is directly attributable to the activities of the societies or agencies.[80]

No natural parent or adoptive parent had come forward to complain to the Committee about their treatment (or that of their child) by any of the adoption societies. For Mr Russell the key question was whether children were 'harmed' by the methods used by the societies. Some cases of ill-treatment of children adopted through societies had been brought to the Committee's attention but he suggested that there were also many children living with their natural parents who were maltreated and the remedy for all was the same – the child protection legislation.

The Adoption of Children (Regulation) Act 1939

The Committee presented its report to the Home Secretary (now Sir Samuel Hoare) on 17 June 1937. Over the next few months MPs sought to find out what was happening to the report and its recommendations but were initially told that he had not had time to consider it,[81] and then a few months later that 'Consultations are in progress … When these consultations have been completed due consideration will be given to the question of the introduction of legislation, but I cannot at the present stage give any undertaking on this point'.[82] In May 1938 the Chairman of the National Council for the Unmarried Mother and Her Child, Mrs H. A. L. Fisher, wrote to the Home Secretary urging action on the Committee's recommendations, in particular those relating to adoption abroad:

> Our Case Committee has heard only recently of two cases in which an unmarried mother proposed to hand over her child to some foreign visitor staying in a London Hotel. So far as we are aware, no legal steps could be taken to prevent these proposals being carried into effect.[83]

The typewritten letter ends with a handwritten postscript: 'This a formal letter – but we are all anxious about the present position. The children are completely unprotected and lost when they leave these shores.'[84]

A few months later in October 1938 the Home Secretary sent a two-page memorandum to the Cabinet, asking his colleagues for approval to introduce a Bill to regulate the activities of adoption societies and other agencies involved in arranging adoptions. He reported that consultation with all the relevant authorities showed general agreement with the Committee's recommendations.[85]

He felt that the Bill would be a comparatively short one and in his view would be a suitable Private Member's Bill. The Cabinet Home Affairs Committee which met a few days later agreed to approve his proposals and it was minuted that the Chancellor of the Exchequer (Sir John Simon, who had set up the Departmental Committee in his earlier role as Home Secretary), and the Lord Chancellor (Lord Maugham) 'strongly supported' them.[86]

Nine days later the Adoption of Children (Regulation) Bill was presented by Miss Florence Horsbrugh as a Private Member's Bill. It was

> to regulate the making of arrangements by adoption societies and other persons in connection with the adoption of children; to provide for the supervision of adopted children by welfare authorities in certain cases; to restrict the making and receipt of payments in connection with the adoption of children; to amend Section 2 of the Adoption of Children Act 1926; and for purposes connected with the matters aforesaid.[87]

When the Bill was debated during its Second Reading, a Conservative MP, H. G. Williams, pointed out that Miss Horsbrugh was 'in almost the unique position of having been the chairman of the Committee which considered the subject and then drawing a place in the Ballot and being able to present a Bill based upon the Report of the Committee'.[88]

Miss Horsbrugh made a heartfelt plea for the legislation when she moved the Bill at the Second Reading. She was concerned for the relinquishing mothers, anxious that they understand their legal position and their right to retrieve their child up until the court order for adoption was made. This was why the legislation included a clause saying that mothers must be given a memorandum explaining their legal position 'in ordinary language' and stipulated that they must sign a document certifying that they had read and understood it. Miss Horsbrugh said that 'some of my legal friends have been rather surprised at this phrase, but I want to stress that this is a human problem'. She gave an example of why such a measure was necessary:

> I know of a pathetic case where a woman went to a society with her baby to be adopted, and within a few hours thought differently about the matter. She went home and told her parents, and her mother told her to fetch it back. She went and was told, 'No, you consented to give up your child for adoption, and you signed the form'. If only that woman had been told, or had been able to get some advice, she might have acted differently. She never saw her child again, as she thought she had given it up legally.[89]

She went on to talk of the importance of the societies, which would have to be registered and stressed the need for full consideration of the potential adopters and not just of their material circumstances.

> Not long ago I saw a woman who brought back an adopted child because she did not like the child. On looking at the woman, I knew that nothing would have induced me ever to give her a child. I asked her why she brought the child back, and how old was he. He was a little boy just under two years old and she gave as her reason for giving him back – 'I do not like him; he is bad-tempered'. I hope that that woman will never have a chance of having any other child.[90]

Miss Horsbrugh went through the clauses of the Bill, which followed closely the recommendations of her Committee's Report. The discussion that followed was amicable and uncontroversial. Every speaker supported the Bill. As the Labour MP, John Joseph Tinker, said, 'This morning I think we have called an amnesty on this matter, because we realise that it is one of those cases in which we ought to get together for what we believe to be the common good of humanity.'[91] Lady Astor, in her usual idiosyncratic way, regretted that the United States could not be included within the British Empire for the purposes of the Bill as she knew 'of the most splendid [American] parents, with Anglo-Saxon blood of course, who want to adopt English, Irish, Scottish and Welsh children'.[92] She went on to pronounce on childlessness and spinsterhood:

> There is nothing in the world more pathetic than a woman without a child who is longing for one. It wrecks her life. I have sat in this House and heard people talking about mothers, as though every

woman was a mother; but our greatest reformers have been unmarried women, and today we have a spinster bringing in a Bill which is going to do a great deal for child life in this country. We ought to be grateful to her.[93]

Indeed Miss Horsbrugh received a great deal of praise throughout the debate. The Labour MP, Edward Dunn said, 'Some of us have always looked upon her as being as hard as granite, and as being entirely the opposite by nature and outlook from what the moving words she has uttered this morning would indicate her to be.'[94] The Conservative, Allan Chapman, claimed that 'thousands of children who may never know her name will have reason to bless her for her humanity, her great industry, and her great sense of duty'.[95] A Government spokesman (the Under-Secretary of State for the Home Department, Mr Geoffrey Lloyd) added his congratulations ('She certainly showed herself to be the master, or perhaps I should say the mistress, of her subject'), and welcomed the Bill on behalf of the Government.[96]

The Bill received Royal Assent on 13 July 1939. The Adoption of Children (Regulation) Act 1939 largely followed the recommendations of the Horsbrugh Report, making it unlawful for 'any body of persons' to make arrangements for the adoption of children unless they were a registered adoption society or local authority (although individuals involved in arranging adoptions were not to be registered – this had been felt too difficult as many adoptions were arranged on a one-off informal basis). Anyone taking part in a society 'existing wholly or in part for the purpose of making arrangements for the adoption of children', which was not registered would be liable to imprisonment or a fine.[97] The Act prescribed conditions for the regulation of adoption societies by local authorities. In keeping with the mention of 'ordinary language', it was an extremely straightforward and practical piece of legislation, laying down strict rules for the safeguarding of children's interests (e.g. a case committee of at least three persons to look into the case of every child considered for adoption through a registered adoption society, and a stipulation that the adopters must be interviewed and their premises inspected, and the ensuing reports considered by the case committee). It set a probationary period of a minimum three months during which the adopter could give up the child and the adoption society could remove it. After the three-month period the adopter had another three months in which to apply for an adoption order for the child. If he or she did not do this (or was turned down by the Court) the adopter had to return the child to the society. Failure to comply meant liability for a fine of up to fifty pounds or a prison sentence of up to six months (or both). Local authorities with registration rights over a society were allowed to require the societies to produce

> such books, accounts and other documents relating to the performance by the society of the function of making arrangements for the adoption of children, as the authority may consider necessary for the exercise of the powers conferred on the authority.[98]

When a child was adopted informally (through neither a society or local authority, and without an adoption order), up to the age of nine it became compulsory (with fines and/or imprisonment for those infringing this) for those involved in arranging it to notify the arrangement to the local welfare authority which then had a duty to ensure that 'child protection visitors ... visit and examine' the child. If the premises or the adopters were unsuitable the welfare authority could apply to a magistrates' court for the removal of the child to a place of safety.[99] Discussion within the civil service while the Act was going through Parliament agreed that in general health visitors would be the people to inspect these adopted children. There was concern about how these unofficial adoptions were defined. The Act excluded adoptions 'for a temporary purpose only'[100] which clearly might encourage avoidance of the provision.

The Act made it illegal for anyone who made arrangements for the adoption of a child (except a local authority) to receive or make any payment or reward in connection with making the arrangements unless a court had agreed to it, or it was made by an adoption society in respect of the maintenance of a child it was responsible for or, it was from the parent of a child to an adoption society which was maintaining it while it awaited placement with an adopter. The penalty for this was again a fine, imprisonment or both. The Act also banned advertising indicating that a parent had a child it wanted adopted, that a person wanted to adopt a child, or that a person was willing to arrange adoptions (except in the case of registered adoption societies or local authorities). A person placing such an advertisement, or knowingly publishing one, would be liable to a fine of up to fifty pounds. The Act also included the limitations on taking children overseas for adoption proposed in the Committee's Report.

It also amended the 1926 Act by allowing the mother of a child to adopt it even if she was under twenty-five years old and permitting people less than twenty-one years older than a child to adopt it where they were 'within the prohibited degree of consanguinity or where husband and wife were applying jointly and either the wife was the mother of the child or the husband the putative father.[101] Both these measures implicitly encouraged the practice of unmarried mothers adopting their own children – either as single women or as part of a married couple – allowing them to keep their own child without the stigma of illegitimacy (see previous chapter).

Six weeks after the Act received Royal Assent the Second World War began. Measures such as this, which involved considerable input from local authorities and central government, were no longer a priority and it was included in the Postponement of Enactments (Miscellaneous Provisions) Act 1939 which postponed a number of recent legislative measures 'until such time as His Majesty may, by Order in Council, appoint'.[102] The only exception was the section amending the 1926 Act to make it easier for parents to adopt their own child, which had no impact on resources.

The death of Miss Clara Andrew

A week before the Adoption of Children (Regulation) Act 1939 received Royal Assent, Clara Andrew, the founder of the National Children Adoption Association, died, aged seventy-seven, at Tower Cressy in Kensington, the hostel through which so many babies had passed on their way to adoption. In her late fifties, an age when many people were thinking of retirement, Miss Andrew had found a cause to which she devoted herself for the rest of her life. Much of the achievement of the NCAA in the interwar years must be attributed to her. From the reports of the Association's Annual Meetings, she appears to have remained closely involved with all aspects of its day-to-day work, and *The Times* said 'she was working up to 12 hours before her death'.[103] She energetically campaigned for adoption issues throughout the 1920s and 1930s, leading deputations and writing letters to politicians and civil service officers. Reporting her death in 1939 the *Evening Standard* stated that she 'spent her time between her office and her London Home, which she shared with laughing babies'. Although the *Standard* described Miss Andrew as 'this busy little spinster ... still working for waifs', it also praised her in more serious terms, as did *The Times*:

> She was largely responsible for the passing of the Adoption of Children Act of 1926. Her last achievement was the success of her representation to the Home Secretary in 1935, resulting in the setting up

of a departmental committee on adoption societies and agencies, and the passing this year of the Adoption of Children Regulation Bill.[104]

At the NCAA's annual meeting which fell a few days later, Princess Alice

> read a few of the many letters of tribute which had been received from associations and from people who had adopted children. From a working-class couple there was sorrow for 'the passing of so grand a lady' and from a well-to-do couple a cheque for £25.[105]

The Viscountess Snowden[106] wrote to The Times as 'Miss Andrew's friend and associate for many years, as were hundreds of others who sympathised with her work'. She went on: 'it is difficult to express our sense of loss' and said that

> Not so much has yet been said of this fine Englishwoman's loveliness of character. Her earnest though humour-loving and ceaseless activity sprang from the possession of a loving heart, which bruised itself over the thought of what small, unwanted children had so often to suffer ... We must be grateful in the knowledge that in the homes where the children are cared for until their permanent homes are discovered, and where Miss Andrew worked till within a few hours of her death, the spiritual presence of a loving and selfless personality will be felt, fit to rank with those other pioneers, Florence Nightingale and Elizabeth Fry, as one of England's noblest daughters.[107]

Despite this comparison, Clara Andrew remains a shadowy figure, rarely mentioned outside the adoption world; the obituaries had few details about her life and I have found out little about her early years. We dimly see an energetic, impatient but sentimental woman, who managed, even by the standards of the time, to maintain an impressively well-connected list of supporters for the NCAA during her twenty-year involvement with it, but who could also empathise with the respectable working- and middle-class couples from the suburbs and new estates who needed babies to create the families they could not produce themselves. She seems to have been remarkably successful in late middle age at acquiring and maintaining strong relationships with a range of people who proved loyal and supportive to her in her work. Although there were occasional tensions with Committee members in the Association (and earlier in Exeter), she inspired great devotion in other people. The letters to her from Princess

Alice (and also from the Princess' private secretary, Janet Harkness) reveal the affection and loyalty they both felt towards her. And at the other end of the NCAA hierarchy there are letters from some of the nursing students expressing their support for her and desire to remain with her at Tower Cressy.[108] Miss Andrew herself remained loyal to those she employed – during the Nursing Committee dispute over Tower Cressy described in Chapter 2 she refused to accept her matron's resignation until overruled by the Committee.

She was remarkably successful in getting grants for her hostels and persuading people to work for legislation she wanted. Possibly she found women easier to work with than men – her letters and notes to Miss Puxley at the Ministry of Health were warm and almost chatty. She finished one with: 'I always enjoy a talk with you and was so glad to see you yesterday.'[109] Her relationships with the senior male civil servants, especially those at the Home Office, were never so intimate. They were dealing with her on policy issues rather than the day-to-day running of the society and the hostels and were concerned about what they considered to be the adoption societies' obsession with secrecy and the consequences it had for the natural mother and the identity of the adopted child. For Clara Andrew, who was above all concerned with finding homes for babies, they just seemed obstructive and bureaucratic.

After Miss Andrew's death, her assistant, Mrs Plummer, took over as general secretary of the NCAA and ran the organisation until 1966. In 1949 the NCAA was one of the inaugural members of the Standing Conference of Societies Registered for Adoption which became the professional body for adoption societies.[110] The NCAA continued its work through the 1950s and 1960s but in 1978 it closed, citing financial pressures and the changing nature of adoption which it did not feel equipped to deal with.[111]

7
The Second World War and Its Aftermath

Dealing with issues arising from the practice of adoption was clearly not a priority in the initial years of the war. Policymakers and practitioners dealing with children had more immediate problems to cope with – organising the successive evacuation programmes and setting up war nurseries. But gradually adoption did again become a topic of concern and the particular problems brought up by wartime will be considered in this chapter. As during the First World War, the number of illegitimate births rose during the war years but this time the general birth rate only declined in the first years of the war, and from 1942 it was higher than it had been from the mid-1930s onwards so the percentage of births that were illegitimate did not go up as much as it might have done. Even so, it reached 9.3 per cent, the highest level it had ever been, in 1945 although then it rapidly started to fall back closer to its pre-war rate.[1] The true rate may have been higher because considerable numbers of married women had babies by men who were not their husbands during the later years of the war. Some were declared as illegitimate births but not all. Accompanying the increase in illegitimacy there was a considerable rise in the number of adoptions, with a peak of over 21,000 in 1946 (most of which would have been babies or children born or conceived during the war). After this the numbers went down during the 1950s until they rose to a peak of nearly 25,000[2] in 1968 and then declined again until the 1990s when they reached the pre-war levels of under seven thousand a year.

The demand for babies and children to adopt was high throughout the war. Every time there was mention of war orphans, ministries and adoption agencies were flooded with requests for children – especially girls. As one woman wrote to the Ministry of Health:

> Last year I felt I would very much like to adopt a little girl of about five years and wrote to several adoption societies, also Church of England Waifs and Strays and Barnardo's. The Church of England Waifs and Strays was the only place where they had any children for adoption and they had a few boys. All the other Societies had a waiting list of people wanting to take children ...
> It is unbelievable that there are no little girls wanting homes, when there are so many Press and Broadcast appeals for funds.[3]

A few months later the Minister of Health, Ernest Brown, made reference in a speech to eleven thousand 'orphans of the world storm' and there was a rush of offers to adopt them. As civil servants pointed out, Brown's phrase had to be interpreted in a very wide sense as meaning

> the thousands of children whose home has been disturbed by war conditions. At present there are approximately 11,000 such children living in residential nurseries and homes under government supervision whose circumstances are such as to make it impossible for them to live with their parents or guardians. Fortunately, only a relatively small proportion of these children are orphans in the strict sense of the word.[4]

Shortly afterwards the Minister of Pensions, Sir William Womersley, whose department was directly responsible for war orphans, clarified the situation in Parliament: his department was paying pensions in respect of about 1700 children who were 'bereft of both parents'. The vast majority of these (c. 1500) were living with relatives or evacuated with the relatives' consent. Almost all the others were settled in schools, naval orphanages or with friends or neighbours. He had received nearly 2000 letters offering to take in these children but only a very few of these could be accepted as so few children needed a home.[5]

The problem was that people were grasping at the chance of adopting 'normal' children from a 'respectable' background. As another woman wrote to the Ministry of Health, the adoption societies

> say they have only illegitimate children and also that they will not have any little girls for adoption for some time ... My husband and I wish to adopt a little girl from either a middle class or professional family.[6]

Implementing the Adoption of Children (Regulation) Act

During the first years of the war the decision to delay the implementation of the Act appears to have been accepted as part of the inevitable dislocation caused by the onset of war – at least no parliamentary questions were raised, and there are no dissenting letters in the civil service files. However by late 1942 there was considerable disquiet. Public meetings on the issue of regulating adoption were held, including a major one at Mansion House in London, organised by the National Children Adoption Association, where the judge Sir Norman Birkett spoke of the 'scandalous abuses which still exist in connection with adoption', and demanded that the 1939 Act be put into operation.[7] The Charity Organisation Society was particularly concerned about a press campaign by the *Sunday Dispatch*'s correspondent, 'Elizabeth Ann', to free up adoption still further. She claimed to organise at least two adoptions a week through the 'Sunday Dispatch Wartime Aunts Scheme'. One of her articles in August 1942 was headlined: 'If You Want to Adopt a Baby – You Will Find a Lot of Red Tape in the Way'. It continued: 'I am looking for someone with a pair of shears sharp enough to cut through a tangle of red tape that is threatening the lives of hundreds, probably thousands of future citizens of Britain … the red tape … is that concerned with the business of adoption.'[8]

B. E. Astbury of the COS wrote to Florence Horsbrugh, who was now Parliamentary Secretary for Health, quoting a case he knew of an unmarried mother in Plymouth who wrote to Elizabeth Ann

> who arranged that the baby should be brought to Paddington and handed over on the station to a couple from Norwich. I took up the matter with Elizabeth Ann and was appalled at the easy manner in which she was handing out children to other people.[9]

And the National Council for the Unmarried Mother and Her Child sent the Home Office a pile of newspaper advertisements for adoption. For example:

> Wanted – some baby-lover to adopt baby girl; love only – Alderson, Flat 3, 182 Lavender Hill, Enfield, Middx (*Kentish Independent*, 22 August 1941).
>
> Offered for Adoption, 4 months old baby girl, all rights forfeited – Write P7428, 'Guardian' Office, Warrington (*Warrington Guardian*, 16 August 1941).[10]

From September 1942 MPs began to ask questions in the House about when the Act would come into operation. In November senior Home Office officials and the Under-Secretary of State for the Home Office, Osbert Peake, received two deputations asking for the Act to be implemented. The first was from the Women Power Committee which apparently consisted of all the backbench women MPs and some other co-opted women. It was led by Miss Irene Ward, a Conservative MP.[11] She argued that the only two objections they could find to bringing the Act into operation were first, that the local authorities should be relieved of the extra work of registering adoption societies, which 'she would have understood ... at the time of evacuation, but now that work had much decreased'; and secondly, the burden of supervision which would be placed on welfare authorities. She felt it would be relatively easy to find personnel for this work. One of the other deputation members, Miss Hawtrey, said she 'knew from Health Visitors that they were anxious to have the Act in force because exceptional cases caused much more trouble than others and it would save work if their supervision of adopted children were put on a regulated basis'. The Under-Secretary was not encouraging. He felt that registration of societies would entail 'a good deal of work' by local authorities and that relatively little evidence had been produced about abuses by societies. In forty cases sent to him by the COS, nineteen showed some evidence of suffering by parent or child but only one case was the result of activities of an adoption society.[12]

The following day the minister and officials received a deputation led by the Charity Organisation Society, with representatives from the NCUMC, NCAA and the Church of England Moral Welfare Council. There was considerable discussion about the activities of 'Elizabeth Ann' and also the proprietress of a nursing home in Redhill who claimed to arrange up to 400 adoptions a year, usually with very little knowledge of the adopting parents. Susan Musson of the NCUMC said:

> Would-be adopters called months ahead to book babies for a definite date. The women confined in the Home did not normally see their babies and if they changed their minds about adoption they were threatened with claims for damages. When it was known that a Ministry of Health inspection was about to take place babies were moved into the Women's Wards to give the impression that they were kept with their mothers.[13]

Miss Stevenson of the NCAA pointed out that if the Act was in operation Mrs James, the owner of the Redhill nursing home, would be unable to register as a society and 'it would not be worth while for her to continue her activities because she would undoubtedly be found to be accepting money'. Mr Peake's reply was as unenthusiastic about implementation as it had been the previous day.[14]

The Home Office was still unenthusiastic in January 1943. A memo from the Home Secretary, Herbert Morrison, on the issue of implementation said that 'It has been represented that as a result of war circumstances there are more illegitimate births and there is increasing need for the protective provisions of the Act', and admitted that the various local authority bodies consulted (the County Councils Association, Association of Municipal Corporation and the London County Council) 'feel to a greater or lesser extent that the Act could/should be brought in now' but that he 'is doubtful the Government would be justified in bringing the Act into operation at the present time, however desirable its provisions may be in themselves'.[15]

However a few days later at a meeting of the Lord President's Committee of the War Cabinet, the Home Secretary's measured argument for retaining the *status quo* was overruled. The Minister of Health, Ernest Brown, said

> that his Department was concerned at the extent to which illegitimate children were being handed over, without proper enquiry and precautions, to persons who were unfit or unable to bring them up under proper conditions. Experience in the last war suggested that this abuse might be expected to increase after three years of war; and the dangers might be enhanced by the increasing pressure for the mobilisation of women for industry. There was some evidence of increasing abuse and growing public anxiety; and there was likely to be criticism if the Act designed to deal with these abuses continued to be left in abeyance.[16]

The Minister added that local authorities generally were willing to undertake these duties and the additional work thrown upon them would not, he thought, be very great. Possibly his Parliamentary Secretary, Miss Horsbrugh, was encouraging him to get the Act working. His arguments succeeded – 'the general feeling of the Committee was … that this additional protection should be provided even at the cost of some increase in the administrative work of local authorities', and it was agreed that the Act should be brought into operation. A few days later when Miss Ward asked about the Act in the Commons she was told that it would be implemented 'as soon as the necessary arrangements can be made'.[17]

These were swiftly set in motion and in mid-March 1943 the local authorities who would be regulating societies and providing welfare services in respect of children adopted through the action of individuals rather than societies were circulated details of their new duties by both the Home Office and the Ministry of Health, together with provisional regulations.[18] It was not swift enough for some campaigners; the press ran some lurid stories such as 'Dodgers rushing to adopt babies – There is evidence to show that as June 1 draws near – when the law will take a hand – more and more unwanted babies are being sold to women anxious to avoid war service'.[19]

The Act came into force on 1 June 1943, introduced to the nation with a radio broadcast by Miss Horsbrugh, who reassured listeners after the 6 p.m. news that although there had been 'a good deal of misunderstanding' about the new Act

> parents will still be able to get their children adopted. People who can provide good homes will still be able to adopt. Those who have been acting as middlemen, or should I say, middlewomen, and doing good work, will be helped to do it better; but those who have been looking upon it as a purely commercial enterprise will, I hope, be put out of business altogether.[20]

By December 1943 the Home Secretary was able to report that thirty two adoption societies had been registered.[21] Local authorities appear to have taken the process of registration seriously. Certainly at the London County Council the initial procedure was not a mere formality; in the last chapter I described how the LCC initially rejected what was eventually called the Church Adoption Society and only approved it for registration after it submitted to a range of the Council's demands.

Servicemen's wives and adoption

One of the frustrations of researching the history of adoption is how few statistics and data were collected about it. Everyone involved in adoption during the Second World War – societies, court officials, civil servants and children's charities – said that a considerable number of married women had babies by men who they were not married to while their husbands were overseas in the services. Some of these were registered as the husband's children, some were not. Some were accepted as part of the family by the returning husband; many were not and were adopted. There is no way of knowing how many mothers and babies were involved but it does appear to have been a substantial number;[22] indeed at the time of writing there have been two accounts in the news within a few weeks of one another. The mother of the novelist Ian McEwan had a son with McEwan's father while still married to her first husband who was serving overseas. She placed an advertisement in a local paper saying 'Wanted, home for baby boy aged one month: complete surrender' and gave the baby to a couple on Reading Station. She later learned that her husband had been killed in the Normandy landings and married the baby's father and subsequently had another son, Ian.[23] And John Lennon's half-sister has described how their mother became pregnant by a Welsh soldier while her husband, John Lennon's father, was away at sea during the war; she too gave her baby up for adoption.[24]

It was a situation which caused the authorities considerable concern, not just because of the moral issues involved but because legally it gave rise to a number of complications. Who should be registered as the father of the child? The legal presumption was that if a woman were married the child must be her husband's. And a court case had confirmed that a wife could not give evidence to bastardise her child.[25] However if she told the registrar – or even implied – that her child was her husband's she was giving false information. And if the husband was registered on the birth certificate as the father his consent was needed if the child was to be adopted. But if he was overseas, perhaps a prisoner of war, he could not be contacted for his consent; and if he was contacted much of the point of covering up the situation by adoption would be lost and in fact he sometimes refused to give consent on the grounds that the child was nothing to do with him. As the secretary of the National Adoption Society explained in a letter to the Lord Chancellor's Office asking for advice: 'In some Courts, when it is explained and there is proof that the husband could not have been the father, the judge will dispense with his consent; in others the case is adjourned for the husband's Consent to be produced'. The NAS pleaded that 'It would clarify the position in assisting these children if it were possible to dispense with the Consent of a husband who is known to have gone abroad before the child, subject to adoption, was conceived'.[26]

This letter was sent on to the Home Office and S. W. Harris was adamant that any such change in the law could not possibly be contemplated as it would imply 'that immoral behaviour by wives of men serving their country overseas was being encouraged or condoned'.[27] However by 1944 the Lord Chancellor's Office staff were taking a more pragmatic line. 'The interest of the child is the main consideration' and if the mother is going to renege on a good adoption for the child if the husband is to be served with notice of the proceedings then that is not helping the child. 'There is no general duty on Courts to aid in the detection of adultery.'[28] This was the kind of advice they sent in response to queries from individual judges and clerks but there was no overall guidance. It is clear from notes between the different ministries that many courts had already been taking this pragmatic approach; courts would accept evidence of the husband's non-access to his wife at the relevant time, or find that he had technically 'deserted' the child, or if he was a Japanese prisoner of war declare that he was incapable of giving consent.

The Ministry of Health and Home Office officials were uneasy, and as one said in a note in 1944: 'It is quite clear that there is a great deal of irregularity by Courts in order to facilitate the adoption of the increasing number of illegitimate children of wives of men serving overseas.'[29] However it appears that the LCO's pragmatic approach continued. The problem with it was that there was no consistent practice across the judicial system.

Unmarried mothers

Unmarried mothers faced particular problems during the war if they were working away from home or in the services. There were problems about their evacuation because many local authorities were reluctant to take them. War workers were in a difficult position: foster mothers were in even shorter supply than before the war, local authorities often did not want women from other areas staying in any voluntary mother and baby homes they might support, and they received no money during the three months they had to be off work. One of the women Elizabeth Roberts interviewed suggested that wide-scale adoption began in her area during the war. It

> only started you could say really, during war time and after the war. When I worked in hospital sometimes it was horrible, they just gave them away like kittens and then beggared off and started all over again. You could see them back more than once, and the baby would go as well.[30]

An incredibly limited and secret scheme set up by the Ministry of Health to help them only assisted 36 women between 1941 and 1948.[31] The situation was better for unmarried servicewomen who became pregnant; if they refused to go home or to a moral welfare home they were admitted to a government hostel and were given help during pregnancy and after the birth by the National Council for the Unmarried Mother and Her Child, and the Soldiers', Sailors' and Airmen's Help Society. According to the official history of social services in the Second World War which documented this programme in some detail, 'every effort was made to enable the mothers to keep their babies and adoption was regarded as a last resort ... Many mothers, who were first determined to have their babies adopted, changed their minds later on, but over one-third went through with the adoption proceedings'.[32] As always, lack of foster mothers and nurseries made it almost impossible for many women to keep their babies if they were not prepared to undertake live-in domestic service. Some residential nurseries run under the Government evacuation scheme took a few of the babies but when the war ended these nurseries gradually all closed down.

The third of unmarried mothers who gave up their children for adoption in the servicewomen's scheme was probably a higher proportion than in the population at large. In 1945 the Ministry of Health surveyed areas with high illegitimacy rates to find out what was happening with services for unmarried mothers. In the first six months of 1945, 7500 illegitimate babies were born in the areas in question. Roughly 81 per cent had remained with their mothers, 12 per cent had been adopted and 4 per cent placed with foster-mothers or in residential nurseries (it is not clear about the remaining 3 per cent).[33] But it was considered by the authors of the official social services history who described the survey that some of those 12 per cent 'were driven to part with their babies and to sign away their maternal rights'[34] because of their lack of resources. At this time it was still believed by most people involved with the children and their mothers that it was better for an unmarried mother to keep her baby than give it away. The Church of England Children's Society (formerly the Waifs and Strays Society) had registered as an adoption society and dealt with 221 adoption cases in 1944 but still said in its annual report that it held

> that every effort should be made to enable a parent to keep a child, before adoption is entertained. Grants are available for maintenance where the chief question is one of money, or a child may be taken into one of the Society's homes until the family circumstances improve.[35]

The Anchorage Mission, a home for unmarried mothers managed by the Children's Aid Society, believed that not only was the mother 'the best person to care for her child' but that 'In many more instances than before the war the parents are not only willing to forgive but ready to have their daughter and her baby home and do all they can to help them.'[36] And in a letter to *The Times*, Augusta Caldecote,[37] the Chairman of the National Children Adoption Association and Lettice Fisher of the National Council for the Unmarried Mother and Her Child, wrote that

> [a]doption is not a solution of [sic] the problem of illegitimacy. We believe that every effort should be made to keep mother and child together, to do everything possible, both before and after the child's birth, to enable the mother to maintain and care for her own child ... Only when it is really impossible that the mother should care adequately for the child should adoption be arranged.[38]

This is surprising. Under the leadership of Miss Andrew the NCAA had always paid lipservice to keeping mother and child together but had advocated adoption and its benefits in forthright terms. Whereas the NCUMC and Mrs Fisher had supported adoption legislation but always maintained that the practice should be seen as a last resort for unmarried mothers. In fact this letter rapidly revealed that there was not a consensus on this issue and over the next twenty years opinion would run against them. Others running adoption societies were certainly unconvinced: the Chairman of the Lancashire and Cheshire Child Adoption Council responded, 'If I thought that adoption was a less desirable fate for a child than to be brought up in the status of an illegitimate child I should not remain chairman of my own adoption society.'[39] She was supported by the Chairman and Vice-Chairman of the other main adoption organisation, the National Adoption Society, who wrote:

> If a girl wishes to keep her illegitimate child with her, nobody should interfere. But there can be no doubt that from the child's point of view it has a better status and receives a better upbringing if adopted ... By putting difficulties in the way of adoption and making every effort to keep mother and child together, as is suggested by some, the child is being punished for its mother's lapse.[40]

A few weeks later Lettice Fisher (this time without the support of Augusta Caldecote whose signing of the earlier letter had probably caused some consternation throughout her organisation) replied to these comments with a more trenchantly critical approach to adoption than she usually employed:

> Sooner or later the adopted child will come to know the truth about its parentage, and may easily receive a psychological shock which may warp its whole existence. It is terrible to discover that one's own mother wanted to get rid of her child, and the most devoted care of adopting parents cannot make up for such a discovery … We do not at all want to attack adoption … What we do want to urge is that it must be something less good than real parentage, if only the real parent can be given the right help.[41]

Renewed pressure for adoption reform

The main thrust of the letter from Mrs Fisher and Viscountess Caldecote was to ask for a review of the Adoption of Children (Regulation) Act which had by then been in force for a year. They said it had 'undoubtedly led to a real diminution of some of the abuses of adoption, but many still remain'.[42] Although societies and organisations were now controlled, they pointed out that individuals could still arrange private adoptions as long as they notified the appropriate local authority and they heard of 'doctors, nurses, midwives and others who, no doubt with the best intentions but without the necessary knowledge and specialised training, offer infants for adoption' often not aware of even the rudimentary regulations affecting private adoption. In fact just a few weeks before this letter was published George Orwell and his wife adopted a baby straight from hospital, which Orwell's sister-in-law, a doctor, had found for them.[43] Eileen, Orwell's wife, had not been well for some years and was not particularly enthusiastic about the idea of adoption although she became very attached to the baby after he arrived. But she died nine months later, having delayed seeing her surgeon until the adoption was through; 'it would have been an uneasy sort of thing to be producing oneself as an ideal parent a fortnight after being told that one couldn't live more than six months or something',[44] and her husband was already suffering from tubercular symptoms. One wonders if an adoption society would have considered the Orwells ideal parental material.

Although the National Adoption Society had taken issue with the less than positive comments on adoption employed in the letter they also were worried about the 'large number of private adoptions being arranged quite casually'[45] and in September 1945 they, and other major adoption societies including the NCAA, attended a conference organised by the National Council of Social Service (NCSS) for them and representatives of courts and local authorities to look at how at how the adoption laws were working. A committee was set up to consider 'the defects of the present adoption code' with a view to asking the Government to amend the adoption laws 'to ensure proper safeguards with regard to adoption in every case by clarifying the regulations and securing greater uniformity of procedure'.[46] Both the conference and the committee were chaired by His Honour Judge Gamon. A year later it reported back to another conference and a report, 'In Loco Parentis', using its findings and recommendations was drawn up by the NCSS and sent to the Lord Chancellor. The essence of the report was that 'the problem ... is no longer to find a home of sorts for an unwanted child, but to find a real home with a real mother and father for a much wanted child'.[47] It proposed a range of measures to improve adoption procedures and bring private adoptions in line with those arranged by societies.

Meanwhile the Gamon Committee and its report had been rather overshadowed by the work of the Curtis Committee. This was an official committee set up in March 1945 by the Government (the Home Secretary, the Ministers of Health and Education jointly) to look at

> existing methods of providing for children who from loss of parents or from any cause whatever are deprived of a normal home life with their own parents or relatives; and to consider what further measures should be taken to ensure that these children are brought up under conditions best calculated to compensate them for the lack of parental care.[48]

Its remit was not to look particularly at adoption, rather the conditions prevailing in the care provided for the 125,000 children without a family home. There had been increasing concern about these conditions: in July 1944 a landscape architect, Lady Allen of Hurtwood,[49] had written a letter to *The Times* calling for an official inquiry into the care given children under the guardianship of Government departments or voluntary organisations. She spoke of 'repressive conditions that are generations out of date'[50] and her letter provoked what *The Times* called an 'exceptionally large correspondence'[51] with writers ranging from George Bernard Shaw to the educational psychologist and psychoanalyst, Dr Susan Isaacs.

In February the following year, Lady Allen published a pamphlet, 'Whose Children?', setting out the situation in more detail. It came after news which had caused widespread shock that Dennis O'Neill, a 12-year-old boy in local authority foster care, had died from injuries received in beatings at the farm where he was boarded out.[52] By then the Government had already announced that it would hold an inquiry along the lines which Lady Allen had campaigned for, and late in February the Home Secretary, Herbert Morrison, listed the committee's membership. It was chaired by Miss Myra Curtis, Principal of Newnham College, Cambridge,[53] and as Stephen Cretney describes, its report 'led directly to the enactment of the Children Act 1948 which remained the foundation of State provision for children in need for the next quarter of a century and ... an integral and important part of machinery of the post-World War II Welfare State.'[54] What concerns us here however is its attitude to adoption.

The Curtis Committee interviewed a number of witnesses about the current state of adoption. Indeed at one point they asked the representative from the Home Office why there were more parents wishing to adopt than children available, which they, like modern politicians, could not understand, 'considering how many destitute children there are in the country?' The reply was:

> There are a number of factors that contribute to that. One of them is that there are a large number of quite unsuitable people always wanting to adopt children, and the letters of complaint that we get written to the Home Office very often reveal quite plainly that they are the most unsuitable people to have children. Then of course there are a great many destitute children who are not available for adoption [because] either their parents are not willing to agree, or their state of health is not suitable. I think mostly the people who want to adopt children want them under the age of two, and I understand from the Societies that the very great majority want girls.[55]

The Committee asked witnesses quite searching questions about the possibility of revoking adoption orders, the role of the guardian *ad litem*, the differing powers of the juvenile and county courts, the age of adopters (people were applying to adopt at 65 and 70, and the Home Office admitted cases had come to their notice 'where adoption Orders have been made in favour of people who are too old'[56]), medical examinations for potential adopters as well as children and inheritance rights.

The Committee talked at length to B. E. Astbury of the Charity Organisation Society who had been a member of the Horsbrugh Committee. Although he was pleased with the way the Adoption of Children (Regulation) Act had worked in ending 'an enormous number of loose adoptions',[57] he was still extremely concerned about the gaps in control, in particular the way that nursing homes evaded all the provisions. The notorious nursing home in Redhill was still going strong, even though in 1939, 'when it came to drafting the regulations every possible attempt was made by various people to try to draw them tight enough to get the Matron within them, and we failed.'[58] The matron succeeded in arguing that as an individual the adoption regulations did not apply to her. In an accompanying memorandum Mr Astbury described the way she and other nursing home proprietors worked, distributing babies all over the country in return for inclusive fees from the birth mothers or sometimes their unpaid labour in the maternity homes. For example, the Sheffield and District Adoption Committee (a registered adoption society) contacted the COS after a couple came to them for advice about a baby they had been given from the Redhill home. The couple had written to the Matron on an acquaintance's recommendation

> asking for information regarding a child whom they wished to adopt. The Sheffield Society saw the Matron's replies, offering a child for adoption and stating that others were available. The letter stated that the child was quite healthy, that a blood test had been taken; it further stated that the mother was a nurse, whereas the birth certificate showed that she was a munitions worker. The putative father was said to be a soldier who was missing. The couple wrote accepting this child, and were then instructed to meet a certain train at Manchester station, where the Matron would arrive with the baby. The Matron arrived by the stated train, and handed over the baby, telling them to apply to the Court for an Adoption Order. This they did, and were referred to the Sheffield Adoption Society for advice. The Matron had told them that she was the guardian of the child, and that she had placed 400 babies in the last year ...
>
> In this case, the home to which the baby was consigned was a good one, but it was pointed out that it might easily have been the reverse. No home visit of any kind had been paid, neither were the couple required to supply any references.[59]

In its final report the Curtis Committee made a number of recommendations about reforming the adoption process. It called for a much more uniform practice for all adoptions irrespective of how they were organised. So in all cases where children were placed for adoption, the local authority must be notified and there must be a probationary period of at least three months before the adopters' application would be dealt with; during this period the child must be placed under the supervision of the local authority's Children's Officer (who would be the guardian *ad litem* unless the adoption was arranged by the local authority), and if necessary could be removed by court order if the placing was 'a detrimental environment'.[60] All private individuals should be prohibited from acting as adoption agencies.

Surprisingly, the Curtis Committee's first preference for substitute care was adoption. Surprisingly, because the discussion provoked by its report was directed elsewhere, and it is not remembered for its advocacy of adoption. The Committee above all emphasised

> the extreme seriousness of taking a child away from even an indifferent home. Every effort should be made to keep the child in its home, or with its mother if it is illegitimate, providing that the home is or can be made reasonably satisfactory. The aim of the authority must be to find something better – indeed much better – if it takes the responsibility of providing a substitute home.[61]

However it went on to say that

> [i]f [adoption] is successful it is the most completely satisfactory method of providing a substitute home. It gives the child new parents, with all the parents' rights and responsibilities, who take the place of the real parents so far as human nature allows.[62]

With the caveat that 'there is no statistical evidence of the percentage of happy results, but in the absence of evidence to the contrary it is reasonable to suppose that in the large majority of cases the connection turns out well'.[63]

Despite its praise of adoption, the Committee's Report gave much more attention to 'boarding out' which was their second choice of substitute care. Adoption by its nature is about a permanent change of family, almost of identity. As the Report admits, it is 'specially appropriate to the child who has finally lost his own parents by death, desertion, or their misconduct, and in a secondary degree to the illegitimate child whose mother is unable or unwilling to maintain him.'[64] They did not spell it out but clearly where parents were still alive, present and possibly contesting their alleged 'misconduct' there would always be problems with using adoption as substitute care in any but the most extreme cases. Stephen Cretney suggests that adoption also took a long time to be seen as a part of social work provision because its official introduction to the United Kingdom had seen it considered in terms of legal status, a means of giving parents legal title to the children they had already acquired, rather than a way of dealing with children in need.[65] This lies at the heart of the many contradictions in adoption: is it a means of giving parents the secure right to a child, or a way of giving a child in need the best possible substitute home? In an ideal world the two are mutually compatible, in practice they are often not. Most potential parents had a vision of their perfect adopted child: it was a child untainted by emotional or physical abuse and deprivation. No wonder the idea of the 'war orphan' was so attractive; a child available for adoption through no fault or flaw in its in its own background or that of its parents.

Adoption legislation

The final legacy of the War and its aftermath was the passing of two Adoption Acts in the late 1940s. The first was a private member's bill introduced by a Conservative MP, Basil Nield, but with the support of the Labour Government. It made a number of changes to adoption practice but did not deal with the major criticism of current adoption that had been made by the Curtis Committee and most of the informed observers – that only an estimated quarter of adoptions were carried out by societies – and apart from the few made through local authorities, the rest were mainly informal arrangements by friends and acquaintances or individual professionals like doctors and matrons. What the 1949 Adoption of Children Act did do was move the 'benefit of the doubt', the favourable treatment, away from the relinquishing mother and over to the adopters. Those supporting the rights of the unmarried mother did not give in immediately in either the Commons or the Lords and concessions were made, but the times were changing and the next twenty years would see much more emphasis on the new family than on the birth mother trying to make her lonely decision.

This was the only time that adoption legislation has been made without following on from a report and recommendations by an official committee[66] (although the Curtis Committee had made recommendations relating to adoption the main emphasis of its Report was elsewhere) and it shows in the fairly chaotic way in which the legislation was formulated, with amendments and alterations being made in both Houses in an almost *ad hoc* manner. Probably the main change to come out of this Act related to the requirement of the natural parent to consent to adoption. The 1926 Act had implicitly said that a mother could not reasonably consent to adoption unless she knew the identity of the adopter, and the Horsbrugh Committee had criticised the practice of some adoption societies in getting mothers to sign away their child on a blank form where the name of the adopter would be later inserted. This was now reversed – the mother was required to give consent to specific adopters – but they were not to be identified unless they wished it. This was taken to mean that a serial number would suffice to replace their name (this was clarified in the consolidating Act the following year because the Chancery Division queried whether this was sufficient description of an applicant).[67] In theory there were new rights for the mother: she could not give consent to adoption before the baby was born and until at least six weeks after the birth to give her time to consider, and her consent must be in writing and witnessed by a JP. The proposal that the mother should give consent in general terms was rejected by the House of Lords but as in practice she had no way of knowing who was behind the number it might as well have been a general consent.

Speakers in the Commons such as Mrs Ayrton Gould MP spoke out against these clauses:

> Even where a woman has a baby under ideal conditions, in happy married life very often for weeks after the birth of the baby she is ill and unfit to make decisions. Fortunately, in ordinary life most women are not called upon to make serious decisions in the first six weeks after the birth of a baby ... I fully appreciate that it is hard on adopting parents if they take a child and the child is snatched from them, but I appreciate still more the importance of protecting the natural mother as much as possible.[68]

But others felt the adopting parents must be protected from the birth mother:

> People who have adopted a child are in constant terror that the natural parent will turn up ... the natural parent can be a very great trouble to the adopter. The natural parent can, and in certain circumstances has, levied blackmail, or tried to get to know the adopted child, or has tried to undermine the affection of the adopted child towards his adopted parents, and a great deal of difficulty has been caused.[69]

It was even suggested that if an initial consent was revoked before the adoption order came through, the birth mother should pay compensation to the adopters. 'It is desirable that there should be some check on the natural mother who wishes to park out a child and get it back later,'[70] although the Home Office Under-Secretary, Mr Younger, felt such cases were 'somewhat rare', and that particular amendment was dropped.[71]

The fear that underlay such comments was that a birth mother would arbitrarily remove a child from its adopting parents after they had bonded with it. Although some of the speakers cited anecdotal evidence that there were many such cases it does not appear that this was the case, although no doubt *In re Hollyman*, reported in early 1945, had exacerbated the concern. The Court of Appeal had allowed the appeal of a mother who had given a written consent to adoption but then attended the child's adoption hearing and said she did not in fact consent. The county court judge said the signed form was sufficient and made the order in spite of the mother's protests. The Appeal judges unanimously agreed that this was wrong, 'the consent must be a continuing consent, and there was no rule that a consent once given could not be retracted. The consent must be operative at the moment when the order was made'.[72] However this was just one legal case and Viscount Caldecote, who as Sir Thomas Inskip had been the Solicitor General when the 1926 Act was passed and was husband of the NCAA Chairman, said in the House of Lords that 'one society' (presumably the NCAA) stated that the number of cases where a mother asked for her child back during the probationary period was very low. He used this as an argument for proposing that all adoptions should be carried out by official agencies.[73]

By the end of the final debate in the Commons on the bill some of the speakers appear quite angry. The playwright Benn Levy, who had supported all the amendments giving adopters more rights, felt that in the 'fields of adoption work and in the related fields, there are opposing factions'[74] and said that adopting parents should be

> warned that they cannot be guaranteed secrecy and that they cannot therefore really be guarded against persecution unless they are rich enough to be able to afford an application through the High Court. That is the most expensive way of doing it, but, unhappily, it is the only secure way. In the county court or the juvenile court adopters are liable to exposure. I bitterly regret that during the passage of this Bill none of us, myself included, devised an Amendment calculated to alter that situation. I realise that it is too late now.[75]

In fact he was wrong, as secrecy and anonymity for adoptive parents were the clear result of this Act.

Opponents of Levy's views were surprisingly thin on the ground by now, although Ernest Thurtle MP ended the debate with a plea 'that the rights of the mother will not be neglected' and said that if the description of the adopter was to be 'so vague and nebulous that no one would be able to identify him' it would not be 'in accordance with the traditions of our British Law that we should adopt a hypocritical proceeding of that kind'.[76] This was not a disagreement on party political lines – all the MPs quoted were Labour, and behind the scenes Government ministers disagreed with each other as well. According to Cretney, the Home Secretary, James Chuter Ede, felt that a proposal made by Benn Levy that there should be a limit on how long the mother could change her mind even though the adopters could still change theirs and return the child to her, was quite unfair. However, the Lord Chancellor thought Levy right.[77]

The Adoption of Children Act 1949 received Royal Assent on 16 December 1949 and came into force, with accompanying rules from the Lord Chancellor, on 1 January 1950. Besides the changes about identifying the adopters already discussed, it said that non-British children could now be adopted by British citizens and would automatically become British citizens themselves and it clarified the right of the mother or father of the child to adopt it either alone or with their spouse; consent could now be given without knowing the identity of the adopter[78] but would be deemed 'unreasonably withheld' if it was then withdrawn on the basis of not knowing the adopter. Once the adopters had put in an application for an adoption order the natural parent (who had already signed consent) would not be allowed to remove the child from the adopter without the court's permission. Husband or wife could now give evidence about whether marital intercourse had taken place to decide the question of paternity; this of course had been a considerable issue during the war.

From 1 April 1950, an adoption order could not be made unless the infant had been continuously in the care of the potential adopters for at least three months and the adopters had to give three months' notice of their intention to apply for the adoption order. So in effect, the adopters could apply for an adoption order as soon as they received the child and thus block the mother from reclaiming her child until the actual hearing, by which time the adopters would have been looking after the child for at least three months and the court would have to decide whether the mother reclaiming the child would be 'to the welfare of the child'.

Marriage between adopted child and adoptive parent was prohibited but not between the adopted child and his or her adopted sibling. There were also measures so that adopted children would now be treated in property and inheritance terms in much the same way as if they were the legitimately born children of the adopters. In other words this amended the parts of the 1926 Act which had left the child linked to the natural parent in terms of wills and intestacy but gave it no rights vis-à-vis its adopting parent. There were various technicalities relating to the Adopted Children Register and the Register of Births, and finally there was a section to amend and extend the Scottish legislation so that the adoption law was co-ordinated across the countries.

Seven months later the Adoption Act 1950 consolidated all the Adoption Acts so far passed. It was introduced in the House of Lords and the only significant alteration brought in was to clarify the use of a serial number for adopters as mentioned above 'as it is often highly desirable that the parent of a child who is proposed to be adopted should not know the identity of the would-be adopter'.[79] Although annual adoption numbers were actually lower during the 1950s than during the late 1940s in many ways the 1949 Act ushered in the two decades of 'classic' adoption – increasing numbers of adopted children were under two years old, illegitimate, and adopted by childless couples rather than single women; and by the time adoption reached its peak in 1968 the majority of placements were made by adoption societies. And after the debates of 1949 there was far less talk about the importance of enabling unmarried mothers to keep their children.

8
Conclusions – And Later Developments

Policies, practices and attitudes in relation to adoption changed enormously during the three decades spanned by this book. After the First World War adoption was seen by many as a last resort for the care of unwanted illegitimate children. By 1950 it was an established way of setting up a family. In 1918 unmarried mothers had been figures of shame to be pitied, helped or despised; by the late 1940s they were increasingly invisible – either the providers of babies for childless couples or silently bringing up their children on their own. The years after the Second World War saw the distillation of a process that began during the interwar years in which the nuclear family – two parents and one or two children – became the dominant model. Adoption of the children of the unmarried fitted neatly into this.

Attitudes to adoption

In the early 1920s there was a general consensus among welfare groups, adoption agencies, and probably those members of the public interested in the subject, that there should be legislation around adoption, although the motives for wanting an adoption law varied. All appeared to agree that orphans should be placed with 'nice' families, rather than institutions, wherever possible. However when it came to unmarried mothers giving up their babies for adoption there was far less agreement. The adoption agencies were firmly in favour of this practice; it was how they received the great majority of their children. As far as they were concerned it was a winning situation for all: the mother had a chance to rebuild her life, the adopting parents were given the child they wanted to create their family and the child was welcomed into the good home which it would never have had with its mother. The societies sought legislation because they wanted the adopting families to have secure possession of their children, free from the fear that their natural parents might reclaim them.

However, in the early 1920s most other organisations dealing with children believed that adoption was occasionally necessary but not really to be encouraged unless there was no chance of family ties being maintained. The NSPCC were particularly suspicious of the practice and were disappointed that the initial legislation did not make obtaining adoption orders compulsory.[1] They saw legislation as a way of attempting to prevent the worst excesses of adoption by bringing it under regulatory control. The major child rescue societies like Barnardo's considered that legalising adoption might protect children from baby farming, although this was in decline anyway and without compulsion it is unlikely that baby farmers would have applied for adoption orders. The organisations dealing with unmarried mothers – both the moral welfare groups and the National Council for the Unmarried Mother and Her Child – were concerned that if it was too easy for unmarried mothers to give away their children they would revert to an immoral life, or at the very least be tempted to sin again when the opportunity arose. Whereas if some way could be found for them to keep their child – through hostel accommodation and child care, subsidised foster parents or an allowance – they would gain maturity and moral stature by looking after their child.

In fairness to many who worked in these agencies, they also thought it was cruel and exploitative to persuade a woman at her most vulnerable to give up her child – a decision they knew many later regretted. There was concern, not least among some of the civil servants, about the attitude of the adoption societies to the relinquishing mothers. They considered that the societies treated the mothers merely as providers of infants, to be dismissed as soon as possible with the minimum of information about the fate of their children. In the 1920s psychoanalytic theories about abandonment and trauma were relatively undeveloped, but clearly there was some understanding that severing mother-child bonds was not such a simple and clear-cut practice as the adoption societies implied.

By 1939 attitudes towards adoption had changed; it was now generally accepted that, for better or worse, it was part of contemporary society. There had been a great deal of criticism in the 1930s about the way some societies and individuals carried out adoptions, but no one suggested that it was possible to ban adoption; the issue was how to improve the practice. The findings of the Horsbrugh Committee and the contents of the Adoption of Children (Regulation) Act 1939 appear to have met with universal agreement, even if it was felt that more legislation to deal with private adoptions might be necessary in future. Gradually agencies which had been ambivalent about adoption became much more involved. At the end of 1934 the Waifs and Strays Society (later the Church of England Children's Society, now the Children's Society), which had previously cared for the thousands of children in its care in institutions or foster-homes, decided that it would start organising its own adoptions. So many of the babies in its homes were being removed by their unmarried mothers and placed for adoption with adoption societies or individuals that they considered it better to keep the whole procedure under their control.[2]

A decade on and adoption was a completely accepted part of British society. In 1947 Barnardo's reversed its previous policy of opposing adoptions in the UK, and became a registered adoption society. Barnardo's Senior Boarding Officer had discovered 'that boarded-out boys and girls growing up in foster-homes under Barnardo's care had come to fear their fourteenth birthday, when they would be taken back to a home for technical or domestic training'.[3] This mirrored the substantial change in attitude towards adoption by the end of the 1940s. It was seen as a force for the good; areas of practice might need reform and improvement but overall it benefited all concerned, especially the child – and the receiving family. It was judged by the Curtis Committee the best form of substitute care for children in need. The birth mother was largely ignored and the NCUMC remained one of the few bodies to stand aside from the general enthusiasm. It was considerably involved in the campaign for the regulation of the adoption societies and for the subsequent implementation of the Act after it was delayed, but it maintained its strong position on adoption and unmarried mothers into the 1940s: 'We take no part in arranging adoptions ourselves, and hold even more firmly as a result of our war experience to our belief in the importance of keeping mother and child together whenever it is humanly possible.'[4]

The rise of adoption

By the 1920s there was a kind of self-consciousness about families; they were smaller than before, their children were increasingly prized for their emotional value and domestic virtues were extolled. Children were not just something that came along; they were an essential part of a lifestyle, to use a modern expression. As Mrs Edwin Gray of the National Council of Women told the Home Secretary in 1920: 'There is a growing desire on the part of parents who are childless to receive a little child within their family life, and they therefore seek a child to adopt.'[5] The decline in family size was really marked; in 1933 the fertility rate sank to the then lowest recorded level, which was not reached again till 1976. Couples were much more conscious of the possibility – and benefit – of deliberately limiting the number of children they had, whether by the use of contraception, or at the very least, abstinence.[6] The ideal family was becoming 'neater'; in Slater and Woodside's survey of wartime couples: 'Two [children] is the overwhelmingly popular number – a "pigeon pair", "two only, and one of each"'.[7] Large families in contrast were 'firmly associated in their minds with poverty, hardship and the lowering of standards' and 'attributed to "lust", to "ignorance" (of birth control), and to lack of outside interests and recreations'.[8]

An adopted family was, in a sense, the ultimate planned family and it was essential that it be as permanently and legally secure as any other planned family. So adoption legislation was vital and the push for it was carried through the 1920s by the newly formed adoption societies; organisations whose only purpose was adoption – not child rescue, or saving fallen women, just putting children together with would-be parents. The societies, particularly the National Children Adoption Association, became a powerful and influential political lobby pressing for what they considered were the interests of the adopters – and the children involved, whose interests they believed were best served by adoption in new families. Working with older-established welfare organisations who also believed – for different reasons – that legislation should be brought in, they were an impressive campaigning body. Without the adoption societies it is debateable whether the campaign to legalise adoption would have kept up its momentum throughout the 1920s (although their campaign was helped by its timing; the 1920s are increasingly seen as an era of quite important domestic legislative reform). The majority of the failed adoption bills between 1921 and 1926 were introduced to Parliament by MPs involved in some way with one or other of the main adoption societies, mainly the NCAA, and the societies kept up a continuing flow of publicity and fund-raising activities to keep the issue in the public eye. They also maintained pressure on the civil servants in the Home Office, the Lord Chancellor's Department and the Ministry of Health, by a stream of letters and visits. It was an effective exercise in lobbying, and even though the societies did not gain all they wanted in terms of secrecy in the 1926 Act they kept up the pressure and eventually achieved most of their agenda of anonymity for the adopting parents in the adoption legislation passed after the Second World War.

Who was adoption for?

The adoption societies always maintained that adoption was in the best interests of all parties involved. Sometimes it may have been, but in general they were uninterested in the welfare of the birth parent; their main concern was for the adopting parents and the children. It is hard to say which of these was the priority. There is no reason to doubt that reputable societies like the NCAA genuinely wished to help the children they placed and sincerely believed in the value of their work for them. When the societies were establishing themselves at the end of the First World War the idea that negative emotional (as opposed to physical) experiences in childhood might cause lasting psychological damage had not yet become a generally accepted concept, and the societies did not feel it was necessary to look at the individual needs of each child, particularly if the child was very young. To the societies such children were a *'tabula rasa'* and what they needed was a home with reasonable parents who would bring them up in their own mould. The historian Janet Fink looked at the issue of blood ties and adoption and suggested that, in contrast to the parliamentary committees and the successive adoption laws which were never quite able to resolve the conflict between natural (blood) family ties and constructed ones, the adoption societies were quite clear in interpreting 'adoption to be a means by which a "new" family was created', and

> adoption was promoted as producing a *natural* (that is, quasi-blood) relationship between the adoptive parent and child to the extent that, it was claimed, adopted children became so much members of their adoptive family that they began to take on their physical characteristics [her italics].[9]

The societies generally claimed that they attempted to match children with parents of a similar class background but this, when it occurred, was the extent of their placing policy in the early years. In her evidence to the Hopkinson Committee in 1920, Miss Andrew of the NCAA was dismissive of potential problems that a child might have in a new home, suggesting that just as children living with unsatisfactory natural parents had to make the best of things so should adopted children – life in such a home would still be preferable to an institution.[10]

This probably just reflects the way in which children were usually regarded at this time – literally to be 'seen and not heard'; their point of view unimportant. However there was discussion in the Hopkinson and Tomlin Reports about the child's rights to be consulted about adoption, and one of the issues debated in Parliament was whether an age should be set for this. Eventually no age was stipulated and it was left to the judge to decide what weight to give the child's opinion, but the Act clearly stated that 'the order if made will be for the welfare of the infant, due consideration being for this purpose given to the wishes of the infant, having regard to the age and understanding of the infant'.[11] However as the societies dealt mainly with children under five it was unlikely that they were ever consulted.

The societies were probably choosier about the babies they offered for adoption than the parents they gave them to. Certainly the NCAA rejected many more babies on grounds of their possible poor health, or their mothers' dubious morals, than it did the parents who were often given only the most perfunctory checks about their home background and their references. Reading through the literature produced by the societies the balance was inevitably towards the interests of the adopters. Obviously the literature was targeted at the potential adopters but it reflected the inevitable reality. They were the ones who came in and chose a child and they were the ones who could return it if things went wrong. Home inspections were cursory or non-existent. A woman adopted through an unnamed adoption society in 1939 wrote about her experience in *Child Adoption*. She described her adoptive mother who had had a mental breakdown after two stillbirths: 'It was suggested to her by the vicar that adopting a baby would be the best answer to her troubles.' She said the society

> could never have checked the family background, as there was great insanity on my [adoptive] mother's side. A sister, a cousin and a niece were permanently in mental homes and the rest of the family were highly eccentric, to put it mildly.

Her summing up expresses the reality of the situation: 'Probably at that time the societies were more interested in providing babies for the applicants than parents for the children.'[12]

Although her adoption was in 1939, on the whole attitudes were beginning to change by then, not towards the relinquishing mother, who was even less considered by the societies, but towards the interests of the child. The Horsbrugh Committee was adamant that every society must have a case committee with trained and experienced members, and that every attempt should be made to place 'the right child in the right home'. By now the NCAA was taking its checking responsibilities more seriously – and it wanted to distinguish itself from the 'rogue' societies. In 1935 Princess Alice, its president, said of the society: 'It would be quite easy to show more spectacular numbers were they to accept a less high standard and were the Case Committee and the physicians less scrupulous in their rules not only of the children but of the adopters.'[13] By the late 1940s the interests of the birth mother had moved firmly into the background and the adoption legislation gave a definite advantage to the interests of the adopters and removed all possibility of the mother knowing who had adopted her child. And although adoptions organised by individuals were still allowed, the adoption process was becoming more regulated to protect the interests of the child.

Only since the late 1970s, with the rise in the adoptions of children from local authority care described below, has adoption, at least as carried out within the United Kingdom (as opposed to the adoption of children brought in from overseas), been carried out with the interests of the children at the forefront of the process. There might be criticism of the way the process is handled or the wisdom of judgements about the children's best interests, but it is clearly the children rather than the adopters or the original parents who are the purpose of the exercise.

Secrecy

The desire for secrecy bordered on obsession among some adopters and societies. There are letters from adopters in the Home Office files explaining that if there was any likelihood of the adoption becoming public they would never apply for an adoption order for their child, even though they had waited for years for this legislation in order to safeguard the child's position in their family.[14] In general those running the main adoption societies felt a great empathy with this point of view. From the evidence of witnesses to the Hopkinson Committee (in particular Clara Andrew of the NCAA), and from the articles and letters they produced, it seems likely that their clientele – or certainly what they liked to believe was their clientele – came chiefly from the 'respectable' upper working, lower middle and middle classes, with a few from the upper middle classes. The kind of people who valued privacy and not letting the neighbours know their business. Those running the main adoption societies appear to have almost instinctively understood this desire and fought persistently for as much secrecy as possible. In 1920 Miss Andrew described the NCAA's ideal adoption system as a legally binding registration process with no court procedure and the minimum interference by the state or the relinquishing mother.

The societies soon accepted the inevitability of a more judicial procedure but sought to minimise the participation of the birth mother, and eradicate any trace of the child's origins. As we have seen, by the 1950s legislative measures had been taken to bring this about, and the general pattern of adoption by strangers was to cover all traces of a child's background. However during the interwar years there was continuing resistance to such a policy: the civil servants involved in adoption legislation were extremely anxious about the loss of all knowledge about the child's original background, and many politicians also expressed concern. There was an awareness that cutting off all trace of a child's origins was a very radical step. M. L. Gwyer, the Ministry of Health's representative on the Tomlin Committee, stressed the danger of relying solely on voluntary agencies to preserve the evidence of a child's identity. Records could so easily be lost or destroyed (as often happened later). The 1926 Adoption Act remained ambivalent about the whole issue. It stated that

> [a]n adoption order shall not deprive the adopted child of any right to or interest in property to which, but for the order, the child would have been entitled under any intestacy or disposition, whether occurring or made before or after the making of the adoption order.[15]

However for this to be put into practice the child or its adopters would have to know about the continuing circumstances of its original family. Later clauses in the Act instruct the Registrar-General to set up a process of 'other registers and books' to link the Adopted Children Register with the register of births but this would not be open to public inspection and information would only be made available by 'an order of a court of competent jurisdiction'.[16] Realistically, very few adopted people were likely to attempt to get a court order, and Haimes and Timms said that 'applications were rarely granted'.[17] Even in Scotland, where adopted people over the age of 17 had the right to see their details without a court order, the figures applying were originally very low.[18]

Secrecy is an important issue in the history of adoption but is not an easy subject for historical research or enquiry. So much investigation about it must be anecdotal – relying on individual autobiographies, interviews, rumours or even gossip – or else remain conjecture; inevitably the nature of secrecy means that many people will not speak of their secrets. The authors of *The Family Story* devoted a chapter to the issue and suggested that looking at the 'silences and secrets which have been constructed by families' may 'enrich our understanding of the history of the family'. They continued:

> Family secrets cluster around what is considered to be the most intimate core of the family – the physical, social and cultural reproduction of its members. They are dominated by the intensely private subjects of sex, money and behaviour, on which, in turn, are focused so many family myths, particularly that of the nuclear family in which couples are devoted and sexually fulfilled, children are loved and wanted, wives are proficient home-makers, and husbands are willing and capable economic providers.[19]

Adoption and women

Was adoption a 'women's' issue in this period? It was not at the time seen particularly in this way but it inevitably affected women in a much more direct way than men. Apart from the children involved, the main people affected by adoption were women – mothers and would-be mothers. Most adopted children were illegitimate and presumably the birth father was rarely present: if he had been there to provide support it is more likely that the mother would have kept her child. In the adoptive family it may sometimes have been the husband who was the driving force for adoption, but the pressure on wives to be mothers during this period meant that women were usually most involved in the process. Certainly the burden of care would have fallen mainly on them in this era of low employment of married women. Even those adopted may have been mainly female; every reference to a preferred gender in adoption during this period makes it clear that girls were markedly favoured above boys, even if adopters settled for what was available.

On the positive side, adoption could offer choices to women which they had not had in such an organised fashion before. Children had been adopted before the 1920s, by strangers as well as relatives, through advertisements and baby-farming networks, but this era saw the start of a relatively secure process, with legal backing. For many of those who gave up their children for adoption in this period it must have meant, as the proponents of adoption claimed, that they were able to make a fresh start or at least move on from what was a potentially desperate situation. The options for low-waged unmarried mothers without family support in the interwar years were incredibly limited despite the efforts of the NCUMC and other welfare groups. There is a growing literature of regret written by relinquishing mothers, mainly in the US, but those who felt they did the right thing in having their child adopted are probably less likely to write about it. Secrecy was not just for the adoptive parents; many birth mothers supported it too. Some of the birth mothers contacted by their natural children since the 1975 Children Act gave adopted children the right to their original details, refuse to see them, perhaps for emotional reasons, but also because they want their past to remain secret.[20]

For those women (and their husbands) who could not have children, adoption offered a chance to create a family, and it also offered the possibility of motherhood to women in an organised fashion unavailable before. As discussed above, this was the first time that large numbers of people felt that they had any control over the shape and size of their family. Declining mortality rates were enormously important in this; there was no point in using unappealing methods of contraception, or abstaining from sex for many years, if the few children you produced were likely to die; similarly, making a conscious decision to adopt a child of unknown genetic and social background was an enormous emotional risk if a statistically high proportion of infants died every year. As Michael Anderson pointed out, only now was mortality beginning to be at 'a sufficiently low level that its possibility of occurrence in any year could more or less be ruled out of the forward thinking of anyone aged between one and late middle age'.[21] The 'possible consequences of this change for a wide range of attitudes and behaviour', he went on, 'still remain largely unexplored', but feeling it was worth taking on the care of an unrelated child for no material reward might be one of the many such consequences.

So wives, and single women and widows, could use adoption to become mothers if they chose. The historian Julie Berebitsky, writing about adoption in the United States, showed how advocates of adoption from the 1920s onwards made a deliberate virtue of this, in a reaction to criticism of adoption as an 'inferior' kind of motherhood. They 'used the vocabulary of choice to underscore adoptive mothers' conscious decision to mother and their unique preparedness for motherhood'.[22] They also felt that the growing emphasis on 'scientific mothering', learned from instruction manuals written by child care 'experts', laying down rules and precepts for child-rearing rather than intuitive maternal instinct, was to the advantage of adoptive mothers because 'if women needed to be educated to motherhood, physical birth no longer gave biological mothers an automatic edge'.[23] Prescriptive writers and lecturers about child care such as Truby King were also extremely influential in England so it is arguable that this was the case here as well. If motherhood was a craft or skill to be learnt there might be less emphasis placed on *who* gave birth and more on the person actually bringing up the baby.

However it was not just in adopting children that women were involved with adoption. They were highly visible during these years both in adoption policy and practice. Women had been involved in welfare work and campaigning groups throughout the nineteenth century so the activity of Miss Clara Andrew and the other female executive members and volunteer workers in her association and the other adoption societies was part of a long tradition. But after gaining a limited and then full franchise, women were increasingly involved as politicians and policy-makers. In the 1920s this was mainly as appointed members of the parliamentary committees or speaking in the adoption bill debates in the House of Commons. By the 1930s their role was stronger; women MPs were in the forefront of pushing for an inquiry into adoption society abuses and Miss Florence Horsbrugh MP was an extremely determined and able chairman of the parliamentary committee which conducted that inquiry. She then successfully steered the resulting legislation through the Commons. During the War it was again women MPs who were particularly vociferous in pressing for the delayed regulatory legislation to be implemented.

***

Adoption since 1950

Finally, a brief account of the major developments after the period covered in this book so we can see how adoption developed after 1950.[24]

In 1954 another Departmental Committee on the Adoption of Children was appointed, chaired by Sir Gerald Hurst who had long been interested in adoption. His report emphasised both the role of the local authority in arranging adoptions, and the contributing importance of adoption societies. In some ways the Committee anticipated later developments in adoption as it suggested that, contrary to much current received opinion, almost any child was adoptable, even if disabled; it also said that it had received evidence from witnesses who believed that adoptees in England and Wales should have rights to information about their origins and it proposed limited measures to introduce this. These were not included in the ensuing Act; prevailing thought in adoption societies and social service departments in general remained strongly in favour of secrecy, and often considered an adoptee's desire for birth information as a sign of emotional immaturity. The 1958 Adoption Act, enacted in response to the Hurst Report, refined and clarified aspects of adoption law but made no major changes.

The next official response to adoption was the establishment of the Houghton Committee in 1969 to review the law, policy and practice of adoption. It reported in 1972 and its recommendations were largely enacted in the Children Act 1975 which was consolidated in the Adoption Act 1976, although the provisions were introduced only gradually, following public expenditure restraints. The Houghton Committee 'was intent on the "professionalisation" of adoption work and its complete regulation'.[25] Adoption would be 'part of a well-supervised and integrated childcare service'[26] in which local authorities would take centre stage. Adoption societies would in future have to work closely with local authorities and would now be subject to much more stringent approval criteria, although once approved they would have more autonomy. Private placements of children for adoption by non-relatives finally became an offence, although this was not implemented until 1982. The Committee recommended restriction of step-parent adoptions which often resulted in a child being completely cut off from one side of its family although its proposed alternative, 'custodianship', was tardily implemented, unsuccessful in practice and subsequently abolished. The Committee also introduced the procedure of 'freeing a child for adoption' which could in certain cases be carried out by court order against parental wishes where an authority believed this would be in a child's best interests. The Committee paid lip service to preserving the natural family but, as Bridge and Swindells suggest, 'on balance, the rights of natural parents were clearly on the way to being relegated to an inferior position in the adoption triangle'.[27]

Probably the most famous recommendation of the Houghton Committee was the proposal that all adopted adults in England and Wales be permitted 'to obtain a copy of their original birth entry'.[28] This was an extremely controversial issue at the time and was debated at length in Parliament. Its retrospective nature meant that birth mothers might be contacted years after relinquishing their children and there was concern that potential adopters would be deterred because adoption no longer meant a 'clean break'. To address some of these concerns, the 1975 Children Act made counselling compulsory before adoptees could be given access to information enabling them to obtain their original birth certificate.

As local authorities became more central to adoption, the work of the voluntary societies began to decline. In 1950 they had set up the

Standing Conference of Societies Registered for Adoption which was open to all agencies registered for adoption.[29] Virtually all voluntary societies had joined and 'it had a powerful influence on the development of adoption'.[30] Throughout the 1950s and 1960s the societies were the major player in adoptions organised by agencies (73 per cent in 1966) but even five years later this was down to 60 per cent, and the next decades saw their influence decline considerably as adoption became more specialised and fewer baby adoptions took place.[31] Many, such as the National Children Adoption Association, closed down.

Adoption throughout the 1950s and 1960s mainly involved illegitimate babies (36 per cent of all adoptions in 1951 were of infants under twelve months, 51 per cent in 1968; 92 per cent of these in 1951 were illegitimate, 97 per cent in 1968), although adoptions by step-parents also increased. The year 1968 was the peak for adoptions in England and Wales with 24,831 orders made. From then on there was a dramatic decrease in adoption as the number of babies offered for adoption rapidly declined. This followed the growing availability of effective contraception and the provision of legal abortion, coupled with a more tolerant attitude to illegitimacy, and policy changes which enabled unmarried mothers to claim social security and housing. The decline was swift; by 1980 the total number of registered adoptions had more than halved (to 10,609), and then halved again to 1998 (4386). Babies made up only 24 per cent of adoptions in 1980 (2599) and four per cent (195) in 1998.[32] In the years since then the figure has varied – declining to 4317 in 1999, rising to nearly 6000 in 2001 and down again to 4980 in 2006. Babies were still only four per cent of the total in 2006 but 52 per cent of those adopted were aged between one and four years compared to 34 per cent in 1998.[33]

Following the legislation of the 1970s and the enormous decrease in the number of babies available, the nature of adoption has changed. The proportion of children adopted out of local authority care rose markedly. In 1952 these made up only 3.2 per cent of adoptions, by 1968 the figure was 8.7 per cent and in the 1990s they accounted for a third or more of all adoptions. There has also been a growing interest in adoption of infants from overseas. In 1998 there were only 258 official intercountry adoptions but recent legal changes mean that local authorities and approved adoption agencies have an obligation to offer an intercountry as well as domestic service, that is they must provide the same assessment and approval process for people wishing to adopt from overseas as for those adopting locally – this is the first official hurdle that potential adopters must surmount if wishing to adopt from overseas.[34] This will probably increase the number of overseas adoptions although as prospective adopters then have to go through complex negotiations in the country of the child's origin the numbers are unlikely to rise substantially in the near future.

The changing nature of adoption led to the establishment of a governmental working group on adoption law in 1989 which published a number of background and discussion papers, and then in 1992 its report, followed by a White Paper and a further consultation paper. Despite all this no legislation ensued. Bridge and Swindells argue that at a point in the Conservative Government's life when family issues were proving extremely controversial it did not wish to introduce another potential battleground which the issues involved – 'race, ethnicity, cohabiting and homosexual adopters, the plight of children in care, and the matter of adoption versus fostering' – were all too likely to provoke.[35] Social work practice in the early 1990s tended to revert to stressing the importance of returning a child in care to its family wherever possible.

The 1997 Labour Government initially steered clear of adoption as an issue but in 2000 the Prime Minister, Tony Blair, announced a personal interest in getting many more 'looked-after' children (i.e. in care) adopted,[36] and a consultation and White Paper followed. This followed a debate stimulated by writers such as Patricia Morgan who argued that adoption should be used far more widely for children in care, suggesting that 'political correctness' which prioritised the rights of natural parents often prevented its use and left children to languish in long-term care.[37] Those working in the field attempted to explain that adopting such children was a much more challenging process than adopting newborn babies as many of the children involved in adoption from care were older children who came from very damaging backgrounds.[38] Following this debate the emphasis was placed on exploring whether looked after children might be permanently removed to an alternative family. Eventually the Adoption and Children Act 2002 was passed with the avowed aim of speeding up the process of adoption for such children and widening the field of potential adopters. Most of its clauses were brought into full effect at the end of 2005.

Final conclusions

Even this brief account of adoption since the Second World War shows that it remains an evolving and controversial concept, its focus continually shifting in different directions depending on the current needs or beliefs of the time. Its strongest supporters in the 1920s might have been surprised at this – they saw adoption as a simple panacea, solving at a stroke the problem of unwanted illegitimate children, desperate unmarried mothers and childless couples. Those who were more sceptical at the time would probably have been far less surprised. They had already raised many of the issues which have emerged in similar or different ways since.

Indeed, looking at current policy and practice around parents and children, it is extraordinary to see how the same issues arise, in different guises, as they did in the interwar years. Once again – with everyone claiming that their solution is 'in the best interests of the child' – the debate surfaces over whether dysfunctional families and lone mothers should be supported and encouraged to keep their children or whether the children should be moved away from them as soon as possible to people who are judged by society to offer a much more positive setting. The Labour Governments led by Tony Blair would not have perhaps subscribed completely to the second viewpoint but they became extremely committed to the idea of encouraging and accelerating adoptions of children in care in contrast to what they perceived as local authority negativity:

> Some social services departments were lukewarm about adoption. They saw it very much as a last resort, whereas it could in fact be a very positive option for many of the children we were talking about. The result was that there were potential adopters, most of whom were aged between 36 and 45 and childless, who in some places had to surmount increasingly high hurdles before receiving a placement.[39]

By 2006 over three-quarters of all adoptions in England and Wales were of 'children looked after' that is, in local authority care,[40] but although the actual number has risen and fallen slightly over the last few years the percentage of children looked after who are adopted each year remains low – usually about six per cent. As many social work experts had pointed out, the process of adopting a child out of care is not an easy or quick one.

A related discussion arises over intercountry adoption. Where once it might have been seen as unquestioningly altruistic to remove children from poverty-stricken countries and disaster areas to comfortable homes in the west there is now increasing awareness that this is not necessarily best for the child, even if it is orphaned, and especially not if it has family in its home country. Apart from moral criticism of what often becomes a cash transaction for a child, there is a potential exacerbation of all the problems of identity which adoptees may suffer even when they are adopted within their own country. Ironically in the 1930s there was also concern about intercountry adoption but then it was about British children being sent overseas to be adopted by wealthy foreign families.

Secrecy in adoption and the resulting loss of identity remain potent issues, and governments and adoption workers are still trying to respond to them: after lobbying, the Adoption and Children Act 2002 gave all birth parents a right to contact their adopted adult children via a registered Intermediary Agency, unless the adoptees had registered a wish not to be contacted (and even if contacted they retain a right to refuse contact or veto disclosure of information).

The debates over the implications of secrecy in adoption have led to an awareness that other forms of constructed families where parentage is unknown may also risk later psychological and emotional problems for the children involved. In 2004, after some years of consultation, the Human Fertilisation and Embryology Authority (Disclosure of Donor Information) Regulations were issued and came into effect from 1 April 2005. These removed anonymity for people donating sperm, eggs or embryos after that date. In future those born as a result of donation will be able to get identifying information when they reach the age of 18. It had become increasingly clear that some of those conceived by donation had the same concerns about the secrecy surrounding their conception and the same need to know about their genetic origins as adopted people. Also, just as birth parents may want to trace their children, the statutory agency regulating infertility treatment says that 'many donors want to know if they have helped an infertile couple to have the family they longed for, and they may wish to tell to [sic] their own children about any genetic siblings or half-sibling(s)' (although they will still not be given identifying information about the children they have helped to create).[41] The arguments surrounding the introduction of these measures have been similar to those around secrecy in adoption. Supporters of anonymity say that people will not donate if they may be later traced, and dismiss as unimportant the identity anxieties of donor-conceived offspring to know about someone who had no physical link with their mother. Once again there are issues at stake about whose interests take precedence – the need of would-be parents to have a child, or of children's right to know about their origins.

The other controversial issue in contemporary adoption which has inspired endless newspaper headlines over the last few years is the question over who is allowed to adopt. The past decade or so has seen a loosening up in the regulations about this – in part due to the need to attract more people to adopt the often disturbed and damaged looked after children who have been removed from abusive or dangerous backgrounds. Single people, unmarried couples – eventually gay couples after prolonged debates in Parliament, the media and among the general public – all are now allowed to adopt. Surprisingly 2006–7 was the first year when details of legal status, gender and number of those adopting were collected (and even this appears to relate only to looked after children who are adopted, not all adopted children). The figures show that 84 per cent of adopters were married couples, four per cent were different sex unmarried couples, nine per cent were single adopters (most of whom were women) and three per cent were same sex couples (one percent being in civil partnerships).[42]

Interestingly, who was allowed to adopt was not such a controversial issue in the early years of legalised adoption in England and Wales. There was debate about the appropriate age gap between adopting parent and child, and rules were made on this, but single men and women were legally allowed to adopt (men only to adopt boys) and, as we saw in Chapter 5, a number of them did so. Homosexuality and cohabitation were not subjects of popular discussion in those years and the questions asked of prospective adopters were not probing; it may well be that some 'single' adopters in the interwar years lived quietly with their adopted child and a friend of the same gender in what may or may not have been a sexual relationship. As usual the lack of detailed statistical information about adoption is frustrating but it may be that the profile of people adopting in the 1930s would have far more in common with that of those adopting in the 2000s than it would have done with that of adopters in the intervening years.

Looking back from the perspective of over eighty years of legal adoption in England and Wales it is quite striking how quickly and effectively the first adoption legislation was effected, even if many of its supporters at the time felt the process was excessively long. The legislation can be criticised for its timid failure to address major issues of inheritance and property rights, compulsory legalisation of adoption or regulation of the procedures of those arranging adoptions; but it was a first step, as is the way with most innovative social legislation in Britain; an initially cautious measure in order to see what problems arise and then deal with them. Since then over 875,000 people have been adopted in England and Wales.[43] If their birth parents, adopting families and relatives are added to that figure one can see the enormous social impact of adoption. Probably several million people are directly affected by it.

Many adoptions in the early years were made without due care and attention, and not all turned out well; moreover the legacy of secrecy has left a long shadow across the lives of many people during the following decades. But those making the policies in the interwar years do appear to have tried hard to think through the implications of what they were doing and to have reacted relatively quickly to failings in the new system. The debates in Parliament occasionally became overly anecdotal or judgemental but in general were thoughtful, and reveal politicians trying to do what was best for the parties involved. The issue of class sometimes arose but party politics appear to have played no part in any of the debates. Even contentious and potentially divisive questions such as what weight a child's religious background should be given in determining its adoptive family were raised mildly. Not till the Parliamentary debates on adoption in the late 1940s was there much evidence of the bitterness and division which have sometimes clouded discussion on adoption in more recent years. Despite all the research on the effect of adoption on children, relinquishing parents, and adopters which has been done since the Second World War it is not clear that the decisions of contemporary policy-makers on adoption are any wiser or more sensitive than those made before the War. If anything, adoption is probably a more contentious and politically sensitive issue now than it was then.

Notes

Introduction

1. *Guardian*, 17 June 1999 – John Hutton, the health minister, was quoted as saying there should be 'radical improvements in adoption services. We will not hesitate to take the necessary action in the future to ensure that looked-after children do not become the innocent victims of misplaced theory or ideology'. And a prospective adopter wrote to the *Evening Standard*, 4 September 2003: 'No first-time natural parent on this planet is, or will ever be, examined and intrusively checked on their parenting capability, as adopters are.'
2. Jenny Keating, 'Struggle for Identity: Issues Underlying the Enactment of the 1926 Adoption of Children Act', *University of Sussex Journal of Contemporary History*, issue 3 (2001), http://www.sussex.ac.uk/history/documents/3._keating_struggle_for_identity.pdf.
3. They could apply to see their original birth certificate when they reached the age of majority but a court order was necessary. During this period very few legally adopted children would have reached the age of majority except for a few whose *de facto* adoptions were made official by the 1926 Adoption Act.
4. See Chapter 6.
5. Murray Ryburn, 'Secrecy and Openness in Adoption: An Historical Perspective', *Social Policy and Administration*, vol. 29, no. 2 (June 1995), pp. 151–68.
6. Ibid., op. cit., p. 166.
7. See Erica Haimes and Noel Timms, 'Access to Birth Records and Counselling of Adopted Persons Under Section 26 of the Children Act, 1975', Final Report to the DHSS (University of Newcastle upon Tyne, May 1983); John P. Triseliotis, 'Obtaining Birth Certificates', in Philip Bean (ed.), *Adoption: Essays in Social Policy, Law and Sociology* (London: Tavistock Publications, 1984).
8. E. Wayne Carp, *Family Matters: Secrecy and Disclosure in the History of Adoption* (London: Harvard University Press, 1998), p. 28.
9. Similar practice in the UK in the 1950s is described in Kathleen Kiernan, Hilary Land and Jane Lewis, *Lone Motherhood in Twentieth-Century Britain: From Footnote to Front Page* (Oxford: Oxford University Press, 1998), pp. 102–10.
10. In contrast Scotland's first Adoption of Children Act, passed in 1930, gave adoptees the right to see their original birth certificate from the age of 17 (see Chapter 5).
11. For more information see J. Rockel and Ryburn, *Adoption Today: Change and Choice in New Zealand* (Auckland: Heinemann/Reed, 1988), pp. 9–10.
12. See Audrey Marshall and Margaret McDonald, *The Many-Sided Triangle: Adoption in Australia* (Melbourne: Melbourne University Press, 2001).
13. Papers in the collection of Patricia Wreford King. Notes, 30 April 1937.

14. A. M. Homes, 'Witness Protection', in Sara Holloway (ed.), *Family Wanted: Adoption Stories* (London: Granta Books, 2005), p. 21.
15. Marshall and McDonald, op. cit., pp. v–vi.
16. Julia Feast, Michael Marwood, Sue Seabrook and Elizabeth Webb, *Preparing for Reunion: Experiences from the Adoption Circle*, New edn (London: The Children's Society, 1998).
17. For example: Feast et al, op. cit.; Sarah Iredale, *Reunions: True Stories of Adoptees' Meetings with Their Natural Parents* (London: The Stationery Office, 1997); Sara Holloway (ed.), *Family Wanted: Adoption Stories* (London: Granta Books, 2005); Amal Treacher and Ilan Katz (eds), *The Dynamics of Adoption: Social and Personal Perspectives* (London: Jessica Kingsley Publishers, 2000).
18. George K. Behlmer, *Friends of the Family: The English Home and Its Guardians 1850–1940* (Stanford: Stanford University Press, 1998); see Chapter 6, 'Artificial Families', pp. 272–315. A couple of the recent popular accounts of adoption have an element of historical background: Sue Elliott in her story of her reunion with her birth mother, *Love Child: A Memoir of Adoption, Reunion, Loss and Love* (London: Vermillion, 2005), and Hunter Davies in *Relative Strangers: A History of Adoption and a Tale of Triplets* (London: Time Warner Books, 2003), which is however more a human interest story of the reunion of triplets born and adopted in 1932 than an actual history of adoption.
19. In particular, G. Roberts, 'Social and Legal Policy in Child Adoption in England and Wales 1913–1958' (PhD thesis, University of Leicester, 1973). Roberts looked in detail at the development of adoption legislation and the changing attitudes to social policy and administration which lay behind the legislative changes. She was able to interview some of the people involved in the independent adoption societies in the early years of adoption and was unconstrained by the data protection legislation which affects everyone now working in the field of adoption or dealing with adoption records.
20. The Horsbrugh Report 1937 (see Chapter 6) said that 'none of the chief adoption societies appears to possess on its staff trained social workers'. (p. 11)
21. Margaret Kornitzer, *Child Adoption in the Modern World* (London: Putnam, 1952).
22. Alexina McWhinnie, *Adopted Children: How They Grow Up: A Study of Their Adjustment as Adults* (London: Routledge & Kegan Paul, 1967). See Chapter 5 for more detail about her survey.
23. John Triseliotis, *Evaluation of Adoption Policy and Practice* (Edinburgh: University of Edinburgh, 1970), pp. 2–7.
24. Eleanor Grey, in collaboration with Ronald M. Blunden, *A Survey of Adoption in Great Britain*, Home Office Research Studies 10 (London: HMSO, 1971).
25. See McWhinnie, op. cit., and John Triseliotis, *In Search of Origins: The Experience of Adopted People* (London: Routledge & Kegan Paul, 1973).

1 Setting the Scene: The Historical and Legal Background

1. Richard Soloway, *Demography and Degeneration: Eugenics and the Declining Birthrate in Twentieth-Century Britain* (Chapel Hill: University of North Carolina Press, 1995), p. 9.

2. Simon Szreter, *Fertility, Class and Gender in Britain, 1860–1940* (Cambridge: Cambridge University Press, 1996). See also Wally Seccombe, 'Starting to Stop: Working-Class Fertility Decline in Britain', *Past and Present*, no. 126 (1990) and *Weathering the Storm: Working-Class Families from the Industrial Revolution to the Fertility Decline* (London: Verso, 1993).
3. Soloway, op. cit., p. 168.
4. Philippe Ariès, *Centuries of Childhood: A Social History of Family Life* (New York: Vintage Books, 1962, translated from the French by Robert Baldick).
5. Jane Lewis, *Women in England 1870–1950: Sexual Divisions and Social Change* (Brighton: Wheatsheaf, 1984), p. 10.
6. Ellen Ross, 'Labour and Love: Rediscovering London's Working-Class Mothers 1870–1918', in Jane Lewis (ed.), *Labour and Love: Women's Experience of Home and Family, 1850–1940* (Oxford: Blackwell, 1986), p. 79.
7. Lewis, 'The Working-Class Wife and Mother and State Intervention, 1870–1918', in Lewis (ed.), *Labour and Love*, op. cit., p. 103.
8. Census for England and Wales, 1901 and 1931, quoted in Diana Gittins, *Fair Sex: Family Size and Structure 1900–39* (London: Hutchinson, 1982), p. 34.
9. For discussion about the emphasis on domesticity during the interwar years see, for example, Carol Dyhouse, *Feminism and the Family in England 1880–1939* (Oxford: Blackwell, 1989); Gittins, op. cit.; Lewis (ed.), *Labour and Love*, op. cit.; Lewis, *Women in England*, op. cit.; Deirdre Beddoe, *Back to Home and Duty: Women between the Wars 1918–1939* (London: Pandora, 1989); Judy Giles, *Women, Identity and Private Life in Britain, 1900–50* (London: Macmillan, 1995); Martin Pugh, *Women and the Women's Movement in Britain 1914–1959* (London: Macmillan, 1992).
10. Pugh, op. cit., p. 83.
11. Gittins, op. cit., p. 56.
12. Cynthia L. White, *Women's Magazines 1693–1968* (London: Michael Joseph, 1970), pp. 96, 100.
13. Ibid.
14. Gittins, op. cit., p. 51.
15. Michael Anderson, 'The Social Implications of Demographic Change' in F. M. L. Thompson, (ed.), *The Cambridge Social History of Britain 1750–1950, Vol. 2: People and their Environment* (Cambridge: Cambridge University Press, 1990), pp. 66–7.
16. Between 1919 and 1939 almost four million new houses were built. In the building boom years 1933–8, an average 334,000 houses were produced each year. John Burnett, *A Social History of Housing 1815–1985* (London: Methuen, 1986), p. 249.
17. Giles, op. cit., p. 68.
18. Alan A. Jackson, *The Middle Classes 1900–1950* (Nairn, UK: David St John Thomas, 1991), p. 36.
19. Burnett, op. cit., p. 237.
20. Naomi Mitchison, 'The Reluctant Feminists', *Left Review*, vol. 1, no. 3 (1934), pp. 93–4, quoted in Dyhouse, op. cit., pp. 186–7.
21. Giles, op. cit., p. 120.
22. Joanna Bourke, *Working-Class Cultures in Britain 1890–1960: Gender, Class and Ethnicity* (London: Routledge, 1994), p. 84.

23. *The Shorter Oxford English Dictionary on Historical Principles* (Oxford: Oxford University Press, 3rd ed, 1973), p. 1809.
24. Geoffrey Crossick, 'The Emergence of the Lower Middle Class in Britain: A Discussion', in Crossick (ed.), *The Lower Middle Class in Britain 1870–1914* (London: Croom Helm, 1977).
25. Lucinda McCray Beier, 'We Were Green as Grass: Learning about Sex and Reproduction in Three Working-Class Lancashire Communities, 1900–1970', *Social History of Medicine*, vol. 16, no. 3 (2003), p. 474.
26. Anderson, op. cit., p. 36.
27. Ibid., p. 475.
28. 'The Registrar-General's Statistical Review of England and Wales for the Years 1938 and 1939 – Text (London: HMSO, 1947), pp. 192, 195.
29. Mr T3P, Social and family life in Preston, 1890–1940. Elizabeth Roberts Archive, Centre for North-West Regional Studies, Lancaster University (ERA).
30. Hugh McLeod, 'White Collar Values and the Role of Religion', in Crossick (ed.), op. cit., p. 72.
31. Leonore Davidoff, Megan Doolittle, Janet Fink and Katherine Holden, *The Family Story: Blood, Contract and Intimacy, 1830–1960* (London: Longman, 1999).
32. Katherine Holden, 'The Shadow of Marriage: Single Women in England 1919–1939' (unpublished PhD thesis, University of Essex, 1996).
33. Anderson, op. cit., p. 28.
34. Christina Hardyment, *Dream Babies: Child Care from Locke to Spock* (London: Jonathan Cape, 1983), p. 123.
35. Ibid., p. 106.
36. Viviana A. Zelizer, *Pricing the Priceless Child: The Changing Social Value of Children*, (Princeton: Princeton University Press, 1985; 2nd ed, 1994), p. 11.
37. Ibid., p. 6.
38. See the Introduction.
39. Zelizer, op. cit., p. 193.
40. Harry Hendrick, *Child Welfare: England 1872–1989* (London: Routledge, 1994), p. 37.
41. Ibid.
42. George K. Behlmer, *Child Abuse and Moral Reform in England, 1870–1908* (Stanford: Stanford University Press, 1982), p. 194.
43. Gittins, op. cit., p. 183.
44. Jean S. Heywood, *Children in Care: The Development of the Service for the Deprived Child* (London: Routledge, 3rd ed, 1978), p. 100.
45. Deborah Dwork, *War Is Good for Babies and Other Young Children: A History of the Infant and Child Welfare Movement in England 1898–1918* (London: Tavistock, 1987), p. 19.
46. Ibid., p. 5. It rose by 6.8 per cent between 1876 and 1897 in contrast to the general mortality rate, which dropped 17.1 per cent during this period.
47. Ibid., p. 114.
48. Ibid., p. 165.
49. Ibid., p. 166.
50. Soloway, op. cit., p. 144.
51. Ibid., p. 152.

52. Royal Free Hospital Archives Centre website, http://www.royalfreearchives. org.uk, accessed 12 March 2003.
53. For example, in 1914, 600 health visitors were employed by local authorities; by 1918 there were 2577 (this included 1044 district nurses acting as part-time visitors but excluded 320 employed by voluntary organisations). There were 650 maternal and child welfare centres in 1915, 1,278 in 1918 (although 578 of these were run by voluntary agencies). See G. F. McCleary, *The Maternity and Child Welfare Movement* (London: P. S. King & Son, 1935), pp. 16–17.
54. Pat Thane, 'Infant Welfare in England and Wales, 1870s to 1930s', in Michael B. Katz and Christoph Sachße (eds), *The Mixed Economy of Social Welfare: Public/Private Relations in England, Germany and the United States* (Baden-Baden: Nomos Verlagsgesellschaft, 1996), p. 258.
55. Dwork, op. cit., p. 214.
56. By John F. J. Sykes, Medical Officer of Health, St Pancras, according to Dwork, op. cit., p. 219.
57. For a detailed account of baby farming and infanticide see Lionel Rose, *The Massacre of the Innocents: Infanticide in Britain 1800–1939* (London: Routledge & Kegan Paul, 1986). Also see Behlmer, *Child Abuse*, op. cit.; Margaret L. Arnot, 'Infant Death, Child Care and the State: The Baby-Farming Scandal and the First Infant Life Protection Legislation of 1872', *Continuity and Change*, vol. 9, part 2 (1994), pp. 271–311.
58. Ivy Pinchbeck and Margaret Hewitt, *Children in English Society, Vol. 2, From the Eighteenth Century to the Children Act 1948* (London: Routledge, 1973), p. 613.
59. Quoted in George K. Behlmer, *Friends of the Family: The English Home and Its Guardians 1850–1940* (Stanford: Stanford University Press, 1998), p. 278; Behlmer, *Child Abuse*, p. 28; Rose, *Massacre*, p. 98. Rose shows that even in this ostensibly clear-cut case there was considerable disquiet about the verdict and the execution among the press, the public and even some of the jurors. The case was seen as an unsuccessful example to frighten off others.
60. Behlmer, *Child Abuse*, p. 36.
61. See Chapter 2 for more details about this.
62. Hansard. House of Lords, vol. 338, p. 502. 16 July 1889. This Adoption of Children Bill was long forgotten and indeed 34 years later the Earl wrote to *The Times* (3 November 1923) to remind readers that there had been earlier parliamentary moves on the issue.
63. Hendrick, op. cit., p. 49.
64. Heywood, op. cit.
65. Hendrick, op. cit., pp. 74–6.
66. See Lionel Rose, *The Erosion of Childhood: Child Oppression in Britain 1860–1918* (London: Routledge, 1991), pp. 98–100; Behlmer, *Friends of the Family*, op. cit., p. 286. In fact there appears to have been a longer history of adoption of children in the care of Boards of Guardians as the London Metropolitan Archive has a bundle of legal agreements from the 1860s to 1918 which relate to children who were 'adopted' by people (presumably wealthy) who gave the St Marylebone Parish Guardians a bond which would be voided if they fulfilled the conditions of feeding, clothing and

educating the children adequately and producing them for inspection when required. The bonds were originally for £300 but in the later years went down to £100. See LMA – STMBG/182/01-20.

67. Rose, *Erosion of Childhood*, p. 99.
68. Behlmer, *Friends of the Family*, op. cit., p. 287.
69. HO 45/11540. Minutes of Evidence to Committee on Child Adoption, Mr A. P. Stanwell Smith, 19 October 1920, p. 29. The apparent lack of supervision and 'red tape' is illustrated by the ease with which the charity worker and writer Miss Edith Sichel 'adopted' a whole series of babies and little girls from the Whitechapel Board of Guardians from 1890 onwards and took them to Surrey. This was not 'adoption' as we know it – the children lived in a separate house from Miss Sichel, had a matron and helpers to look after them and were raised to become servants themselves. Alison Light, *Mrs Woolf and the Servants: The Hidden Heart of Domestic Service* (London: Penguin, 2007), pp. 97–108.
70. HO 45/11540. Minutes of Evidence, Mr Tom Percival, written evidence, 19 October 1920, p. 26.
71. Nigel Middleton, *When Family Failed: The Treatment of Children in the Care of the Community during the First Half of the Twentieth Century* (London: Victor Gollancz, 1971), pp. 224–36.
72. LABG 185, 'Register of Adoptions'.
73. Hendrick, op. cit., p. 48.
74. For example, William Woodruff describes how his mother was sent to friends when her mother was widowed and fell on hard times. Later she is described as 'adopted'. It was not a good example of informal adoption. Neglected and possibly abused she eventually fled home. William Woodruff, *The Road to Nab End: An Extraordinary Northern Childhood* (London: Abacus, 2002), p. 272.
75. P. H. Pettit, 'Parental Control and Guardianship', in R. H. Graveson and F. R. Crane (eds), *A Century Of Family Law* (London: Sweet & Maxwell, 1957), p. 67.
76. Ibid., p. 60.
77. Pinchbeck and Hewitt, op. cit., p. 584.
78. Heywood, op. cit., p. 16.
79. For more detail of the earlier history of the illegitimate child see Pinchbeck and Hewitt, op. cit., Chapter XIX; Mary Hopkirk, *Nobody Wanted Sam: The Story of the Unwelcomed Child, 1530–1948* (London: John Murray, 1949). For the Foundling Hospital see Ruth K. McClure, *Coram's Children: The London Foundling Hospital in the Eighteenth Century* (London: Yale University Press, 1981). C. Oliver and P. Aggleton *Coram's Children: Growing Up in the Care of the Foundling Hospital 1900–1955* (London: Thomas Coram Research Unit, 2000); Val Molloy, 'Identity, Past and Present, in an Historical Child-Care Setting', *Psychodynamic Practice*, vol. 8, no. 2 (2002); Tanya Evans, *Unfortunate Objects: Lone Mothers in Eighteenth-Century London* (Basingstoke: Palgrave Macmillan, 2005).
80. Kathleen Kiernan, Hilary Land and Lewis, *Lone Motherhood in Twentieth-Century Britain: From Footnote to Front Page* (Oxford: Oxford University Press, 1998), p. 74. See Chapter 2 for more about attitudes to unmarried mothers during the First World War.

81. Ibid., p. 98.
82. Mr B1B, Social Life in Barrow and Lancaster, 1890–1940, ERA.
83. Of course not all unmarried mothers were poor – and there were some from the middle classes who kept their children although they were usually discreet about it.
84. Ginger Frost, '"The Black Lamb of the Black Sheep": Illegitimacy in the English Working Class, 1850–1939', *Journal of Social History*, vol. 37, no. 2 (Winter 2003), p. 295.
85. Ibid., p. 296.
86. Carl Chinn, *They Worked All Their Lives: Women of the Urban Poor in England, 1880–1939* (Manchester: Manchester University Press, 1988), p. 31. Ada Haskins, one of the interviewees in Steve Humphries, *A Secret World of Sex: Forbidden Fruit: The British Experience 1900–1950* (London: Sidgwick & Jackson, 1988), describes exactly this situation. Her illegitimate baby was brought up by her mother who pretended it was hers. Her son always knew her as his sister. He was by then 57 years old; she longed to tell him the truth but feared that she would never be able to.
87. Chinn, op. cit., p. 145.
88. B. R. Mitchell, in collaboration with Phyllis Deane, *British Historical Statistics* (Cambridge: Cambridge University Press, 1988), pp. 42–4. Figures have been rounded to nearest thousand.
89. Matthew Thomson, *The Problem of Mental Deficiency: Eugenics, Democracy, and Social Policy in Britain 1870–1959* (Oxford: Clarendon Press, 1998), p. 20.
90. Humphries, op. cit., p. 51.
91. Thomson, op. cit., p. 22.
92. Humphries, op. cit., p. 64.
93. Thomson, op. cit., p. 250.
94. Ibid., p. 251.
95. Ibid., p. 299.
96. Mrs H4P, Social and family life in Preston, 1890–1940, ERA.
97. Mrs C5P, Family and social life in Barrow, Lancaster and Preston, 1940–1970, ERA.
98. Mrs C3P, Family and social life in Barrow, Lancaster and Preston, 1940–1970, ERA.
99. Deborah Derrick (ed.), *Illegitimate: The Experience of People Born outside Marriage* (London: NCOPF, 1986), pp. 37–40. However, Stephen Cretney points out that the public knowledge of illegitimacy did not necessarily lead to social disadvantage. Not only did various illegitimate aristocrats have successful careers but both Keir Hardie and Ramsay MacDonald survived the revelation of their illegitimacy. Stephen Cretney, *Family Law in the Twentieth Century: A History* (Oxford, Oxford University Press, p. 545.
100. Jane Marcus, (selected and introduced), *The Young Rebecca: Writings of Rebecca West 1911–17* (London: Macmillan, 1982), pp. 140–1; 146–7.
101. Constance Rover, *Love, Morals and the Feminists* (London: Routledge & Kegan Paul, 1970), p. 136.
102. Patricia W. Romero, *E. Sylvia Pankhurst: Portrait of a Radical* (New Haven: Yale University Press, 1987), pp. 164–77.

103. For example, Stephen Spender's widow, the pianist Natasha Litvin, was illegitimate; she lived with foster parents until, aged nearly 12, she returned to her actress mother. Interview in *Observer*, 9 May 2004.
104. Sheila Ferguson and Hilda Fitzgerald, *Studies in the Social Services: History of the Second World War, UK Civil Series* (London: Longmans and HMSO, 1954), pp. 85–6. Despite the lack of detailed information the authors manage to provide a useful survey of the accommodation and treatment available to unmarried mothers who kept their babies in this period.
105. M. M. Geikie Cobb, 'Parent and Child', in G. Evelyn Gates (ed.), *The Woman's Year Book 1923–24* (London: Women Publishers, 1923), p. 182.
106. Figures from 'The Registrar-General's Statistical Review of England and Wales' for the years 1927–36.

2 Developments in the Voluntary Sector

1. Claire Tomalin, *Jane Austen: A Life* (London: Viking, 1997), pp. 25, 37.
2. George Eliot, *Silas Marner*; Charles Dickens, *Great Expectations*; Frances Hodgson Burnett, *A Little Princess*.
3. Pat Turner and Jenny Elliott, *Adoption: Reviewing the Record* (London: NCH Ashwood Project, 1992), p. 7; Mary E. Crutcher, 'Eighty-Seven Years of Adoption Work', *Child Adoption*, no. 19 (Summer 1956).
4. Pinchbeck and Hewitt quote a girl telling Andrew Doyle, a government inspector who was sent out to Canada in 1874 to investigate the situation of the emigrated children, that: "Doption, sir, is when folks get a girl to work without wages'. Ivy Pinchbeck and Margaret Hewitt, *Children in English Society, Vol 2, From the Eighteenth Century to the Children Act 1948* (London: Routledge, 1973), p. 568.
5. Joy Parr, *Labouring Children: British Immigrant Apprentices to Canada, 1869–1924* (London: Croom Helm, 1980), p. 88.
6. Ibid., p. 91.
7. Ibid.
8. Gillian Wagner, *Children of the Empire* (London: Weidenfeld and Nicolson, 1982), p. 234.
9. Ibid., p. 241. For more information about the child migrant schemes see Parr and Wagner op. cit.; also Gillian Wagner, *Barnardo* (London: Weidenfeld and Nicolson, 1979); J. Wesley Bready, *Doctor Barnardo: Physician, Pioneer, Prophet* (London: George Allen & Unwin, 1st ed. 1930); P. Bean and J. Melville, *Lost Children of the Empire: The Untold Story of Britain's Child Migrants* (London: Unwin Hyman, 1989); Margaret Humphreys, *Empty Cradles* (London: Doubleday, 1994). There are also useful articles by Geoffrey Sherington, Patrick A. Dunae, Shurlee Swain and Kathleen Paul on child migration to Canada and Australia, in Jon Lawrence and Pat Starkey (eds), *Child Welfare and Social Action in the Nineteenth and Twentieth Centuries* (Liverpool: Liverpool University Press, 2001).
10. Barnardo v McHugh, 1891, and Barnardo v Ford, 1891. See Wagner, *Barnardo*, op. cit., Chapter 13.
11. June Rose, *Inside Barnardos: 120 Years of Caring for Children* (London: Futura, 1987), p. 199.

12. HO45/11540. Minutes of Evidence to Committee on Child Adoption, 1921. Miss R. S. M. Peto, 5 October 1920.
13. Ibid., Lady Henry Somerset, 2 November 1920.
14. Other than a brief entry in *Hutchinson's Woman's Who's Who* (London: Hutchinson, 1934), p. 35, I have found no biographical accounts of Clara Andrew. The information here is gathered from birth and death certificates in the Family Records Centre, the 1901 Census, material in the Devon Records Office (DRO), newspaper items, notes and correspondence in files at the National Archive, and letters and NCAA papers in the collection of Patricia Wreford King. According to Westminster City Council, which holds some of the individual records of the NCAA, its organisational records no longer exist.
15. At Wiesbaden according to *Hutchinson's Woman's Who's Who*.
16. MH 57/53. Letter from Miss Andrew to Mr Stutchbury, 15 January 1918.
17. DRO, Exeter. Letter from Lord Fortescue to Mr Sidney Andrew, 1 March 1915.
18. DRO. Report – *The Devon & Cornwall War Refugees Committee* (undated, c1920).
19. See Biographical Notes.
20. MH 57/53. Letter from Miss Andrew to Mr Stutchbury, 15 January 1918.
21. Ibid. There are notes on the letter suggesting people she might be in touch with but it is not clear if she was sent this information.
22. MH 57/53. Letter from Mrs England to Mr Stutchbury, 20 February 1918.
23. *Western Evening Herald*, 23 February 1918.
24. Papers in the collection of Patricia Wreford King. 'Any Baby's Mother', undated typescript by Clara Andrew, mid-1930s, p. 2.
25. *Western Morning News*, 3 July 1918.
26. MH 57/53. Undated NCAA leaflet, p. 2 (probably 1918 as it says 'Further details are from Mrs England at Exeter'). Mrs England ceased to be prominent in the NCAA once it moved to London in early 1919.
27. Ibid., p. 1.
28. Ibid., p. 2.
29. MH 57/53. NCAA Agreement.
30. MH 57/53. Undated NCAA leaflet, p. 2.
31. Ibid., p. 3.
32. See Biographical Notes.
33. MH 57/53. Note by Miss Puxley, 17 January 1919.
34. At 19, Sloane Street, London SW1.
35. Princess Alice came from the heart of the royal establishment (see Biographical Notes). In her autobiography she says she joined the NCAA 'soon after its foundation in 1917 at the instance of Lady Northcote, herself an adopted child of Lord and Lady Mountstephen'. Princess Alice, *For My Grandchildren: Some Reminiscences of Her Royal Highness Princess Alice* (London: Evans Bros, 1966), p. 211.
36. According to *The Times*, 3 May 1923, Princess Alice inaugurated 'Women's Hour' on BBC Radio by addressing listeners 'on the subject of the adoption of babies'.
37. *The Times*, 2 December 1919. Tower Cressy was used by the NCAA until the war. It was damaged by a bomb and later 'demolished by enemy action' in 1944. NCAA Annual Report, 1946.

38. MH 57/53. Memo from Miss Puxley to Mr Maude, 16 April 1924.
39. Ibid. Notes by Miss Puxley of meeting with Miss Andrew, 7 October 1922.
40. See Biographical Notes.
41. LCC/CH/M/25/1. NCAA's Memorandum of Association, 15 March 1926.
42. MH 57/53. Booklet – 'The National Children Adoption Association' undated but c.December 1919, p. 10.
43. Ibid., p. 14.
44. Ibid., p. 16.
45. Ibid., p. 16.
46. Minutes of Evidence to Committee on Child Adoption, op. cit., Miss Clara Andrew, 5 October 1920, p. 5. The National Children's Home & Orphanage (now NCH) had a similar experience. In Turner and Elliott, op. cit., p. 8, the authors say the NCH said in 1936 that 'the demand for baby girls far exceeds supply'. They suggested: 'Girls were probably seen as easier to manage or more domestically useful than boys'. In 1947, the NCAA Annual Report says that for the first time boys were more popular than girls but this was possibly an effect of war because the NCCA 1952–53 Annual Report says girls are back in favour: 'The Association is, unfortunately, unable to offer a second girl where one has already been placed, for so many applicants still wish to adopt girls that the Case Committee has felt bound to "ration" them so to speak!'
47. Minutes of Evidence to Committee on Child Adoption, op. cit., Miss Clara Andrew, 5 October 1920, p. 7.
48. Ibid., p. 6.
49. Ibid., p. 9.
50. 'Forty Years of Adoption Work, Part Two', *Child Adoption*, no. 23 (Summer 1957), p. 14
51. NCAA Booklet, op. cit., p. 12.
52. Minutes of Evidence to Committee on Child Adoption, op. cit., Miss Andrew, 5 October 1920, p. 23.
53. *The Times*, 13 March 1920.
54. *The Times*, 18 March 1920.
55. MH 57/53. Memo from Miss Puxley to Mr Maude, 16 April 1924.
56. During her appearance before the Hopkinson Committee Miss Andrew was questioned on adverse publicity about the NCAA. In May 1920 the *News Chronicle* reported that eight babies had been sent to Cardiff. Miss Andrew said it had all been checked out but admitted that it 'gave the impression of wholesale planting of babies without any preparation'. She denied a story in *Daily Mail* about 50 babies being sent to Scotland. Minutes of Evidence to Committee on Child Adoption, op. cit., Miss Clara Andrew, 5 October 1920, p. 20.
57. *John Bull*, 18 November 1922.
58. Ibid.
59. MH 57/53. Letter from Miss Andrew to W. Walton Dunn, Chief Constable of Durham, 16 June 1920.
60. Ibid. Letter from Dunn to Miss Andrew, 6 July 1920.
61. Ibid. Notes of meeting between Ministry of Health officials and Miss Andrew, 1 December 1922.

62. Although it was claimed in the report of a public meeting organised by the NAS that this work started 'in a smaller way' in 1911 (*The Times*, 29 October 1923). Later on the NAS letterhead said the organisation was established in 1913. See Chapter 6 and Biographical Notes for more information.
63. Gwyneth Roberts, 'Social and Legal Policy in Child Adoption in England and Wales 1913–1958', PhD thesis, University of Leicester, 1973, p. 32.
64. 'Prebendary Buttle and the Buttle Trust', The Buttle Trust, 1978, p. 5.
65. *The Times*, 12 January 1924.
66. *The Times*, 3 July 1925.
67. MH 57/53. Memo from Miss Puxley to Dr Campbell, 26 November 1922.
68. Even the pamphlet about him produced by the successful trust he established admits this. 'Prebendary Buttle', op. cit., p. 6.
69. HO 45/11540. Leaflet – 'The National Adoption Society', undated but c1918–19, p. 3
70. Ibid.
71. *The Times*, 25 May 1921; 1 June 1921.
72. Ibid.
73. Mrs Harry Barlow, (Organising Secretary, NAS), 'Child Adoption', *Woman's Year Book 1923–1924* (London: Women Publishers, 1923), p. 539.
74. 'The National Adoption Society: Early Adoption Work in Britain', *Child Adoption*, no. 26 (Spring 1958), p. 10.
75. MH 57/53. Memo to Dr Campbell, 25 November 1922.
76. *The Times*, 14 January 1924.
77. MH 57/53. Letter from Miss Andrew to Miss Puxley, 21 March 1923.
78. *The Times*, 16 March 1933. This building, Castlebar, was converted to a mother and baby home in 1947 when its size and staffing difficulties made its earlier functions impossible to sustain (NCAA Annual Report 1947). A few years later it became economically unviable and was closed (NCAA Annual Report 1952–53).
79. *The Times*, 8 July 1937. Presumably Queen Elizabeth rather than Queen Mary who opened Castlebar.
80. Papers in the collection of Patricia Wreford King. Minutes of NCAA Executive Committee meeting, 4 January 1933.
81. Ibid.
82. Ibid.
83. Ibid.
84. PWK Papers. Letter from Miss Andrew to Lady Inskip, 8 February 1933.
85. PWK Papers. Letter from Sidney Andrew to Miss Andrew, 27 February 1933.
86. PWK Papers. Letter from the Earl of Athlone to Miss Andrew, 2 March 1933.
87. PWK Papers. Letter from Princess Alice to Miss Andrew, 10 April 1933.
88. PWK Papers. Letter from Sir Thomas Inskip to Princess Alice, 19 May 1933.
89. PWK Papers. Letter from Princess Alice to Sidney Andrew, 22 May 1933.
90. PWK Papers. Minutes of the Nursing Committee, 15 June 1933.
91. PWK Papers. Letter from Miss Andrew to Sidney Andrew, 20 July 1933
92. PWK Papers. Minutes of the Executive Committee, 3 January 1934.

224 Notes

93. E. W. Hope, *Report on the Physical Welfare of Mothers and Children: England and Wales, Volume 1* (Liverpool: The Carnegie United Kingdom Trust, 1917), p. 48. This was a comprehensive contemporary report on the condition of mothers and children, discussing the available services, and making recommendations for improvements and reform. The first volume was written by Hope, the Medical Officer of Health (MOH) for Liverpool; the second by Janet M. Campbell, a Senior Medical Officer at the Board of Education.
94. Kathleen Kiernan, Hilary Land and Jane Lewis, *Lone Motherhood in Twentieth-Century Britain: From Footnote to Front Page* (Oxford: Oxford University Press, 1998), p. 74.
95. Lydia Murdoch, *Imagined Orphans: Poor Families, Child Welfare, and Contested Citizenship in London* (New Brunswick, NJ: Rutgers University Press, 2006), pp. 148, 221.
96. The NCUMC Manifesto (London 1918) gave its original full title as 'The National Council for the Unmarried Mother and Her Child (and for the Widowed or Deserted Mother in Need)'.
97. NCUMC Manifesto, p. 1.
98. See Biographical Notes.
99. Lettice Fisher, *Twenty-One Years and After, 1918–1946: The Story of the National Council for the Unmarried Mother and Her Child* (London: NCUMC, 2nd ed, 1946), p. 9. For more information about the NCUMC see Sue Graham-Dixon, *Never Darken My Door: Working for Single Parents and Their Children 1918–1978* (London 1981): Hilary Mackaskill, *From the Workhouse to the Workplace: 75 Years of One-Parent Family Life 1918–1993* (London: NCOPF, 1993); also see a forthcoming book by Pat Thane and Tanya Evans provisionally entitled *Sinners? Scroungers? Saints? Unmarried Motherhood in Modern England.*
100. NCUMC evidence to Associated Societies for the Care and Maintenance of Infants (see Chapter 3).
101. By 30 April 1939 the Council had handled 17,405 cases. Fisher, op. cit., p. 8.
102. Mackaskill, op. cit., p. 11.
103. Ibid.
104. NCUMC Manifesto 1918, p. 6.
105. HO 45/11540. 'Statement on Adoption' by NCUMC (undated but mid-1921). In the 1940s Miss Susan Musson, the long-term General Secretary of the NCUMC (1920–42) and then a Vice-President, was listed in the annual reports of the National Children Adoption Association as one of their 'Honorary Interviewers'.
106. NCUMC Manifesto, pp. 5–6.

3 Pressure for Government Action

1. This illegitimacy rate was at a peak, rapidly declining to the pre-war level but obviously contemporary commentators did not know this.
2. HO 45/11540. Minutes of Evidence to Committee on Child Adoption, Mrs Edwin Gray, National Council of Women, 2 November 1920, written evidence, p. 40.

3. *The Times*, 24 February 1919.
4. *The Times*, 22 September 1919.
5. National Archive, MH 55/276. 'Report of the Proceedings of the Conference on Child Adoption'.
6. Associated Societies for the Care and Maintenance of Infants, 'Report of Select Committee appointed to examine the principle and practice of Child Adoption', (London, cApril 1920).
7. Ibid., p. 33.
8. *The Times*, 6 July 1920.
9. *Time and Tide*, vol. 2, no. 21 (27 May 1921).
10. ASCMI Committee on Child Adoption. Evidence of Woman's Mission to Women, and Children Aid Society, p. 21.
11. Ibid. Evidence of Miss Clara Andrew, NCAA, p. 31.
12. Ibid. Evidence of Mr Drysdale Woodcock, NAS, p. 13.
13. Ibid., Report, p. 8.
14. Ibid., p. 9.
15. Ibid., p. 9.
16. Ibid., p. 9.
17. The National Council of Women was formed in 1895 as the Union of Women Workers to bring together women who worked, mostly voluntarily, in the social sector, and to campaign for improvements in the quality of life for all and, in particular, in the status of women. It changed its name to NCW in 1918.
18. See Biographical Notes.
19. The National Council of Women of Great Britain & Ireland, Occasional Paper, no. 86, p. 20.
20. MH 55/276, 'Deputation to the Home Secretary', 17 March 1920, p. 3.
21. Ibid., p. 10.
22. Reported in *The Times*, 18 March 1920.
23. *The Times*, 8 May 1920.
24. The Committee on Child Adoption (hereafter the Hopkinson Committee).
25. Report of the Committee on Child Adoption 1921, Cmd 1254 (hereafter the Hopkinson Report), p. 3.
26. HO 45/11540. Minutes of Evidence to Committee on Child Adoption, Miss Clara Andrew, 5 October 1920, p. 5.
27. Ibid., Mrs H. A. L. Fisher, 27 October 1920, p. 13.
28. Ibid., Mrs H. A. L Fisher, 27 October 1920, p. 15.
29. Ibid., Mr S. Cohen, 4 October 1920, pp. 32–7.
30. Ibid., Commissioner Adelaide Cox, 5 October 1920, pp. 46–57.
31. Ibid., Dr Frederick Norton Kay Menzies, 1 November 1920, p. 8.
32. Although Miss Andrew of the NCAA claimed that she only knew of one case where a child had been adopted and the mother had possibly 'fallen again'. Ibid., Miss Clara Andrew, 5 October 1920, p. 16.
33. Ibid., Lady Henry Somerset, 2 November 1920, p. 14.
34. Ibid., Miss Amelia Scott, 2 November 1920, p. 27.
35. Ibid., Mrs Edwin Gray, 2 November 1920, p. 33.
36. Ibid., Tom Percival, written evidence, 19 October 1920, p. 26.
37. Ibid., Miss Z. L. Puxley, 27 October 1920, p. 2.

38. Ibid.
39. Ibid., Miss Z. L. Puxley, 27 October 1920, p. 3.
40. Ibid., Dr Frederick Norton Kay Menzies, 1 November 1920, p. 8.
41. Ibid., Mr W. Clarke Hall, 26 October 1920, pp. 29–37.
42. NCUMC Manifesto, London 1918, pp. 3–4.
43. John Macnicol, *The Movement for Family Allowances 1918–1945: A Study in Social Policy Development* (London: Heinemann, 1980), pp. 150–3.
44. See Macnicol, op. cit.
45. For example, Eleanor Rathbone, *The Ethics and Economics of Family Endowment* (London: Epworth Press, 1927); *The Case for Family Allowances* (London: Penguin Books, 1940). Also see, Hugh Vibart, *Family Allowances in Practice* (London: P. S. King & Son, 1926).
46. Eleanor Rathbone, *The Disinherited Family* (Bristol: Falling Wall Press, 1986), pp. 369–70.
47. Minutes of Evidence to Committee on Child Adoption, op. cit., Mr Cecil M. Chapman, 12 November 1920, p. 4.
48. Ibid., Miss Clara Andrew, 5 October 1920, p. 14.
49. Ibid., p. 23.
50. Ibid.
51. Ibid., pp. 7–8.
52. Ibid., Miss R. S. M. Peto, 5 October 1920, p. 41.
53. HO 45/12642. Letter from Charles Singer to the Duchess of Atholl DBE, MP, 19 March 1926.
54. Minutes of Evidence to Committee on Child Adoption, op. cit. Mr W. Clarke Hall, 26 October 1920, p. 25.
55. Ibid., Mr R. Newton Crane, 19 November 1920, pp. 19–20.
56. Ibid., Mrs R. P. Wethered, 4 October 1920, p. 17.
57. Ibid., p. 24.
58. Murray Ryburn, 'Secrecy and Openness in Adoption: An Historical Perspective', *Social Policy & Administration*, vol. 29, no. 2 (June 1995), p. 155.
59. Minutes of Evidence to Committee on Child Adoption, op. cit. His Hon. Judge Edward Abbott Parry, 20 October 1920, p. 3.
60. Ibid., H. B. Drysdale Woodcock, 19 November 1920, p. 13.
61. Ibid., Ernest J. Schuster, 4 October 1920, p. 16.
62. Ibid., Miss Clara Andrew, 5 October 1920, p. 14.
63. Ibid., p. 12.
64. Ibid., W Clarke Hall, 26 October 1920, p. 28.
65. Ibid., Miss Clara Andrew, 5 October 1920, p. 22.
66. Ibid., Mr Seddon during evidence of Miss Clara Andrew, 5 October 1920, p. 22.
67. Ibid., Miss Clara Andrew, 5 October 1920, p. 22.
68. Ibid., p. 16.
69. Ibid., Miss Clara Andrew, 5 October 1920, p. 18.
70. Ibid., Mrs Edwin Gray, written evidence, Appendix N, p. 43.
71. Ibid., Miss RSM Peto, 5 October 1920, p. 37.
72. Ibid., Mr Tom Percival/Mr A. P. Stanwell Smith, 19 October 1920, p. 20.
73. Ibid., Memorandum, Mr R. P. Parr, NSPCC, 16 November 1920.
74. Ibid., Miss Z. L. Puxley, 27 October 1920, pp. 6–7.

75. Hansard, House of Commons, vol. 140, p. 903, 12 April 1921.
76. Ibid., vol. 143, p. 1549, 23 June 1921.
77. Hopkinson Report, op. cit, p. 4.
78. An endorsement of Zelizer's thesis about the 'priceless child' discussed in the Chapter 1.
79. Hopkinson Report, op. cit., p. 10.
80. Ibid., p. 12.
81. Ibid., p. 3.
82. Ibid., p. 5.
83. Ibid.
84. Ibid., p. 7.
85. Ibid., p. 8.
86. Ibid., p. 9.
87. A. J. P. Taylor, *English History 1914–1945* (Oxford: Oxford University Press, 1965). This may simply reflect the interest of earlier historians of the period. Sir Gerald Hurst, an MP, lawyer and judge who was involved with adoption policy (see later chapters) was clear in his 1942 autobiography that 'The "twenties" were a period of social reforms', and went on to list his involvement in the campaigns to introduce legitimation by subsequent marriage, the equal guardianship of infants and the Criminal Law Amendment Act as well as the legalisation of adoption. See Sir Gerald Hurst, *Closed Chapters* (Manchester: Manchester University Press, 1942), p. 105.
88. Joanne Workman, 'Wading through the Mire: An Historiographical Study of the British Women's Movement between the Wars', *University of Sussex Journal of Contemporary History*, issue 2 (April 2001), p. 1.
89. Winifred Holtby, quoted in Dale Spender, *Time and Tide Wait for No Man* (London: Pandora Press, 1984), p. 103.
90. Pat Thane, 'What Difference Did the Vote Make?' in Amanda Vickery (ed.), *Women, Privilege and Power: British Politics 1750 to the Present* (Stanford: Stanford University Press, 2001), p. 279.
91. Pat Thane, 'What Difference Did the Vote Make? Women in Public and Private Life in Britain since 1918', *Historical Research*, vol. 76, no. 192 (May 2003), p. 273.
92. Ibid., p. 272.
93. Martin Pugh, *Women and the Women's Movement in Britain 1914–1959* (London: Macmillan, 1992), p. 114.
94. Taylor, op cit, p. 262.
95. *Time and Tide*, vol. 2, no. 21, (27 May 1921).
96. Ibid., vol. 6, no. 32, (7 August 1925).
97. Hansard, House of Commons, vol. 150, p. 816, 14 February 1922.
98. Stephen Cretney, *Family Law in the Twentieth Century: A History* (Oxford: Oxford University Press, 2003), p. 600.
99. HO 45/11540. Home Office Departmental Comment, 7 April 1921.
100. HO 45/11540. Home Office Departmental Comment (unsigned), 20 July 1921.
101. See Biographical Notes.
102. HO 45/11540. S. W. Harris, 22 July 1921.
103. Ibid.
104. See Biographical Notes.

105. HO 45/11540. 'Conference on Child Adoption,' 28 November 1921.
106. Ibid. Memo from S. W. Harris, initialled as seen and commented on by various people, 24 October 1921.
107. Ibid. 'Conference on Child Adoption', 28 November 1921.
108. See Biographical Notes.
109. 'Conference on Child Adoption', op cit.
110. Ibid.
111. See Biographical Notes.
112. HO 45/11540. Home Office Departmental Comment, undated but c1922.
113. See Hansard, House of Commons, vol. 162, p. 1879, 17 April, 1923. See Biographical Notes about Sir Leonard Brassey.
114. See Hansard, House of Commons, vol. 164, p. 248, 15 May 1923. Gerald Hurst (later knighted) was the son in law of Sir Alfred Hopkinson. See Biographical Notes.
115. HO 45/11540. Home Office Departmental Comment (initials unclear), 26 May 1923.
116. Ibid. Note, 5 June 1923.
117. Ibid. Letter from Robert Parr, Director, NSPCC, to S. W. Harris, 31 May 1923.
118. Ibid. 10 prosecutions for neglect, three for ill-treatment, one for criminal assault.
119. Hansard, House of Commons, vol. 166, p. 1885, 16 July 1923.
120. Hansard, House of Commons, vol. 168, p. 29, 13 November, 1923.
121. Ibid. 'Notes on Lord Gorell's Question in regard to Child Adoption', mid-March 1924.
122. See Biographical Notes.
123. HO 45/12642. 'Notes on the Duke of Atholl's Bill', 17 March 1924.
124. Sir Gerald Hurst, *Closed Chapters* (Manchester: Manchester University Press, 1942), p. 146.
125. *The Times*, 19 January 1924.

4 Legislation Takes Shape

1. HO 45/12642. Home Office notes, 8 March 1924.
2. Ibid. Letter from Sir John Anderson to Sir Claud Schuster, 17 March 1924.
3. Permanent Secretary 1922–32. See Biographical Notes.
4. HO 45/12642. 'Notes on the Duke of Atholl's Bill'.
5. History of the Home Office 1782–1982 – extracts on Home Office website, http://www.homeoffice.gov.uk/webwork/hohist.html, accessed 2 April 2002.
6. HO 45/12642. 'Notes on the Duke of Atholl's Bill', 17 March 1924.
7. Ibid. 'Notes on the Duke of Atholl's Bill', 17 March 1924.
8. HO 45/11540. 'Notes on Lord Gorell's Question in Regard to Child Adoption', mid-March 1924.
9. The Child Adoption Committee (hereafter the Tomlin Committee), 4 April 1924.
10. *Dictionary of National Biography, 1931–1940* (Oxford: Oxford University Press, 1949), p. 866. See Biographical Notes.

11. Adoption of Children (Scotland) Bill 1924, 28 March 1924.
12. Child Adoption Committee 1924–25, First Report. Cmd 2401 (hereafter known as the Tomlin Report), p. 4.
13. Ibid., p. 5.
14. Ibid.
15. Ibid.
16. Ibid., p. 4.
17. Ibid., p. 1.
18. Ibid., p. 5.
19. HO 45/12642. Draft First Report, Tomlin Committee, p. 10.
20. Ibid.
21. Ibid. Undated note (1925) from M. L. Gwyer to S. W. Harris.
22. Ibid. Undated memorandum (1925) prepared by M. L. Gwyer, p. 3.
23. Ibid., p. 1.
24. Ibid., p. 2.
25. Ibid., p. 2.
26. Ibid.
27. Ibid.
28. Ibid., p. 3.
29. Georgina Stafford (compiled), *Where to Find Adoption Records: A Guide for Counsellors* (London: British Agencies for Adoption and Fostering, 1992).
30. HO 45/11540. Minutes of Evidence to Committee on Child Adoption 1921, H. B. Drysdale Woodcock, 19 November 1920, p. 13.
31. Tomlin report, op. cit., p. 9.
32. Ibid., p. 6.
33. Ibid., p. 7.
34. Child Adoption Committee, Second Report. Cmd 469. Clause 3b.
35. Ibid. Clause 9.
36. Ibid. Clause 10.
37. Ibid. Clause 11(6) and (7).
38. HO 45/12642. Draft First Report, Tomlin Committee, p. 10. 'The topic is one which we think will have to be discussed under the new terms of reference which you have committed to us, and we therefore propose to deal with it more fully in our report under that reference'.
39. Child Adoption Committee, Third & Final Report 1926. Cmd 2711, p. 4.
40. Ibid. Second Schedule.
41. See Biographical Notes.
42. HO 45/12642. Note, 3 April 1925.
43. Hansard. House of Commons, vol. 182, p. 1721, 3 April 1925.
44. Ibid., pp. 1730–1.
45. Ibid., pp. 1739–40.
46. Ibid., p. 1746.
47. HO 45/12642. Note, April 1925.
48. See Biographical Notes.
49. HO 45/12642. 15 July 1925.
50. Hansard. House of Commons, vol. 191, p. 243, 3 February 1926.
51. See Biographical Notes.
52. HO 45/12642. Handwritten note (unreadable initials), 8 February 1926.
53. Hansard. House of Commons, vol. 192, p. 924, 26 February 1926.

54. Ibid., p. 929.
55. Ibid., p. 931.
56. Ibid., p. 932.
57. Ibid., p. 933.
58. Ibid., p. 937.
59. Ibid.
60. Ibid., p. 939.
61. Ibid., p. 941.
62. Ibid., p. 944.
63. Ibid., p. 945.
64. Ibid., p. 950.
65. Ibid., p. 951.
66. Ibid., p. 952.
67. Ibid., p. 967.
68. Ibid., p. 958.
69. Hansard. Report of Standing Committee A, 16 March 1926.
70. HO 45/12642. Memos, March–June 1926.
71. *Times Educational Supplement*, 20 March 1926.
72. Hansard. House of Commons, vol. 196, p. 2674, 18 June 1926.
73. Adoption of Children Act, 1926. Clause 2(1)(b).
74. Conservative MP; member, founding committee of NCAA.
75. Hansard. House of Commons, vol. 196, pp. 2648–9, 18 June 1926.
76. Adoption of Children Act, 1926. Clause 2(2).
77. Hansard. House of Commons, vol. 196, p. 2652, 18 June 1926.
78. Ibid., p. 2663.
79. Ibid., p. 2664.
80. Ibid.
81. Ibid., p. 2666.
82. Adoption of Children Act, 1926. Clause 3(b).
83. Hansard. House of Lords, vol. 65, p. 128, 21 July 1926.
84. Hansard. House of Commons, vol. 198, p. 2954, 3 August 1926.
85. Ibid., vol. 196, p. 2680, 18 June 1926.
86. *Manchester Guardian*, 6 November 1926.
87. The Tomlin Report, op. cit., p. 5.
88. Hansard. House of Commons, vol. 182, p. 1725, 3 April 1925.
89. Ibid., p. 1726.
90. The Hon. Treasurer of the National Adoption Society admitted in 1927 that in over 1400 adoptions arranged by his Society no relinquishing parent had ever tried to obtain the details of the adopter from the Society, but he argued that if they were given such details as of right they would be unable to resist contacting the adopting family. HO 45/12695. Letter from Lt Col. A. C. H. Kennard to Sir Claud Schuster, 7 April 1927.
91. Gail Savage, *The Social Construction of Expertise: The English Civil Service and Its Influence 1919–1939* (Pittsburgh: University of Pittsburgh Press, 1996), pp. 18–23.
92. The Civil Service was also notable for its lack of senior women. In 1938 Hilda Martindale reviewed the position of women in the civil service but had to admit that despite the large increase in female civil servants they were not well-represented in the higher levels (*Women Servants of the State 1870–1938:*

A History of Women in the Civil Service (London: George Allen & Unwin, 1938). R. K. Kelsall pointed out that in 1930 in the whole Administrative Class (the highest level of civil servants) there were only twenty women, or about two per cent of the total. Even by 1939 only 43 women (just over 3 per cent) were in this Class (*Higher Civil Servants in Britain: From 1870 to the Present Day* (London: Routledge & Kegan Paul, 1955), p. 170). The only visible woman civil servant dealing with adoption was Miss Zoe Puxley at the Ministry of Health who was a Principal and later Assistant Secretary.
93. See Biographical Notes.
94. Stephen Cretney, *Family Law in the Twentieth Century: A History* (Oxford: Oxford University Press, 2003), p. 792.

5 The First Years of Legally Sanctioned Adoption

1. Report of the Committee on Child Adoption 1921 (the Hopkinson Report), p. 5, suggested that adoption had recently grown extensively and would continue to do so. The Child Adoption Committee 1924–25 – First Report (the Tomlin Report) said that 'the war led to an increase in the number of 'de facto' adoptions but that increase has not been wholly maintained. The people wishing to get rid of children are far more numerous than those wishing to receive them …', p. 4. Neither suggested potential figures for adoptions.
2. HO 45/14188. Fourth Report on the Work of the Children's Branch (October 1928), p. 81.
3. *Daily Express*, 3 January 1927.
4. Report of the Departmental Committee on Adoption Societies and Agencies, Cmd 5499, 1937 (The Horsbrugh Report), p. 4.
5. Hansard. House of Commons, vol. 282, p. 377, 13 December 1933.
6. A. E. Stanley Smith, 'The Adoption of Children Act 1926, The Benefit and Some Disadvantages of the Present Law', *The Child Welfare Worker*, Vol. VIII, no. 29 (Spring & Summer 1927), p. 6.
7. Formerly the main non-militant suffrage organisation, the National Union of Women's Suffrage Societies.
8. HO 45/12695. Note, 22 September 1926.
9. Ibid. Letter from A. E. A. Napier to Mrs E. Hubback, 11 January 1927.
10. Ibid. Note from NCAA, 23 February 1927.
11. Ibid. However by 1933 the NCAA had made it part of its rules that adopters must get an adoption order within 18 months of adopting through the Association. 'Forty Years of Adoption Work', *Child Adoption*, no. 23 (Summer 1957), p. 14.
12. Ibid. Letter from Lt-Col. A. C. H. Kennard, National Adoption Society, 7 April 1927.
13. Annual Report of the NSPCC, 1927–28, p. 17.
14. Annual Report of the NSPCC, 1930–31, p. 14.
15. Ibid. Letter from Sir John Anderson to local authorities, enclosing a copy of the Adoption of Children Act 1926 and of the Adoption of Children (Summary Jurisdiction) Rules, 1926, p. 1.
16. Ibid. Letter from Sir John Anderson to Clerks to the Justices, enclosing a copy of the Adoption of Children Act 1926 and of the Adoption of Children (Summary Jurisdiction) Rules, 1926, p. 3.

17. Ibid., p. 2.
18. Ibid., p. 2.
19. Ibid.
20. The Horsbrugh Report, op. cit., p. 4. N.B. A few of the High Court and County Court orders apply to more than one child which is why these numbers fall slightly short of the total number of adopted children, which was 42,011.
21. Hansard. House of Commons, vol. 247, p. 612, 26 January 1931.
22. Bath Records Office – Register Office 'Minute Book: Adoption of Children Act 1926', 1927–33.
23. Ibid. Case dated 17 December 1930.
24. Ibid. Case dated 30 April 1930.
25. Ibid. Case dated 3 July 1929.
26. J 84/152; 172; 179; 194; 197.
27. HO 45/14188. Fourth Report on the Work of the Children's Branch (October 1928), p. 80. The amount of information given for each tier of court varies.
28. Ibid., p. 82.
29. Ibid., p. 83.
30. Ibid., p. 83.
31. Ibid., p. 84.
32. Ibid., p. 84.
33. James Wedgwood Drawbell, *Experiment in Adoption* (London: Victor Gollancz, 1935), p. 136.
34. *The Times*, 3 December 1930.
35. *Daily Telegraph*, 3 December 1930.
36. *The Times*, 3 December 1930. The mother was awarded the writ of *habeas corpus* and it was ordered that the child be handed over to her the day following the judgement.
37. Ibid.
38. 'The Adoption of Children Act in Working', *The Solicitor's Journal* (14 February 1931), listed a number of these issues.
39. Hansard. House of Commons, vol. 211, p. 2103, 13 December 1927.
40. HO 45/17061. Letter from the Home Office to the NAS, 14 June 1934.
41. Ibid. Letter from the Home Office to Hibbert & Pownall, Ashton-under-Lyne, 11 April 1934.
42. Ibid. Letter from the Home Office to Mr Blaxill, Chairman, Colchester Juvenile Court Panel, 3 May 1934.
43. HO 144/16063. Note, 4 June 1930.
44. Hansard. House of Commons, vol. 237, p. 2737, 15 April 1930.
45. Ibid.
46. RG 48/1424. Adoption of Children (Scotland) Bill 1930 – Standing Committee amendments.
47. John Triseliotis, *In Search of Origins: The Experience of Adopted People* (London: Routledge & Kegan Paul, 1973), p. 1.
48. Ibid.
49. LCC – CH/M/20/7. Report of Education Officer to Special Services Subcommittee, 21 January 1927.
50. Ibid. General Purposes Committee, 7 February 1927.

51. Ibid. Report of Special Section appointed to deal with cases under Adoption of Children Act 1926, figures dated 14 December 1927.
52. 'Adoption of Children', *Charity Organisation Quarterly*, Vol. II, no. 1 (Jan 1928), p. 19.
53. HO 45/20467. London County Council Minutes, p. 170 – Joint report of the Central Public Health Committee, the Education Committee and the Public Assistance Committee, 13 & 14 July 1932.
54. Ibid., p. 169.
55. Ibid.
56. Ibid.
57. Ibid.
58. LCC – CH/M/20/1. Letter from G. H. Gater, Education Officer LCC, to The Chief Clerk, Juvenile Courts, Bow St. Police Court, 29 November 1932.
59. Ibid. Draft circular from G. H. Gater, Education Officer to Divisional Officers in Districts, 28 October 1932.
60. Ibid. Unsigned hand-written memorandum, November 1932.
61. Ibid.
62. Ibid. Typed memorandum to the Medical Officer, 21 November 1932.
63. Ibid. Letter from Education Officer, 20 December 1932.
64. Ibid. Report by Education Officer to Managing Committee on adoption, 24 January 1933.
65. The Horsbrugh Report, op. cit., p. 9.
66. Ibid., p. 40.
67. Ibid., p. 41.
68. Ibid., p. 41.
69. Ibid., p. 42.
70. MEPO 2/4237. Letter from C. R. Bradburne, Official Solicitor, to S. W. Harris, Home Office, 12 January 1928.
71. John Triseliotis, *Evaluation of Adoption Policy and Practice* (Edinburgh: University of Edinburgh, 1970), p. 9.
72. Mrs C8P, Family and social life in Barrow, Lancaster and Preston, 1940–1970. Elizabeth Roberts Archive, Centre for North-West Regional Studies, Lancaster University. In fact, one of the interviewees in Roberts' earlier survey (Mr F1P, Preston) did adopt an unrelated child and went on to foster and adopt more after the war, but the few other adopters all adopted relatives' children.
73. Robina S. Addis, Francesca Salzberger and Elizabeth Rabl, *A Survey based on Adoption Case Records* (London: National Association for Mental Health, 1955).
74. Ibid., p. 18. Their conclusion was: 'The proportion of problem cases is significantly greater where the adopter's work status is more than one category higher than that of the natural parents. It would seem that it is not advisable to move a child too far up the social ladder. This may impose too great a strain on him and the adopters may be disappointed if the child does not come up to their high expectations.'
75. Alexina McWhinnie, *Adopted Children: How They Grow Up* (London: Routledge & Kegan Paul, 1967), p. 69.
76. See Chapter 2.
77. Pat Turner and Jenny Elliott, *Adoption: Reviewing the Record* (London: NCH Ashwood Project, 1992), p. 9.

78. See Naomi Pfeffer, *The Stork and the Syringe: A Political History of Reproductive Medicine* (Cambridge: Polity Press, 1993).
79. For example, see the selection of letters sent to the sex education and birth control campaigner, Marie Stopes. Ruth Hall (ed.), *Dear Dr Stopes: Sex in the 1920s* (London: Andre Deutsch, 1978).
80. Elliot Slater and Moya Woodside, *Patterns of Marriage: A Study of Marriage Relationships in the Urban Working Classes* (London: Cassell & Company, 1951), p. 188.
81. Pfeffer, op. cit., p. 98.
82. Ibid., p. 100.
83. Michael Anderson, 'The Social Implications of Demographic Change' in F. M. L. Thompson (ed.), *The Cambridge Social History of Britain 1750–1950, Vol. 2: People and their environment* (Cambridge: Cambridge University Press, 1990), p. 40.
84. Ross McKibbin, *Classes and Cultures: England 1918–1951* (Oxford: Oxford University Press, 1998), p. 80.
85. 4.8 per cent in 1931 compared to 6.3 per cent in 1901 – figures from the Census for England and Wales, 1901 and 1931, quoted in Diana Gittins, *Fair Sex: Family Size and Structure 1900–39* (London: Hutchinson 1982), p. 34. However, these figures would not include much of the casual and part-time labour by married women which went unreported in the census.
86. All figures from 'The Registrar-General's Statistical review of England & Wales' (London: HMSO) through the 1950s.
87. Basil Nield quoted in N. V. Lowe, 'English Adoption Law: Past, Present, and Future', in Sanford N. Katz, , John Eekelaar and Mavis Maclean (eds), *Cross Currents: Family Law and Policy in the United States and England* (Oxford: Oxford University Press, 2000), p. 315.
88. Barbara Reynolds, *Dorothy L Sayers: Her Life and Soul* (London: Hodder & Stoughton, 1993), p. 244, says Anthony was officially adopted. David Coomes, *Dorothy L Sayers: A Careless Rage for Life* (Oxford: Lion, 1992), p. 111, says she would not adopt officially as she would have had to produce a birth certificate with her name as sole parent.
89. Victoria Glendinning, *Rebecca West: A Life* (London: Weidenfeld, 1987); Bonnie Kime Scott (ed.), *Selected Letters of Rebecca West* (New Haven, CT: Yale University Press, 2000), p. 112.
90. 'The Registrar-General's Statistical Review of England & Wales for the Year 1950', Part II (London: HMSO, 1952), pp. 82–3.
91. Katherine Holden discusses the experience of single people adopting and fostering, in Katherine Holden, *The Shadow of Marriage: Singleness in England, 1914–60* (Manchester: Manchester University Press, 2007), Chapter 6, pp. 140–63.
92. Olive Renier, *Before the Bonfire* (Warwickshire: P. Drinkwater, 1984), p. 2.
93. *The Guardian*, 27 November 2003.
94. Caroline Moorehead, *Martha Gellhorn: A Life* (London: Chatto, 2003).
95. Holden, 'The Shadow of Marriage: Single Women in England 1919–1939' (unpublished PhD thesis, University of Essex 1996), pp. 274–5. Ironically 'aunt' was also what some illegitimate children living with their grandparents called their real mother (e.g. the novelist Catherine Cookson),

although unlike the cases mentioned by Holden they were usually unaware that this was an adoptive relationship.
96. From Rosamund Essex, *A Woman in a Man's World* (London: Sheldon Press, 1977), quoted in Mary Abbott, *Family Affairs: A History of the Family in Twentieth Century England* (London: Routledge, 2003), p. 34.
97. 'A Spinster Adopter Speaks', *Child Adoption*, no. 18 (Spring 1956), p. 14.
98. 'Self-Portrait of an Adopting Mother', *Child Adoption*, no. 33 (Spring 1960), p. 14.
99. NCAA Annual Report, 1952–53, p. 6.
100. McWhinnie, op. cit., p. 200.

6 Action on the Adoption Societies

1. MEPO 2/4237. Letter from C. R. Bradburne, official solicitor, to S. W. Harris, Home Office, 12 January 1928.
2. PC 12/73. Letter from W. J. Allen, Home Office, to Privy Council Office, 22 May 1930.
3. Ibid. Letter from S. W. Harris, Home Office, to Colin Smith, 9 December 1930.
4. See Biographical Notes.
5. House of Commons, vol. 261, p. 1010, 11 February 1932.
6. Ibid., p. 1196, 12 February 1932.
7. See Biographical Notes.
8. HO 45/20466. Notes of meeting 24 February 1932 sent to S. W. Harris at the Home Office by A. B. Maclachlan, 17 March 1932.
9. Ibid.
10. S. Margery Fry, 'Women as JPs' in G. Evelyn Gates (ed.) & NUSEC (compiled), *The Woman's Year Book 1923–24* (London: Women Publishers Limited, 1923), p. 120.
11. HO 45/20466. Letter from S. W. Harris to A. B. Maclachlan, quoting requests from the Magistrates' Association, 11 March 1932.
12. Soon substantially amended by the Children and Young Persons Act 1933 but not in the sections mentioned above.
13. HO 45/20466. Paper re 'Adoption Societies' to S. W. Harris from unnamed civil servant, 23 March 1932.
14. *John Bull*, 4 June 1932.
15. *Sunday Dispatch*, 3 July 1935.
16. *News Chronicle*, 27 March 1931.
17. HO 45/20467. Letter from NSPCC and others to Sir John Gilmour, 4 March 1933.
18. Ibid. Cases: Northwich; Middlesbrough.
19. HO 144/22596. Home Office Children's Branch Report on Hutchison House, 2 April 1931, p. 3. Some of the information in this file has been released under the Freedom of Information Act rules but some has been removed under FOI S40 exemption.
20. Ibid. Evidence of E. T. Beesley, HCAAS, to Tomlin Committee, 15 December 1924.

21. Ibid. Letter from B. E. Astbury to J. F. Henderson , the Home Office, 19 December 1932.
22. Ibid. Note from A. C. Slater, Home Office, 21 July 1942.
23. HO 45/20467. Letter from NSPCC and others, 4 March 1933. Case: High Wycombe.
24. Ibid. Memorandum from A. B. Maclachlan to Home Office, 4 April 1933.
25. Eileen Younghusband, 'Report on the Employment and Training of Social Workers' (Edinburgh: Carnegie United Kingdom Trust, 1947), p. 81.
26. Eileen Younghusband, 'Social Work in Britain: A Supplementary Report on the Employment and Training of Social Workers' (Edinburgh: Carnegie United Kingdom Trust, 1951), p. 55.
27. HO 45/17061. Letter from Cecil M. Chapman to the Home Secretary, 21 May 1935.
28. *The Times*, 3 July 1935.
29. Ibid.
30. *The Times*, 22 October 1935.
31. HO 45/17115. Letter dated 27 November 1935.
32. Ibid. Home Office note signed 'R R J' dated 26 November 1935.
33. Hansard. House of Commons, vol. 308, p. 1164, 13 February 1936.
34. Report of the Departmental Committee on Adoption Societies and Agencies: Copy of Warrant of Appointment – 31 January 1936.
35. *The Dictionary of National Biography, 1961–70* (Oxford: Oxford University Press, 1981), p. 541.
36. Report of the Departmental Committee on Adoption Societies and Agencies 1936–37, Cmd 5499 (hereafter known as the Horsbrugh Report), p. 1.
37. Ibid., p. 6.
38. Ibid., p. 9.
39. Ibid., p. 10.
40. Ibid.
41. Ibid., p. 11.
42. Ibid.
43. Ibid.
44. Ibid., p. 12.
45. Ibid., p. 13.
46. Ibid., p. 14.
47. Ibid.
48. Ibid., p. 15.
49. Ibid., p. 14.
50. Lois Raynor, *The Adopted Child Comes of Age* (London: George Allen & Unwin, 1980), p. 41.
51. Ibid.
52. The Horsbrugh Report, op. cit., p. 16.
53. Ibid., p. 17.
54. Ibid., p. 18.
55. Ibid., p. 21.
56. Ibid., p. 20.
57. Ibid., p. 20.
58. Ibid., p. 21.
59. Ibid., p. 22.

60. Ibid., p. 23.
61. Ibid., p. 25.
62. Ibid., p. 27.
63. LCC/CH/M/24/3 – Report of the Education Officer to the Adoption Section of the General Sub-Committee of the Education Committee, LCC, 9 July 1943, p. 6.
64. Ibid. Meeting of LCC officials with new Adoption Society Chairman, Herbert Reynolds, 5 August 1943.
65. LCC/CH/M/24/4 – Re-registration of the Church Adoption Society, 26 July 1945.
66. 'Prebendary Buttle and the Buttle Trust' (The Buttle Trust, 1978).
67. The Horsbrugh Report, op. cit., p. 30.
68. Ibid., p. 31.
69. Ibid., p. 32.
70. Ibid., p. 35.
71. Ibid., p. 36.
72. Ibid., p. 39.
73. Ibid., p. 40.
74. Ibid., p. 9.
75. Ibid., p. 44.
76. Ibid., p. 50.
77. Ibid.
78. In the Children Act 1908, and Children and Young Persons Act 1932, incorporated in the Public Health Act 1936, to come into force 1 October 1937.
79. The Horsbrugh Report, op. cit., p. 52.
80. Ibid., p. 55.
81. Hansard. House of Commons, vol. 326, p. 866, 12 July 1937.
82. Ibid., vol. 331, p. 553, 4 February 1938.
83. HO45/18243. Letter dated 23 May 1938.
84. Ibid.
85. Ibid. Memorandum dated 27 October 1938.
86. Ibid. 'Extract from Conclusions of a Meeting of the Home Affairs Committee', 2 November 1938.
87. Hansard. House of Commons, vol. 341, p. 459, 11 November 1938.
88. Ibid., vol. 342, p. 2406, 16 February 1938.
89. Ibid., p. 2358, 16 December 1938.
90. Ibid., p. 2360.
91. Ibid., p. 2382.
92. Ibid., p. 2383.
93. Ibid., p. 2384.
94. Ibid., p. 2385.
95. Ibid., p. 2394.
96. Ibid., p. 2413.
97. 'Adoption of Children (Regulation) Act 1939' Section 1 (1) & (2).
98. Ibid., Section 5 (1).
99. Ibid., Section 7.
100. Ibid., Section 7 (8) (a).
101. Ibid., Section 8 (1).

102. MH 55/1635. Adoption of Children (Regulation) Act 1939.
103. *The Times*, 10 July 1939.
104. *Evening Standard*, 8 July 1939.
105. *The Times*, 14 July 1939.
106. Writer, suffragist, Labour Party activist, a vice president of the NCAA. Widow of Philip Snowden, Viscount Snowden the former Chancellor of the Exchequer in the 1924, 1929–31 Labour Governments and 1931 National Government.
107. *The Times*, 29 July 1939.
108. Papers in the collection of Patricia Wreford King.
109. MH 57/53. Letter from Miss Clara Andrew to Miss Zoe Puxley, 21 March 1923.
110. Now the British Agencies for Adoption and Fostering (BAAF).
111. Hilary Halpin, 'Why We Closed', *Child Adoption*, no. 94 (1978), pp. 27–29; 'Opting Out', editorial in the same issue.

7 The Second World War and Its Aftermath

1. B. R. Mitchell, with collaboration of Phyllis Deane, *Abstract of British Historical Statistics* (Cambridge: Cambridge University Press, 1962), p. 44. These figures refer to England and Wales.
2. From 1954 to 1969, over a third, rising to 60 per cent in 1969, of adoptions were by one of their own natural parents, usually with their partner, the child's step-parent, but this includes both legitimate and illegitimate children. See 'The Registrar-General's Statistical Reviews of England & Wales' and Eleanor Grey, in collaboration with Ronald M. Blunden, *A Survey of Adoption in Great Britain*, Home Office Research Studies 10 (London: HMSO, 1971).
3. MH 55/1636. Letter dated 29 April 1942.
4. MH 55/1636. Unsigned note dated 9 June 1942.
5. Hansard. House of Commons, vol. 381, pp. 518–9, 2 July 1942.
6. MH 55/1636. Letter dated 12 July 1942.
7. NCAA Annual Report to 31 January 1943, p. 11.
8. *Sunday Dispatch*, 23 August 1942.
9. HO 45/19299. Letter dated 14 July 1942.
10. Ibid. October 1942.
11. See Biographical Notes.
12. MH 55/1635. 'Notes of a Deputation from the Woman Power Committee', 24 November 1942.
13. Ibid. 'Notes of a Deputation from the Charity Organisation Society', 25 November 1942.
14. Ibid.
15. HO 45/19299. Memo from Home Secretary, 21 January 1943.
16. MH 55/1635. 'Extract from Conclusions of a Meeting of the Lord President's Committee', 25 January 1943.
17. Hansard. House of Commons, vol. 386, p. 608, 28 January 1943.
18. East Sussex County Record Office. Letters to Welfare Authorities (England) and the London County Council from Ministry of Health (Circular 2790) 18 March 1943; to County Councils and County Borough Councils from

the Children's Branch, Home Office, 18 March 1943. The regulations were issued in permanent form on 8 September 1943 but were unchanged from the March version.
19. *Sunday Chronicle*, 11 April 1943.
20. HO 45/19300. Miss Horsbrugh's BBC Postscript, 1 June, 1943.
21. Hansard. House of Commons, vol. 395, p. 986, 8 December 1943. It appears to have been a smooth process for most societies – the LCC registered the NCAA on the day the Act came into force, having received all its documentation in advance. However the LCC initially rejected the registration of the Church Adoption Society.
22. In Birmingham the public health department followed up almost all the mothers of children registered as illegitimate and during the last two years of the war a third of all illegitimate children were born to married women although in 1945 only 283 of the 520 such women had husbands in the services. The remainder were divorced, widowed or living apart from their husbands. See Sheila Ferguson and Hilda Fitzgerald, *Studies in the Social Services: History of the Second World War*, UK Civil Series (London: Longmans & HMSO, 1954), p. 98.
23. *Evening Standard*, 16 January 2007; *Guardian*, 17 January 2007.
24. Julia Baird, *Imagine This: Growing Up with My Brother John Lennon* (London: Hodder & Stoughton, 2007), p. 20.
25. Russell v Russell (1924).
26. LCO 2/2642. Letter from Helen M. Blackburne, Secretary of the National Adoption Society (NAS), to the Chief Clerk, Lord Chancellor's Office, House of Lords. 21 January 1942.
27. Ibid. Letter from S. W. Harris, Home Office, to G. P. Coldstream, Lord Chancellor's Office. 18 April 1942.
28. Ibid. Letter from A. E. A. Napier, Lord Chancellor's Office, to His Hon. Judge Sir Gerald Hargreaves. 30 May 1944. Similar sentiments repeated in other letters to inquiries from judges and magistrates.
29. MH 102/1364. Note from Home Office. 16 May 1944.
30. Mrs F1L, Family and social life in Barrow, Lancaster and Preston, 1940–70, Elizabeth Roberts Archive, Centre for North-West Regional Studies, Lancaster University.
31. Ferguson & Fitzgerald, op. cit., p. 113.
32. Ferguson & Fitzgerald, op. cit., p. 124. Details in CAB 102/771. 'Notes for the Official History'.
33. Described in Ferguson & Fitzgerald, op. cit., p. 130.
34. Ibid.
35. LCC/CH/M/24/2. Church of England Children's Society – Registration of Adoption Societies 1945–49. Report of Executive Committee for Year ended 31 December 1944, p. 7.
36. LCC/CH/M/23/4. Children's Aid Society – Anchorage Mission Annual Report, Year ending, 31 December 1943.
37. Formerly Lady Inskip. See Biographical Notes.
38. *The Times*, 4 July 1944.
39. *The Times*, 11 July 1944.
40. *The Times*, 17 July 1944.
41. *The Times*, 3 August 1944.
42. *The Times*, 4 July 1944.

43. Bernard Crick, *George Orwell: A life* (London: Secker & Warburg, 1980), p. 319.
44. Ibid, quoted, p. 330.
45. National Adoption Society Annual Report, 1944, p. 8.
46. National Adoption Society Annual Report, 1945, p. 8.
47. 'In Loco Parentis' (London: National Council of Social Service, June 1947), p. 5.
48. Report of the Care of Children Committee, September 1946, Cmd 6922 (hereafter the Curtis Report), p. 5.
49. See Biographical Notes.
50. *The Times*, 15 July 1944.
51. *The Times*, 31 July 1944.
52. The foster father later received six years penal servitude for manslaughter, the foster mother six months imprisonment for neglect. *The Times*, 20 March 1945.
53. Hansard. House of Commons, vol. 408, pp. 940–2, 22 February 1945.
54. Stephen Cretney, *Family Law in the Twentieth Century: A History* (Oxford: Oxford University Press, 2003), p. 672.
55. MH 102/2256. Notes of Meeting held at the Home Office, 27 August 1945, p. 6.
56. Ibid., p. 12.
57. MH 102/2260. Notes of Meeting held at the Home Office, 10 September 1945, p. 11.
58. Ibid., p. 13.
59. Ibid. Memorandum on the Working of the Adoption of Children (Regulation) Act by B. E. Astbury, p. 1.
60. Curtis Report, op. cit., p. 179.
61. Ibid., p. 148.
62. Ibid.
63. Ibid.
64. Ibid.
65. Cretney, op. cit., pp. 675, 685.
66. Ibid., p. 611.
67. The Lord Chancellor, Hansard, House of Lords, vol. 167, p. 645, 13 June 1950.
68. Hansard. House of Commons, vol. 466, p. 679, 24 June 1949.
69. Ibid.,vol. 470, p. 1608, 5 December 1949.
70. Ibid., p. 1611.
71. Ibid., p. 1614.
72. *The Times*, 23 January 1945.
73. Hansard. House of Lords, vol. 163, pp. 1080–1, 11 July 1949.
74. Hansard. House of Commons, vol. 470, p. 1615, 5 December 1949.
75. Ibid., p. 1619.
76. Ibid., p. 1620.
77. Cretney, op. cit., p. 613.
78. The parent was allowed to set conditions 'with respect to the religious persuasion in which the infant is to be brought up'. Adoption of Children Act, 1949. Clause 3 (2).
79. The Lord Chancellor, Hansard, House of Lords, vol. 167, p. 645, 13 June 1950.

8 Conclusions – And Later Developments

1. The NSPCC kept statistics about the cases it dealt with involving adopted children (see Chapter 6 for some case studies). Between 1924 and 1936 it dealt with 2698 such cases (involving 2969 children), from which 36 prosecutions resulted leading to 35 convictions and 1485 people being 'warned'. (Annual Report of the NSPCC, 1935–36, p. 46).
2. Mildred de M. Rudolf, *Everybody's Children: The Story of the Church of England Children's Society 1921–48* (London: Oxford University Press, 1950), p. 96.
3. June Rose, *Inside Barnardo's: 120 Years of Caring for Children* (London: Futura, 1987), p. 200.
4. Lettice Fisher, *Twenty One Years and After, 1918–1946, The Story of the National Council for the Unmarried Mother and Her Child* (London: NCUMC, 2nd ed, 1946), p. 19.
5. MH 55/276, Deputation to the Home Secretary, 17 March 1920.
6. See Hera Cook, 'The Long Sexual Revolution: British Women, Sex and Contraception in the Twentieth Century' (DPhil thesis, University of Sussex 1999).
7. Elliot Slater and Moya Woodside, *Patterns of Marriage: A Study of Marriage Relationships in the Urban Working Classes* (London: Cassell & Company, 1951), p. 179.
8. Ibid., pp. 181–2.
9. Janet Fink, 'Private Lives, Public Issues: Moral Panics and "The Family" in 20th-Century Britain', *Journal for the Study of British Cultures*, vol. 9/2 (2002), p. 139.
10. Minutes of Evidence to Hopkinson Committee, Miss Clara Andrew, 5 October 1920, p. 18.
11. Adoption of Children Act, 1926, Clause 3 (b).
12. 'Mine Was Not a "Failed" Adoption', *Child Adoption*, no. 80 (1975), p. 59.
13. *The Times*, 3 July 1935.
14. For example, the letter quoted in Chapter 3. HO 45/12642, from Charles Singer to the Duchess of Atholl, 19 March 1926.
15. Adoption of Children Act, 1926. Clause 5 (2).
16. Ibid., Clause 11 (7).
17. Erica Haimes and Noel Timms, *Adoption, Identity and Social Policy: The Search for Distant Relatives* (Gower, Hants 1985), p. 3.
18. Between 1961 and 1970 an average of 42 Scottish adoptees a year applied for their original birth certificates. This is 1.5 per thousand of adopted people over 17 years old. See John Triseliotis, *In Search of Origins : The Experience of Adopted People* (London: Routledge & Kegan Paul, 1973), p. 2.
19. Ibid.
20. Not surprisingly there are no overall figures for this but in Howe & Feast's study of adopters who search for their parents 7 per cent were rejected outright by the birthparent (i.e. 19 out of 274 people; 17 by their mother, 2 by their father) and another 9 per cent (24 people) had the contact terminated by the birth parent within a year. David Howe and Julia Feast, *Adoption, Search & Reunion: The Long Term Experience of Adopted Adults* (London: The Children's Society, 2000), pp. 108, 111.

21. Michael Anderson, 'The Social Implications of Demographic Change' in F. M. L. Thompson (ed.), *The Cambridge Social History of Britain 1750–1950, Vol. 2: People and their environment* (Cambridge: Cambridge University Press, 1990), p. 27.
22. Julie Berebitsky, *Like Our Very Own: Adoption and the Changing Culture of Motherhood 1851–1950* (Lawrence, KS: University Press of Kansas, 2000), p. 76.
23. Ibid., p. 85.
24. For this account I have used N. V. Lowe, 'English Adoption Law: Past, Present, and Future, in Sanford N. Katz, John Eekelaar and Mavis Maclean (eds), *Cross Currents: Family Law and Policy in the United States and England* (Oxford: Oxford University Press, 2000); Caroline Bridge and Heather Swindells, *Adoption: The Modern Law* (Bristol: Family Law, 2003); NCVO Briefing, 'The Changing Role of Voluntary Agencies in Adoption' (1982); S. Cretney, *Family Law in the Twentieth Century: A History* (Oxford: Oxford University Press, 2003); David Howe and Julia Feast, *Adoption, Search & Reunion: The Long Term Experience of Adopted Adults* (London: The Children's Society, 2000); Erica Haimes and Noel Timms, *Adoption, Identity and Social Policy: The Search for Distant Relatives* (Gower, Hants 1985); John Triseliotis, *Evaluation of Adoption Policy and Practice* (Edinburgh: University of Edinburgh, 1970).
25. Bridge & Swindells, op. cit., p. 9.
26. Ibid., p. 8.
27. Ibid., p. 11.
28. The Committee proposed raising the age in Scotland at which this access was allowed to 18 rather than the existing 17 to equalise the situation but this was not implemented.
29. Local authorities were not invited to join even if they undertook adoption. In 1969 the Standing Conference was reconstituted as the Association of British Adoption Agencies (now BAAF – the British Association for Adoption and Fostering) and equal membership was offered to local authorities and voluntary adoption agencies. NCVO Briefing, op. cit., p. 5.
30. Ibid., p. 3.
31. Lowe, op. cit., says exact figures are not available, p. 324.
32. Figures quoted in Lowe, op. cit., pp. 316–20.
33. Figures from http://www.statistics.gov.uk/downloads/theme_compendia/adoptions_2006.xls, accessed 1 February 2008. These are adoptions placed on the Adopted Children Register after a court order. Figures for court orders are slightly lower and there is frequent confusion between the two sets of statistics.
34. Provisions in the Adoption (Intercountry Aspects) Act 1999 and Adoption and Children Act 2002.
35. Bridge & Swindells, op. cit., p. 24.
36. *Guardian*, 24 April 2000, quoted Mr Blair saying, 'I want to make it easier for children to be placed quickly. The most important thing is that children are in a loving family rather than a care home, however well it is run'.
37. Patricia Morgan, *Adoption and the Care of Children: The British and American Experience* (London: The IEA Health and Welfare Unit, 1998).
38. For example, Kendra Inman, 'Looking for Love', *Guardian*, 31 May 2000, pointed out the high breakdown of permanent placements for children from care: one in five for over-threes, 50 per cent for 10–12 year olds. She also

quoted figures suggesting that 30–40 per cent of adoptions now involve some form of ongoing contact with birthparents, illustrating another change in the nature of adoption.
39. http://www.pm.gov.uk/output/page2094.asp, accessed 3 February 2008. Press briefing from the Prime Minister's Official Spokesman, 17 February 2000.
40. http://www.dcsf.gov.uk/rsgateway/DB/SFR/s000691/SFR44-2006.pdf http://new.wales.gov.uk/docrepos/40382/40382313/statistics/health/health-2006/sdr155-2006.pdf?lang=en, both accessed 3 February 2008. First shows figures from England, second from Wales.
41. http://www.hfea.gov.uk/en/1183.html, accessed 3 February 2008.
42. http://www.dcsf.gov.uk/rsgateway/DB/SFR/s000741/SFR27-2007rev.pdf, accessed 8 February 2008.
43. http://www.opsi.gov.uk/SI/em2005/uksiem_20050890_en.pdf, accessed 10 February 2008.

Biographical Notes

1. *Dictionary of National Biography, 1931–1940* (Oxford: Oxford University Press), p. 444.
2. *Dictionary of National Biography, 1981–1985* (Oxford: Oxford University Press), p. 9.
3. Olive Banks, *The Biographical Dictionary of British Feminists, Vol. 2: A Supplement, 1900–1945* (Herts: Harvester Wheatsheaf, 1990), p. 201.

Biographical Notes

Allen, Lady (Marjory) of Hurtwood, 1897–1976 (campaigner for rights of children in care)
Educated at Bedales and University College, Reading. Garden designer. Elected first fellow of the new Institute of Landscape Architects in 1930. Married Clifford Allen, socialist politician and pacifist (later Lord Allen of Hurtwood), who died in 1939. Increasingly interested in the well-being of children and in 1944 started a campaign to expose the conditions under which children in institutions were living. This led to the establishment of the Curtis Committee and the passing of the 1948 Children Act.

Anderson, Sir John, 1882–1958 (head of the Home Office during the 1920s)
Civil servant and politician (Independent Nationalist MP, Scottish Universities 1938–50). Educated at George Watson's College, Edinburgh University and Leipzig University. Joined the civil service in 1905, working first at the Colonial Office, then at the National Health Insurance Commission, 1912–17. Permanent Under-Secretary at the Home Office, 1922–32. After a period as Governor of Bengal returned to the UK and became the only Permanent Secretary to be appointed Home Secretary (in 1939–40). Chancellor of the Exchequer, 1943–5. Created Viscount Waverley in 1952.

Andrew, Clara, 1862–1939 (founder of the National Children Adoption Association)
Educated at Maynard's School, Exeter and Wiesbaden, Germany. Member, Exeter National Insurance Committee. During First World War was Hon. Secretary and Vice-President for the Devon and Cornwall War Refugees Committee; Assistant Lady Supervisor at the Arsenal at Woolwich; and Lady Superintendent at Newbury & Swindon Munitions Works. In February 1918 set up the Children Adoption Association in Exeter. It rapidly became a National Association and moved to London. She remained Hon. Director of the NCAA until her death, living in the Association's main hostel in Kensington.

Astbury, B. E. (Benjamin), died 1969 (member of the Horsbrugh Committee)
General Secretary of the Family Welfare Association (formerly the Charity Organisation Society) for many years, retiring in 1956. Served on many governmental committees (e.g. on legal aid, intestacy, the law and practice relating to charitable trusts), charitable trusts and on the Appeals Committee of the BBC. After the death of Rev Buttle, he was Secretary of the Buttle Trust (1953–63).

Atholl, Duchess of (Katharine Stewart-Murray), 1874–1960 (original member of the Tomlin Committee)
Conservative MP (Kinross and West Perthshire 1923–38), government minister and campaigner. Educated at Wimbledon High School and the Royal College of Music. Married future 8th Duke of Atholl in 1899. Parliamentary Secretary to the

Board of Education (first Conservative woman minister), 1924–9. Campaigned against female circumcision in Kenya; visited Spain during the Civil War and spoke out against her government's policies towards the conflict. Resigned her parliamentary seat in opposition to appeasement in 1938.

Atholl, Duke of (J. G. Stewart-Murray), 1871–1942 (introduced adoption bill in 1924)
Soldier and Conservative MP (West Perthshire 1910–17). Educated at Eton. Served in Kitchener's Sudan campaign, in the Boer War, and during the First World War. Succeeded as 8th Duke in 1917. Lord Chamberlain 1921–2.

Barker, Sir W. R. (Wilberforce Ross), 1874–1957 (member of Tomlin Committee)
Civil servant and lawyer. Educated at Marlborough College and Oxford. Joined Board of Education in 1903; legal adviser 1918–25; Chairman, Indian Public Service Commission, 1926–32.

Blackwell, Sir Ernley (Robertson Hay), 1868–1941 (Home Office legal adviser during the 1920s)
Lawyer and civil servant. Educated at Glenalmond. Called to the Bar in 1892. Legal Assistant Under-Secretary of State, Home Office, 1906–31 and engaged in advisory duties during the Second World War.

Brassey, Sir Leonard (Henry Leonard Campbell), 1870–1958 (introduced adoption bill in 1923)
Conservative MP (Northamptonshire North 1910–18, Peterborough, Northamptonshire 1918–29). Educated at Eton and Oxford. Created Baron Brassey of Apethorpe in 1938.

Butler, Sir Geoffrey, 1887–1929 (introduced adoption bill in 1925)
Historian and Conservative MP (Cambridge University 1923–9). Educated at Clifton College and Cambridge. Librarian and lecturer at Corpus Christi College, specialising in modern diplomatic history. Joined Foreign Office in 1915; Director of British Bureau of Information in New York 1917–19. As an MP he served on various governmental committees and in 1925 became Parliamentary Secretary to Sir Samuel Hoare, the then Secretary of State for Air.

Buttle, Rev. Frank (William Francis), 1878–1953 (founder of National Adoption Society)
Clergyman, adoption worker and fund-raiser. Educated at Whitgift Grammar School, Croydon, Durham University, and Cambridge. Ordained 1906. Curate in Bethnal Green, Cambridge, and later a vicar in Haggerston, East London. Started to arrange adoptions in Cambridge with help of Church League of Women's Suffrage. In London during the war again involved with adoption and c. 1917 set up the National Adoption Society. Enormously interested in raising monies for the societies he was involved with and his business practices led to some controversy. Left the NAS and formed the Church Adoption Society. Later set up the Buttle Trust (helped by Benjamin Astbury – see above) to assist deprived children, particularly those who were adopted, illegitimate and from the professional

classes. He raised nearly a million pounds for it and since his death it has become a substantial charity.

Chamberlain, Rt. Hon. (Arthur) Neville, 1869–1940 (member of Hopkinson Committee)
Government minister and Conservative MP (Ladywood, Birmingham 1918–29; Edgbaston, Birmingham 1929–40). Educated at Rugby and Mason Science College, Birmingham. Birmingham councillor and Lord Mayor. Various ministerial positions including Minister of Health 1923, 1924–9, 1931; Chancellor of Exchequer 1923–4, 1931–7; Prime Minister 1937–40; Lord President of Council 1940. Although known for his policy of appeasement in the late 1930s he was interested in social issues; a long-term supporter of the National Council for the Unmarried Mother and Her Child (its President 1928–31), and a reforming Minister of Health.

Curtis, Dame Myra, 1886–1971 (chaired Curtis Committee)
Civil servant and Principal of Newnham College, Cambridge. Educated at Winchester School for Girls and Cambridge. Worked across the civil service, moving to the Treasury as assistant secretary and director of women's establishments in 1937 before retiring in 1941. Then elected as Principal of her old college, Newnham. Also took on various public appointments both during and after the War, including heading an interdepartmental committee to inquire into the care of deprived children, better known as the Curtis Committee, which reported in 1946.

Fisher, Lettice (Mrs H. A. L), 1875–1956 (founder member and chairman of the National Council for the Unmarried Mother and Her Child)
Campaigner, writer and academic. Educated at Francis Holland School and Oxford. Married H. A. L. Fisher, the historian, vice-chancellor of Sheffield University, and education minister in the 1916–22 coalition government. Taught history and economics at St Hugh's, Oxford, and wrote several books on these and other issues. Instrumental in founding the National Council for the Unmarried Mother and Her Child in 1918, served as its chairman for over 30 years, and continued to support it after her retirement.

Galbraith, His Hon. Judge James Francis Wallace, 1872–1945 (introduced Adoption of Children Act 1926)
Lawyer and Conservative MP (East Surrey 1922–35). Educated at Blackheath Proprietary School and Oxford. Called to the Bar in 1895. County Court Judge 1935–45.

Gamon, His Hon. Judge Hugh Reece Percival, 1880–1953 (chaired Gamon Committee on adoption)
Barrister and judge. Educated at Harrow and Oxford. Called to the Bar in 1906. County Court Judge from 1936. Interested in social issues. Chaired a committee to look at revising the adoption laws, set up by a conference of interested parties organised by the National Council of Social Service in 1945. It produced a report, 'In Loco Parentis', in 1947.

Biographical Notes 247

Gwyer, M. L. (Sir Maurice Linford), 1878–1952 (member of Tomlin Committee)
Lawyer and civil servant. Educated at Highgate, Westminster and Oxford. Called to the Bar in 1903. Joined legal staff of National Health Insurance Commission in 1912. In 1919 appointed legal adviser and solicitor to the Ministry of Health; in 1926 he became Treasury solicitor and King's proctor. In 1937 he was appointed Chief Justice of India.

Harris, John Henry, 1875–1962 (member of Horsbrugh Committee)
Metropolitan Police Magistrate (Thames Police Court 1930–45). Educated at St Paul's School and Oxford. Called to the Bar in 1900.

Harris, S. W. (Sir Sidney West), 1876–1962 (Home Office civil servant involved with adoption issues and member of Tomlin Committee)
Civil servant. Educated at St Paul's School and Oxford. Joined Home Office in 1903; was Private Secretary to successive Home Secretaries, 1909–19; Assistant Secretary in charge of the Children's Branch, 1919–34. After retiring from the civil service was President of the British Board of Film Censors, 1947–60, and chaired a departmental committee on the development of marriage guidance.

Hopkinson, Sir Alfred, 1851–1939 (chaired Hopkinson Committee)
Lawyer and Liberal Unionist MP (Cricklade, Wiltshire 1895–8; Combined English Universities 1926–9). Educated privately, Owen's College, Manchester and Oxford. Called to the Bar in 1873. Appointed the first Vice Chancellor of Victoria (Manchester) University in 1900, retired 1913 to devote 'himself unstintingly to public service'.[1]

Horsbrugh, Baroness Florence Gertrude, 1889–1969 (chaired Horsbrugh Committee and introduced Adoption of Children (Regulation) Act 1939)
Conservative MP (Dundee 1931–45; Moss Side, Manchester 1950–9). Educated at Lansdowne House, Edinburgh, and St. Hilda's, Folkestone. Parliamentary Secretary, Ministry of Health 1939–45, and did much preparatory work for the National Health scheme. Parliamentary Secretary, Ministry of Food 1945. Minister for Education 1951–4 (first woman to be a Cabinet Minister in a Conservative Government). Delegate to three League of Nations Assemblies and the meeting in San Francisco where the UN Charter was drafted. Made a life peer in 1959.

Hurst, Sir Gerald Berkeley, 1877–1957 (introduced adoption bill in 1923)
Lawyer and Conservative MP (Moss Side, Manchester 1918–23, 1924–35). Educated at Bradford Grammar School and Oxford. Called to the Bar in 1902. Practised in Chancery Division till 1937. County Court Judge 1937–52. Served as soldier 1914–18. Son-in-law of Sir Alfred Hopkinson. Chaired 1954 Departmental Committee on the Adoption of Children whose findings are known as the Hurst Report.

Inskip, Lady Augusta, 1876–1967 (Chairman of the National Children Adoption Association)
Daughter of the 7th Earl of Glasgow, and widow of Charles Orr Ewing, Unionist MP. Married Thomas Inskip in 1914. Involved with the NCAA for many years and Chairman in the 1940s.

Inskip, Sir Thomas, 1876–1947 (introduced adoption bill in 1924)
Lawyer, Conservative MP and government minister (Central division, Bristol 1918–29; Fareham 1931–9). Educated at Clifton College and Cambridge, called to the Bar in 1899. Served in naval intelligence during the First World War. Held legal positions throughout the Conservative governments during the 1920s and 1930s (solicitor general and attorney-general). Brought up in deeply religious evangelical environment and played major role in defeating proposed revisions to the Prayer Book in 1927 and 28. In 1936 appointed Minister for Co-ordination of Defence, in 1939 Lord Chancellor and in 1940, Lord Chief Justice. Created Viscount Caldecote of Bristol in 1939.

Jewson, Dorothy, 1884–1964 (member of Tomlin Committee)
Labour MP (Norwich 1923–4). Educated at Norwich High School and Cambridge. Teacher, Independent Labour Party activist. With Dora Russell founded Workers' Birth Control Group in 1924. Norwich City Councillor 1927–36.

Joynson-Hicks, Sir William 'Jix', 1865–1932 (Home Secretary when 1926 Adoption Act passed)
Lawyer, Conservative MP and government minister (North-West division, Manchester 1908–10; Brentford 1911–18; Twickenham 1918–29). Educated at Merchant Taylors School, admitted as a solicitor 1887. Held various government positions in the 1922–4 Conservative government and was Home Secretary throughout the 1924–9 administration, where was responsible for the 1929 Act which finally gave the vote to all citizens over 21. Like his colleague, Sir Thomas Inskip, he was a religious evangelical and active in the campaign to defeat a revised Prayer Book. Created Viscount Brentford of Newick in Sussex in 1929.

Maclachlan, A. B. (Alan Bruce), 1874–1955 (Ministry of Health official involved with establishment of Horsbrugh Committee)
Civil servant. Educated at Merchant Taylor's School and Cambridge. Joined Local Government Board in 1897; Assistant Secretary, 1919–28, and Principal Assistant Secretary, Ministry of Health, 1928–37.

Macnaghten, Hon. Sir Malcolm, 1869–1955 (introduced adoption bill in 1924)
Lawyer and Ulster Unionist MP (North Derry 1922, Londonderry 1922–8). Educated at Eton and Cambridge. Called to the Bar in 1894. High Court Judge 1928–47.

Mallon, James Joseph, 1875–1961 (member of Horsbrugh Committee)
Warden of Toynbee Hall 1919–54. Educated at Owens College, Manchester. Member of thirteen of the first Trade Boards set up after 1909 and involved with many committees and public organisations throughout his life.

Manning, Brian O'Donoghue, 1891–1964 (member of Horsbrugh Committee)
Chartered accountant. Educated at St Stephen's Green School, Dublin and Dover College. Director of several companies and member of various governmental bodies.

Nield, Sir Basil Edward, 1903–96 (introduced Adoption of Children Act 1949)
Lawyer and Conservative MP. Educated at Oxford. Called to the Bar in 1925. MP for Chester 1940–59. Appointed Recorder of Manchester in 1956 and to the High

Court in 1960. In 1949 introduced the Adoption Bill which eventually became the Adoption of Children Act 1949.

Nicholson, Reginald, 1869–1946 (introduced adoption bill in 1922)
Coalition Liberal MP (Doncaster division, Yorkshire 1918–22). Educated at Charterhouse. Worked for Bengal Nagpur Railway 1894, manager of *The Times* 1910–15.

Norman, Lady Priscilla Montagu, 1899–1991 (member of Horsbrugh Committee)
Member London County Council 1925–8, 1931–5. Wife of the Governor of the Bank of England, Montagu Collet Norman. A founder of the National Association for Mental Health (later Mind) and chairman of its executive committee for 15 years. Mother of the journalist Sir Peregrine Worsthorne.

Norman, The Hon. Lady Priscilla, died 1964 (member of Hopkinson Committee)
During First World War established, with her husband Sir Henry Norman, the British Hospital at Wimereux which treated 3600 officers and men. Mentioned in dispatches, awarded 1914 Star, British War and Allied Victory medals. Trustee of the Imperial War Museum. Committee member Women's Liberal Federation, Liberal Women's Suffrage Union. Women's Volunteer Service driver during Second World War. Chairman, National Adoption Society for five years.

Pimlott, John Alfred Ralph (John), 1909–69 (secretary to Horsbrugh Committee)
Civil servant. Educated at Hele's School, Exeter and Oxford. Joined Home Office 1932. Various positions in civil service. Assistant Under-Secretary of State, Department of Education and Science from 1960.

Princess Alice, Countess of Athlone, 1883–1981 (President of National Children Adoption Association)
Born at Windsor Castle and died in Kensington Palace. The daughter of Queen Victoria's son, Prince Leopold Saxe-Coburg, the Duke of Albany, she married Queen Mary's brother, the Earl of Athlone. When she died she was Queen Victoria's last surviving grandchild. Her husband was Governor-General of South Africa 1924–31 so for much of the 1920s she was away. Active patron of many institutions as well as the NCAA and was also 'the first member of the royal family publicly to advocate birth control'.[2]

Puxley, Zoë Lavallin, 1882–1970 (Ministry of Health official involved with adoption issues)
Civil servant. Formerly General Secretary of Ranyard House (mission which provided district nurses across London). Appointed to the Local Government Board (which became the Ministry of Health), and was a Principal in the Maternal and Child Welfare department. Subsequently Assistant Secretary of the Public Health Division of the Ministry of Health. Involved with many organisations – chairman of National Council for the Unmarried Mother and Her Child management committee in the 1950s, of the Chadwick Trust in the 1940s, and on the executive committee of the Central Council for District Nursing in London.

Russell, Geoffrey W., 1877–1956 (member of both Tomlin and Horsbrugh Committees)
Lawyer. Admitted as solicitor in 1903. Stayed in private practice until his retirement in 1939, and from 1918 was a partner in Parker, Garrett & Co . Lifelong Liberal. Appointed to several government committees.

Russell, Mrs Lilian (C. E. B), 1875–1949 (member of Hopkinson Committee)
Civil servant and voluntary worker. Educated at Queen's College. Inspector for the Children's Department, Home Office 1917–23. Was Dr Albert Schweitzer's first British woman helper and assisted him at his hospital at Lambaréné in French Equatorial Africa. Also worked in leper colonies in SE Nigeria, 1937–8 and 1946, and in Siam, 1939.

Schuster, Baron Claud, 1869–1956 (head of Lord Chancellor's Office throughout 1920s and 1930s)
Civil servant. Educated at Winchester and Oxford, called to the Bar in 1895. Secretary to London Government Act Commission 1899–1902; then worked in various legal advisory posts for Sir Robert Morant at the Board of Education, 1903–11. Went with Morant to National Insurance in 1911, and in 1915 became Clerk of the Crown in Chancery and Permanent Secretary in the Lord Chancellor's Office where he advised ten successive chancellors until his retirement in 1944. Created Baron in 1944.

Seddon, James Andrew, 1868–1939 (member of Hopkinson Committee)
Labour MP (Newton, Lancs 1906–10); National Democratic and Labour Party MP (Hanley 1918–22); unsuccessful Conservative candidate for Hanley, 1923. Educated at schools in Huyton and Prescot. Trade Union organiser. President of the Trades Union Congress, 1914.

Sherwood, Frederic William, 1864–1931 (member of Hopkinson Committee)
Lawyer. Educated at Reading School and Oxford. Called to the Bar in 1890. Recorder of Worcester. A founding member of National Council for the Unmarried Mother and Her Child.

Shortt, Edward, 1862–1935 (Home Secretary who set up Hopkinson Committee)
Lawyer, Liberal MP and government minister (Newcastle-upon-Tyne 1910–22). Educated at Durham School, Durham University, called to the Bar 1890. Recorder of Sunderland 1907–18. Appointed Chief Secretary of Ireland 1918 and Home Secretary 1919–22. Later appointed to several governmental committees and appointed 2nd President of the British Board of Film Censors in 1929.

Stutchbury, H. O. (Harold Owen), c. 1875–1966 (Ministry of Health official involved with adoption issues)
Civil servant. Educated at Oxford. Principal at the Local Government Board and subsequently Ministry of Health. Member, original executive committee of National Council for the Unmarried Mother and Her Child, representing the LGB. Also executive committee member of the Central Council for District Nursing in London.

Biographical Notes 251

Tate, Mavis Constance, 1893–1947 (campaigned for inquiry into adoption societies)
National Conservative MP (West Willesden 1931–5; Frome, Somerset 1935–45). Educated at St. Paul's Girls' School. 'One of the few women MPs of this period who was prepared to call herself a feminist in the House of Commons.'[3] Strong supporter of equal pay, birth control and abortion law reform. President of the Women's Freedom League during the War. Led ultimately successful campaign against the Civilian War Injuries legislation which provided unequal compensation to single men and women.

Tomlin, Thomas James Cheshyre, 1867–1935 (chaired Tomlin Committee)
Judge. Educated at Harrow and Oxford, called to the Bar 1891. Appointed junior equity counsel to various government departments and after taking silk engaged in a wide variety of cases in the House of Lords and the Privy Council. In 1923 appointed a High Court judge and in 1929 a lord of appeal, with a life peerage as Baron Tomlin of Ash in Kent. Chaired several commissions, the most famous of which was on the civil service 1929–31.

Ward, Dame Irene, 1895–1980 (campaigned for Adoption of Children (Regulation) Act 1939 to be implemented)
Conservative MP (Wallsend 1931–45, Tynemouth 1950–74). Created Baroness Ward of North Tyneside 1974. Educated at Newcastle Church High School. Chairman of the Woman Power Committee during the war. Concerned with issues affecting women such as equal pay and working conditions and campaigned against sex discrimination throughout her parliamentary career. The longest-serving woman MP (38 years).

Wilson-Fox, Hon. Mrs Eleanor Birch, c. 1871–1963 (member of Tomlin Committee)
Educated at Graham Street High School. Widow of Henry Wilson-Fox, MP. Chaired many committees such as Hackney War Pensions Committee, South African Comforts Committee 1914–18, Women's Advisory Committee League of Nations Union, 1931–5; Vice Chairman, Joint Parliamentary Advisory Council.

Bibliography

Archival sources

The National Archives – files substantially consulted:
Cabinet Office
CAB 102/771 – Illegitimacy and Unmarried Mothers

Home Office
HO 45/11540 – CHILDREN: Adoption of Children Bills 1922 and 1923. Report of Committee on Child Adoption
HO 45/12642 – CHILDREN: Adoption of Children Bills, 1924–1926. Report of the Tomlin Committee, 1925
HO 45/12695 – CHILDREN: Adoption of Children Act, 1926: operation of the Act. Adoption of Children (Summary Jurisdiction) Rules, 1926
HO 45/14188 – CHILDREN: Children's Branch Reports, 1923–1928.
HO 45/14607 – CHILDREN: Child adoption; protection of infant life. The inspection of voluntary homes
HO 45/17061 – CHILDREN: Adoption of Children Act 1926: general papers
HO 45/17115 – CHILDREN: Report of the Departmental Committee on Adoption Societies and Agencies 1937
HO 45/18243 – CHILDREN: Adoption of Children (Regulation) Bill, 1938
HO 45/19299 – CHILDREN: Adoption of Children (Regulation) Act, 1939
HO 45/19300 – CHILDREN: Adoption of Children (Regulation) Act, 1939
HO 45/20466 – CHILDREN: Adoption of Children Act, 1926: points of law and practice
HO 45/20467 – CHILDREN: Adoption of Children Act, 1926: points of law and practice
HO 144/16063 – CHILDREN: Adoption of Children Act, 1926: operation of the Act 1927–1932
HO 144/22596 – CHILDREN: Homeless Children's Aid and Adoption Society, 1931–1946

Supreme Court of Judicature
J 84/172: J 84/159: J 84/179: J 84/197: J 84/194

Ministry of Health
MH 51/591 – Adoption of Children Act 1926; Adoption of Children [Regulation] Act 1939
MH 55/276 – Child Adoption: Home Office Committee
MH 55/1635 – Adoption of Children (Regulation) Act 1939: Departmental committee on adoption societies
MH 55/1636 – Adoption of Children (Regulation) Act, 1939: miscellaneous enquiries 1941–47

MH 57/53 – National Children Adoption Association; application for licence
MH 102/1364 – Adoption of Children: legal aspects
MH 102/2256 – Adoption of Children: notes of meeting held at Home Office Care of Children Committee
MH 102/2260 – Adoption of Children: copy of evidence given by Mr B. E. Astbury
MH 102/2261 – Adoption of Children: Judge Gamon's unofficial committee

General Register Office
RG 41/20 – Adoption of Children Act 1926
RG 48/131 – Solicitors still drawing up deeds of adoption despite the Adoption Act 1926
RG 48/1422 – Adoption of Children Act 1926: interpretation of Section II
RG 48/1424 – Adoption of Children (Scotland) Bill 1930: correspondence and papers
RG 48/1428 – Adoption of Children Act 1926: suggested amendment regarding search of index to Adopted Children Register
RG 48/1431 – Issue of original birth certificates of adopted children
RG 48/1434 – Adoption order set aside: 1944–5

Lord Chancellor's Office
LCO 2/1159 – Adopted Children Register, directions for recording of birth dates and names in: memoranda and legal opinions on
LCO 2/1162 – Adoption Societies and Agencies, Committee of inquiry into activities of: evidence for, and report
LCO 2/2642 – Adoption of Children Act 1926: 1939–1945

Metropolitan Police Office
MEPO 2/4237 – Home Office enquiry into methods pursued by Adoption Societies or other agencies

Privy Council
PC 12/73: Charter: National Children Adoption Association

London Metropolitan Archives

LABG 185 – Lambeth Board of Guardians: Register of Adoption, 1901–30
LCC/CH/M/1/29 – Adoption of Children Act – 1926
LCC/CH/M/12/11 – Adoption of Children (Regulation) Act – 1939
LCC/CH/M/20/1 – Adoption of Children Correspondence from the Education Officer – 1932–6
LCC/CH/M/20/2 – Adoption of Children – Paper re 'The Working of Children Act', 1926 read at conference of superintendents of school attendance Depts – 1929
LCC/CH/M/20/4 – Adoption of Children in Council Institutions – General Policy – 1930–2
LCC/CH/M/20/6 – Adoption of Children Bill & Act 1926
LCC/CH/M/20/7 – Adoption of Children Act 1926 – 'Ad Litem' Functions – Cases Section of Special Services sub-committee – General Papers – 1926–34
LCC/CH/M/22/6 – Registration of Adoption Societies – Crusade of Rescue, 1941–59

LCC/CH/M/23/2 – Registration of Adoption Societies – Southwark Catholic Rescue Society, 1943–58
LCC/CH/M/23/4 – Registration of Adoption Societies – Children's Aid Society, 1945–58
LCC/CH/M/24/2 – Registration of Adoption Societies – Church of England Children's Society (formerly, Waifs and Strays Society), 1945–9
LCC/CH/M/24/3 – Registration of Adoption Societies – Church of England Children's Society (formerly, Waifs and Strays Society) – The Church Adoption Society – 1943–4
LCC/CH/M/24/4 – Registration of Adoption Societies – Church of England Children's Society (formerly, Waifs and Strays Society) – The Church Adoption Society – 1944–9
LCC/CH/M/25/1 – Registration of Adoption Societies – National Children Adoption Association – 1943–57
LCC/CH/M/25/2 – Registration of Adoption Societies – Baptist Union Adoption Society, 1948–59
LCC/CH/M/25/3 – Registration of Adoption Societies – National Children Adoption Association – National Children's Home & Orphanage – 1944–51
STMBG/182/01-20 – Agreements for Adoption of Children – 1867–1918

Elizabeth Roberts Archive, Centre for North-West Regional Studies, Lancaster University

Social and family life in Preston, 1890–1940
Social life in Barrow and Lancaster, 1890–1940
Family and social life in Barrow, Lancaster and Preston, 1940–70

The Women's Library

NCUMC records and press cuttings

Bath Records Office

Register Office 'Minute Book – Adoption of Children Act 1926', 1927–33

Devon Record Office, Exeter

Files relating to Miss Clara Andrew

East Sussex County Records Office, Lewes

Various files

Family Records Centre

Births and deaths records

Papers in the Collection of Patricia Wreford King

Letters, notes, reports, minutes relating to Miss Clara Andrew and the National Children Adoption Association

Parliamentary material

Publications

Report of the Committee on Child Adoption, 1921. Cmd 1254.
Child Adoption Committee – First Report, 1924–5. Cmd 2401.
Child Adoption Committee – Second Report, 1924–5. Cmd 2469.
Child Adoption Committee – Third & Final Report, 1926. Cmd 2711.
Report of the Departmental Committee on Adoption Societies and Agencies, 1936–7. Cmd 5499.
Report of the Care of Children Committee, 1946. Cmd 6922.
Department of Health, *Adoption: The Future* (HMSO 1993).
Hansard.
The Registrar-General's Statistical Reviews of England & Wales.

Legislation

Adoption of Children Act, 1926
Adoption of Children (Regulation) Act, 1939
Adoption of Children Act, 1949
Adoption Act, 1950
Adoption and Children Act, 2002
Children and Young Persons Act, 1932
Children and Young Persons Act, 1933
Guardianship of Infants Act, 1925
Legitimacy Act, 1926

Secondary sources

Books and reports

Abbott, Mary, *Family Affairs: A History of the Family in 20th Century England.* London: Routledge, 2003.
Addis, Robina S., Salzberger, Francesca, Rabl, Elizabeth, *A Survey Based on Adoption Case Records*. London: National Association for Mental Health, 1955.
Ariès, Philippe, *Centuries of Childhood: A Social History of Family Life.* Translated from the French by Robert Baldick, New York: Vintage Books, 1962.
Associated Societies for the Care and Maintenance of Infants, 'Report of Select Committee Appointed to Examine the Principle and Practice of Child Adoption'. London: c. April, 1920.
Baird, Julia, *Imagine This: Growing Up with My Brother John Lennon.* London: Hodder & Stoughton, 2007.
Banks, Olive, *The Biographical Dictionary of British Feminists*, vol. 2: A Supplement, 1900–1945. Herts: Harvester Wheatsheaf, 1990.
Bean, Philip (ed.), *Adoption: Essays in Social Policy, Law and Sociology.* London: Tavistock, 1984.
Bean, P. & Melville, J., *Lost Children of the Empire: The Untold Story of Britain's Child Migrants*. London: Unwin Hyman, 1989.
Beddoe, Deirdre, *Back to Home and Duty: Women between the Wars 1918–1939.* London: Pandora, 1989.

Behlmer, George K., *Child Abuse and Moral Reform in England, 1870–1908*. Stanford, CA: Stanford University Press, 1982.
Behlmer, George K., *Friends of the Family: The English Home and Its Guardians, 1850–1940*. Stanford, CA: Stanford University Press, 1998.
Benet, Mary Kathleen, *The Character of Adoption*. London: Cape, 1976.
Berebitsky, Julie, *Like Our Very Own: Adoption and the Changing Culture of Motherhood, 1851–1950*. Lawrence, KS: University Press of Kansas, 2000.
Berridge, David, *Children's Homes*. Oxford: Blackwell, 1985.
Blythe, Ronald, *The Age of Illusion: England in the Twenties and Thirties 1919–40*. London: Penguin Books, 1963.
Bock, Gisela & Thane, Pat (eds), *Maternity and Gender Policies: Women and the Rise of the European Welfare States, 1880s–1950s*. London: Routledge, 1991.
Bortolaia Silva, Elizabeth (ed.), *Good Enough Mothering? Feminist Perspectives on Lone Motherhood*. London: Routledge, 1996.
Bourke, Joanna, *Working-Class Cultures in Britain 1890–1960: Gender, Class and Ethnicity*. London: Routledge, 1994.
Bready, J. Wesley, *Doctor Barnardo: Physician, Pioneer, Prophet*. 1st ed. London: George Allen & Unwin, 1930.
Bridge, Caroline & Swindells, Heather, *Adoption: The Modern Law*. Bristol: Family Law, 2003.
Burnett, John, *A Social History of Housing 1815–1985*. London: Methuen, 1986.
Butler, David & Butler, Gareth, *British Political Facts 1900–1994*. 7th ed. London: Macmillan, 1994.
The Buttle Trust, 'Prebendary Buttle and the Buttle Trust'. 1978.
Campbell, Janet M., *Report on the Physical Welfare of Mothers and Children: England & Wales*, vol. 2. Liverpool: The Carnegie United Kingdom Trust, 1917.
Carp, E. Wayne (ed.), *Adoption in America: Historical Perspectives*. Ann Arbor: University of Michigan Press, 2002.
Carp, E. Wayne, *Family Matters: Secrecy and Disclosure in the History of Adoption*. London: Harvard University Press, 1998.
Chinn, Carl, *They Worked All Their Lives: Women of the Urban Poor in England, 1880–1939*. Manchester: Manchester University Press, 1988.
Clarke Hall, W. & Clarke Hall, Justin, *The Law of Adoption and Guardianship of Infants*. London, 1928.
Coomes, David, *Dorothy L. Sayers: A Careless Rage for Life*. Oxford: Lion, 1992.
Cooter, Roger (ed.), *In the Name of the Child: Health and Welfare, 1880–1940*. London: Routledge, 1992.
Crawford, Anne, et al.(eds), *The Europa Biographical Dictionary of British Women*. London: Europa Publications, 1983.
Cretney, Stephen, *Family Law in the Twentieth Century: A History*. Oxford: Oxford University Press, 2003.
Crick, Bernard, *George Orwell: A Life*. London: Secker & Warburg, 1980.
Crossick, Geoffrey (ed.), *The Lower Middle Class in Britain 1870–1914*. London: Croom Helm, 1977.
Cunningham, Hugh, *Children and Childhood in Western Society since 1500*. London: Longman, 1995.
Davidoff, Leonore, Doolittle, Megan, Fink, Janet & Holden, Katherine, *The Family Story: Blood, Contract and Intimacy, 1830–1960*. London: Longman, 1999.
Davies, Hunter, *Relative Strangers: A History of Adoption and a Tale of Triplets*. London: Time Warner Books, 2003.

Davin, Anna, *Growing Up Poor: Home, School and Street in London 1870–1914*. London: Rivers Oram, 1996.
Derrick, Deborah (ed.), *Illegitimate: The Experience of People Born Outside Marriage*. London: NCOPF, 1986.
Douglas, Anthony and Philpot, Terry (eds), *Adoption: Changing Families, Changing Times*. London: Routledge, 2003.
Drawbell, James Wedgwood, *Experiment in Adoption*. London: Victor Gollancz, 1935.
Dwork, Deborah, *War Is Good for Babies and Other Young Children: A History of the Infant and Child Welfare Movement in England 1898–1918*. London: Tavistock, 1987.
Dyhouse, Carol, *Feminism and the Family in England 1880–1939*. Oxford: Blackwell, 1989.
Ellison, Mary, *The Deprived Child and Adoption*. London: Pan Books, 1963.
Else, Anne, *A Question of Adoption: Closed Stranger Adoption in New Zealand 1944–1974*. Wellington: Bridget Williams Books, 1991.
Evans, Tanya, *Unfortunate Objects: Lone Mothers in Eighteenth-Century London*. Basingstoke: Palgrave Macmillan, 2005.
Feast, Julia, Marwood, Michael, Seabrook, Sue, Webb, Elizabeth, *Preparing for Reunion: Experiences from the Adoption Circle*. New ed. London: The Children's Society, 1998.
Feldman, David & Stedman Jones, Gareth (eds), *Metropolis London: Histories and Representations since 1800*. London: Routledge, 1989.
Ferguson, Sheila and Fitzgerald, Hilda, *Studies in the Social Services: History of the Second World War*, UK Civil Series. London: Longmans & HMSO, 1954.
Fisher, Lettice, 'Twenty-One Years and After, 1918–1946: The Story of the National Council for the Unmarried Mother and Her Child'. 2nd ed. London: NCUMC, 1946.
Giles, Judy, *Women, Identity and Private Life in Britain, 1900–50*. London: Macmillan, 1995.
Gittins, Diana, *Fair Sex: Family Size and Structure 1900–39*. London: Hutchinson, 1982.
Gittins, Diana, *The Family in Question: Changing Households and Familiar Ideologies*. London: Macmillan, 1985.
Glendinning, Victoria, *Rebecca West: A Life*. London: Weidenfeld, 1987.
Gloversmith, Frank (ed.), *Class, Culture and Social Change: A New View of the 1930s*. Brighton: Harvester Press, 1980.
Gordon, Linda, *Heroes of Their Own Lives: The Politics and History of Family Violence: Boston 1880–1960*. New York: Viking, 1988.
Graham-Dixon, Sue, 'Never Darken My Door: Working for Single Parents and Their Children 1918–1978'. London: NCOPF, 1981.
Graveson, R. H. & Crane, F. R. (eds), *A Century of Family Law*. London: Sweet & Maxwell, 1957.
Grey, Eleanor, in collaboration with Blunden, Ronald M, *A Survey of Adoption in Great Britain*, Home Office Research Studies 10, London: HMSO, 1971.
Haimes, Erica & Timms, Noel, *Adoption, Identity and Social Policy: The Search for Distant Relatives*. Hants: Gower, 1985.
Haimes, Erica & Timms, Noel, 'Access to Birth Records and Counselling of Adopted Persons Under Section 26 of the Children Act, 1975', Final Report to the DHSS, University of Newcastle upon Tyne, May 1983.

Hall, Lesley A. *Hidden Anxieties: Male Sexuality, 1900–1950*. Cambridge: Polity Press, 1991.

Hall, Penelope M. & Howes, Ismene V., *The Church in Social Work: A Study of Moral Welfare Work undertaken by the Church of England*. London: Routledge & Kegan Paul, 1965.

Hall, Ruth (ed.), *Dear Dr Stopes: Sex in the 1920s*. London: Andre Deutsch, 1978.

Halsey, A. H. (ed.), *Traditions of Social Policy: Essays in Honour of Violet Butler*. Oxford: Basil Blackwell, 1976.

Halsey, A. H., *British Social Trends since 1900*. Basingstoke: Macmillan, 1988.

Hardyment, Christina, *Dream Babies: Child Care from Locke to Spock*. London: Jonathan Cape, 1983.

Haste, Cate, *Rules of Desire: Sex in Britain: World War One to the Present*. London: Chatto & Windus, 1992.

Hendrick, Harry, *Child Welfare: England 1872–1989*. London: Routledge, 1994.

Heywood, Jean S., *Children in Care: The Development of the Service for the Deprived Child*. 3rd ed. London: Routledge, 1978.

Hoksbergen, R. A. C., *Adoption in Worldwide Perspective: A Review of Programs, Policies and Legislation in 14 Countries*. Den Haag: Swets & Zeitlinger, 1986.

Holden, Katherine, *The Shadow of Marriage: Singleness in England, 1914–60*. Manchester: Manchester University Press, 2007.

Holloway, Sara (ed), *Family Wanted: Adoption Stories*. London: Granta Books, 2005.

Hope, E. W., *Report on the Physical Welfare of Mothers and Children: England & Wales*, vol. 1, Liverpool: The Carnegie United Kingdom Trust, 1917.

Hopkinson, Sir Alfred, *Penultima*. London: Martin Hopkinson, 1930.

Hopkirk, Mary, *Nobody Wanted Sam: The Story of the Unwelcomed Child, 1530–1948*. London: John Murray, 1949.

Howe, David & Feast, Julia, *Adoption, Search & Reunion: The Long-Term Experience of Adopted Adults*. London: The Children's Society, 2000.

Humphreys, Margaret, *Empty Cradles*. London: Doubleday, 1994.

Humphries, Steve, *A Secret World of Sex: Forbidden Fruit: The British Experience 1900–1950*. London: Sidgwick & Jackson, 1988.

Humphries, Steve & Gordon, Pamela, *A Labour of Love: The Experience of Parenthood in Britain 1900–1950*. London: Sidgwick & Jackson, 1993.

Hurst, Sir Gerald, *Closed Chapters*. Manchester: Manchester University Press, 1942.

Hutchinson's Woman's Who's Who. London: Hutchinson, 1934.

Iredale, Sarah, *Reunions: True Stories of Adoptees' Meetings with Their Natural Parents*. London: The Stationery Office, 1997.

Jackson, Alan A., *The Middle Classes 1900–1950*. Nairn: David St John Thomas, 1991.

Jeffreys, Sheila, *The Spinster and Her Enemies: Feminism and Sexuality 1880–1930*. London: Pandora, 1985.

Katz, Michael B. & Sachβe, Christoph (eds), *The Mixed Economy of Social Welfare: Public/Private Relations in England, Germany and the United States* Baden-Baden: Nomos Verlagsgesellschaft, 1996.

Katz, Sanford N., Eekelaar, John & Maclean, Mavis (eds), *Cross Currents: Family Law and Policy in the United States and England*. Oxford: Oxford University Press, 2000.

Kelsall, R. K., *Higher Civil Servants in Britain: From 1870 to the Present Day*. London: Routledge & Kegan Paul, 1955.
Kellmer Pringle, M. L. *Adoption Facts and Fallacies: A Review of Research in the United States, Canada and Great Britain between 1948 and 1965*. London: Longmans, 1967.
Kiernan, Kathleen, Land, Hilary & Lewis, Jane, *Lone Motherhood in Twentieth-Century Britain: From Footnote to Front Page*. Oxford: Oxford University Press, 1998.
Kornitzer, Margaret, *Child Adoption in the Modern World*. London: Putnam, 1952.
Lane-Claypon, Janet E., *The Child Welfare Movement*. London: G Bell, 1920.
Lawrence, Jon & Starkey, Pat (eds), *Child Welfare and Social Action in the Nineteenth and Twentieth Centuries*. Liverpool: Liverpool University Press, 2001.
Lewis, Jane, *The Politics of Motherhood: Child and Maternal Welfare in England, 1900–1939*. London: Croom Helm, 1980.
Lewis, Jane, *Women in England 1870–1950: Sexual Divisions and Social Change*. Brighton: Wheatsheaf Books, 1984.
Lewis, Jane (ed.), *Labour and Love: Women's Experience of Home and Family, 1850–1940*. Oxford: Blackwell, 1986.
Lewis, Jane, *The End of Marriage? Individualism and Intimate Relations*. Cheltenham: Edward Elgar, 2001.
Lewis, Roy & Maude, Angus, *The English Middle Classes*. London: Phoenix House, 1949.
Light, Alison, *Forever England: Femininity, Literature and Conservatism between the Wars*. London: Routledge, 1991.
Light, Alison, *Mrs Woolf and the Servants: The Hidden Heart of Domestic Service*. London: Penguin, 2007.
McCleary, G. F., *The Maternity and Child Welfare Movement*. London: PS King & Son, 1935.
Mackaskill, Hilary, 'From the Workhouse to the Workplace: 75 Years of One-Parent Family Life 1918–1993'. London: NCOPF, 1993.
Macnicol, John, *The Movement for Family Allowances 1918–1945: A Study in Social Policy Development*. London: Heinemann, 1980.
McClure, Ruth K., *Coram's Children: The London Foundling Hospital in the Eighteenth Century*. London: Yale University Press, 1981.
McKibbin, Ross, *Classes and Cultures: England 1918–1951*. Oxford: Oxford University Press, 1998.
McLeod, Hugh, 'White Collar Values and the Role of Religion'. In *The Lower Middle Class in Britain 1870–1914*, edited by Geoffrey Crossick. London: Croom Helm, 1977.
McWhinnie, Alexina, *Adopted Children: How They Grow Up: A Study of Their Adjustment as Adults*. London: Routledge & Kegan Paul, 1967.
Magnusson, Magnus (ed.), *Chambers Biographical Dictionary*. Edinburgh: Chambers, 1990.
Marcus, Jane (selected and introduced). *The Young Rebecca: Writings of Rebecca West 1911–17*. London: Macmillan, 1982.
Marshall, A. & McDonald, M., *The Many-Sided Triangle: Adoption in Australia*. Melbourne: Melbourne University Press, 2001.
Martindale, Hilda, *Women Servants of the State 1870–1938: A History of Women in the Civil Service*. London: George Allen & Unwin, 1938.

Melosh, Barbara, *Strangers and Kin: The American Way of Adoption*. Cambridge, MA: Harvard University Press, 2002.

Middleton, Nigel, *When Family Failed: The Treatment of Children in the Care of the Community during the First Half of the Twentieth Century*. London: Victor Gollancz, 1971.

Mitchell, B. R., with collaboration of Phyllis Deane. *Abstract of British Historical Statistics*. Cambridge: Cambridge University Press, 1962.

Moorehead, Caroline, *Martha Gellhorn: A Life*. London: Chatto, 2003.

Morgan, Patricia, *Adoption and the Care of Children: The British and American Experience*. London: IEA Health and Welfare Unit, 1998.

Mowat, Charles Loch, *Britain between the Wars 1918–1940*. 1968 edition. London: Methuen.

Murdoch, Lydia, *Imagined Orphans: Poor Families, Child Welfare, and Contested Citizenship in London*. New Brunswick, NJ: Rutgers University Press, 2006.

The National Council of Women of Great Britain & Ireland, Occasional Paper, No. 86.

NCUMC Manifesto, 'The National Council for the Unmarried Mother and Her Child (and for the Widowed or Deserted Mother in Need)'. London, 1918.

NCVO Briefing, 'The Changing Role of Voluntary Agencies in Adoption'. 1982.

Normanton, Helena, *Everyday Law for Women*. London: Ivor Nicholson & Watson, 1932.

NSPCC – Annual Reports.

Oliver, C. & Aggleton, P., *Coram's Children: Growing Up in the Care of the Foundling Hospital 1900–1955*. London: Thomas Coram Research Unit, 2000.

Oxford Dictionary of National Biography, various volumes. Oxford: Oxford University Press, various dates.

Parr, Joy, *Labouring Children: British Immigrant Apprentices to Canada, 1869–1924*. London: Croom Helm, 1980.

Pearce, Nasreen, *Adoption: The Law and Practice*. London: Fourmat, 1991.

Peel, Robert A. (ed.), *Essays in the History of Eugenics*. London: Galton Institute, 1998.

Peele, Gillian & Cook, Chris (eds), *The Politics of Reappraisal 1918–1939* London: Macmillan, 1975.

Pettit, P. H. 'Parental Control and Guardianship'. In *A Century of Family Law*, edited by R. H. Graveson and F. R. Crane. London: Sweet & Maxwell, 1957.

Pfeffer, Naomi, *The Stork and the Syringe: A Political History of Reproductive Medicine*. Cambridge: Polity Press, 1993.

Pinchbeck, Ivy & Hewitt, Margaret, *Children in English Society, vol. 2: From the Eighteenth Century to the Children Act 1948*. London: Routledge, 1973.

Princess Alice, *For My Grandchildren: Some Reminiscences of Her Royal Highness Princess Alice*. London: Evans Bros, 1966.

Pugh, Martin, *Women and the Women's Movement in Britain, 1914–1959*. London: Macmillan, 1992.

Puxon, Margaret, *The Family and the Law: The Laws of Marriage, Separation and Divorce*. London: Macgibbon, 1967.

Rathbone, Eleanor, *The Disinherited Family*. London: Allen & Unwin, 1924.

Rathbone, Eleanor, *The Ethics and Economics of Family Endowment*. London: Epworth Press, 1927.

Rathbone, Eleanor, *The Case for Family Allowances*. London: Penguin Books, 1940.
Raynor, Lois, *The Adopted Child Comes of Age*. London: George Allen & Unwin, 1980.
Renier, Olive, *Before the Bonfire*. Warwickshire: P. Drinkwater, 1984.
Reynolds, Barbara. *Dorothy L. Sayers: Her Life and Soul*. London: Hodder & Stoughton, 1993.
Richards, Margaret, *Adoption*. Bristol: Family Law, 1989.
Roberts, E., *A Woman's Place: An Oral History of Working-Class Women, 1890–1940*. Oxford: Blackwell, 1984.
Rockel, J. and Ryburn, M., *Adoption Today: Change and Choice in New Zealand*. Auckland: Heinemann/Reed, 1988.
Romero, Patricia W., *E. Sylvia Pankhurst: Portrait of a Radical*. New Haven, CT: Yale University Press, 1987.
Rose, June, *Inside Barnardos: 120 Years of Caring for Children*. London: Futura, 1987.
Rose, Lionel, *The Massacre of the Innocents: Infanticide in Britain 1800–1939*. London: Routledge & Kegan Paul, 1986.
Rose, Lionel, *The Erosion of Childhood: Child Oppression in Britain, 1860–1918*. London: Routledge, 1991.
Ross, Ellen, *Love and Toil: Motherhood in Outcast London, 1870–1918*. Oxford: Oxford University Press, 1993.
Rover, Constance, *Love, Morals and the Feminists*. London: Routledge & Kegan Paul, 1970.
Rudolf, Mildred de M., *Everybody's Children: The Story of the Church of England Children's Society 1921–48*. London: Oxford University Press, 1950.
Savage, Gail, *The Social Construction of Expertise: The English Civil Service and Its Influence, 1919–1939*. Pittsburgh: University of Pittsburgh Press, 1996.
Schwieso, Josh, and Pettit, Peter (eds), *Aspects of the History of British Social Work*. Reading: Faculty of Education & Community Studies, University of Reading, 1995.
Scott, Bonnie Kime (ed.), *Selected Letters of Rebecca West*. New Haven, CT: Yale University Press, 2000.
Seccombe, Wally, *Weathering the Storm: Working-Class Families from the Industrial Revolution to the Fertility Decline*. London: Verso, 1993.
Seglow, Jean, Kellmer Pringle, Mia & Wedge, Peter, *Growing Up Adopted: A Long-term Study of Adopted Children and Their Families*. National Foundation for Educational Research in England and Wales, 1972.
Shorter, Edward, *The Making of the Modern Family*. New York: Basic Books, 1977.
The Shorter Oxford English Dictionary on Historical Principles. 3rd ed. Oxford: Oxford University Press, 1973.
Skeggs, Beverley, *Formations of Class and Gender: Becoming Respectable*. London: Sage, 1997.
Slater, Elliot & Woodside, Moya, *Patterns of Marriage: A Study of Marriage Relationships in the Urban Working Classes*. London: Cassell & Company, 1951.
Smart, Carol, (ed.), *Regulating Womanhood: Historical Essays on Marriage, Motherhood and Sexuality*. London: Routledge, 1992.

Soloway, Richard, *Demography and Degeneration: Eugenics and the Declining Birthrate in Twentieth-Century Britain*. Chapel Hill, NC: University of North Carolina Press, 1995.
Spender, Dale, *Time and Tide Wait for No Man*. London: Pandora Press, 1984.
Stafford, Georgina (compiled). *Where to Find Adoption Records: A Guide for Counsellors*. London: British Agencies for Adoption and Fostering (BAAF), 1992.
Steedman, Carolyn Kay, *Landscape for a Good Woman: A Story of Two Lives*. London: Virago, 1986.
Stenton, Michael & Lees, Stephen (eds), *Who's Who of British Members of Parliament, Vol. III, 1919–1945; Vol. IV, 1945–1979*. Brighton: Harvester Press, 1979/1981.
Stone, Olive, *Family Law*. London: Macmillan, 1977.
Szreter, Simon, *Fertility, Class and Gender in Britain, 1860–1940*. Cambridge: Cambridge University Press, 1996.
Taylor, A. J. P., *English History 1914–1945*. Oxford: Oxford University Press, 1965.
Thane, Pat, *Foundations of the Welfare State*. 2nd ed. London: Longman, 1996.
Thane, Pat, 'What Difference Did the Vote Make?' In *Women, Privilege and Power: British Politics 1750 to the Present*, edited by Amanda Vickery. Stanford, CA: Stanford University Press, 2001.
Thompson, F. L. M., *The Rise of Respectable Society: A Social History of Victorian Britain 1830–1900*. London: Fontana Press, 1988.
Thompson, F. M. L. (ed.), *The Cambridge Social History of Britain 1750–1950, Vol. 2: People and Their Environment*. Cambridge: Cambridge University Press, 1990.
Thompson, Paul, *The Edwardians: The Remaking of British Society*. 2nd ed. London: Routledge, 1992.
Thomson, Matthew, *The Problem of Mental Deficiency: Eugenics, Democracy, and Social Policy in Britain c1870–1959*. Oxford: Clarendon Press, 1998.
Tizard, Barbara, *Adoption: A Second Chance*. London: Open Books, 1977.
Tomalin, Claire, *Jane Austen: A Life*. London: Viking, 1997.
Treacher, Amal, and Katz, Ilan (eds), *The Dynamics of Adoption: Social and Personal Perspectives*. London: Jessica Kingsley, 2000.
Triseliotis, John, *Evaluation of Adoption Policy and Practice*. Edinburgh: University of Edinburgh, 1970.
Triseliotis, John, *In Search of Origins: The Experience of Adopted People*. London: Routledge & Kegan Paul, 1973.
Turner, Pat & Elliott, Jenny, *Adoption: Reviewing the Record*. London: NCH Ashwood Project, 1992.
Uglow, Jennifer (ed.), *The Macmillan Dictionary of Women's Biography*. London: Macmillan, 1999.
United Nations Department of Social Affairs, *Study on Adoption of Children*. New York, 1953.
Vibart, Hugh, *Family Allowances in Practice*. London: PS King & Son, 1926.
Vickery, Amanda (ed.), *Women, Privilege and Power: British Politics 1750 to the Present*. Stanford, CA: Stanford University Press, 2001.
Wagner, Gillian, *Barnardo*. London: Weidenfeld and Nicolson, 1979.
Wagner, Gillian, *Children of the Empire*. London: Weidenfeld and Nicolson, 1982.

Walton, Ronald G., *Women in Social Work*. London: Routledge & Kegan Paul, 1975.
Weeks, Jeffrey, *Sex, Politics and Society: The Regulation of Sexuality since 1800*. London: Longman, 1981.
Wells, Sue, *Within Me, Without Me – Adoption: An Open and Shut Case?* London: Scarlet Press, 1994.
White, Cynthia L., *Women's Magazines 1693–1968*. London: Michael Joseph, 1970.
Who's Who, various volumes. London: A&C Black, various dates.
Who Was Who, various volumes. London: A&C Black, various dates.
Williams, Susan A, *Ladies of Influence: Women of the Elite in Interwar Britain*. London, Allen Lane: Penguin Press, 2000.
Woman's Year Book 1923–1924. London: Women Publishers, 1923.
The Women's Who's Who 1934–35. London: Shaw Publishing, 1934.
Woodruff, William, *The Road to Nab End: An Extraordinary Northern Childhood*. London: Abacus, 2002.
Yeo, Eileen Janes, *The Contest for Social Science: Relations and Representations of Gender and Class*. London: Rivers Oram Press, 1996.
Younghusband, Eileen, *The Newest Profession: A Short History of Social Work*. Surrey: IPC Business Press, 1981.
Younghusband, Eileen, 'Report on the Employment and Training of Social Workers'. Edinburgh: Carnegie United Kingdom Trust, 1947.
Younghusband, Eileen, 'Social Work in Britain: A Supplementary Report on the Employment and Training of Social Workers', Edinburgh: Carnegie United Kingdom Trust, 1951.
Zelizer, Viviana A., *Pricing the Priceless Child: The Changing Social Value of Children*. 2nd ed. 1994. Princeton: Princeton University Press, 1985.
Zweiniger-Bargielowska, Ina (ed.), *Women in Twentieth-Century Britain*. Harlow: Pearson Educational, 2001.

Theses

Cook, Hera, 'The Long Sexual Revolution: British Women, Sex and Contraception in the Twentieth Century'. DPhil thesis, University of Sussex, 1999.
Fink, Janet, 'Condemned or Condoned? Investigating the Problem of Unmarried Motherhood in England 1945–1960'. PhD thesis, University of Essex, 1997.
Holden, Katherine, 'The Shadow of Marriage: Single Women in England 1919–1939'. PhD thesis, University of Essex, 1996.
Keating, Jennifer, 'Chosen Children? The Legalisation of Adoption in England and Its Aftermath, 1918–1939'. DPhil thesis, University of Sussex, 2005.
Roberts, G, 'Social and Legal Policy in Child Adoption in England and Wales 1913–1958'. PhD thesis, University of Leicester, 1973.
Tanner, K. F., 'The Life History of Adoption: A Social-Psychological Perspective'. DPhil/MPhil thesis, University of Reading, 1987.
Teague, A. J., 'Social Change, Social Work, and the Adoption of Children', PhD thesis, LSE, University of London, 1987.

Journal articles

'A Spinster Adopter Speaks'. *Child Adoption*, no. 18 (Spring 1956).
'Adoption of Children'. *Charity Organisation Quarterly*, vol. 2, no. 1 (Jan 1928).

'Forty Years of Adoption Work'. Parts 1 & 2, *Child Adoption*, no. 22 (Spring 1957); no. 23 (Summer 1957).

'Mine Was Not a "failed" Adoption'. *Child Adoption*, no. 80 (1975).

'Self-Portrait of an Adopting Mother'. *Child Adoption*, no. 33 (Spring 1960).

'The Adoption of Children Act in Working'. *Solicitor's Journal* (14 Feb 1931).

'The National Adoption Society'. Parts I & II, *Child Adoption*, no. 26 (Spring 1958); no. 27 (Summer 1958).

Anderson, Michael, 'The Emergence of the Modern Life Cycle in Britain'. *Social History*, vol. 10, no. 1 (Jan 1985).

Arnot, Margaret L., 'Infant Death, Child Care and the State: The Baby-Farming Scandal and the First Infant Life Protection Legislation of 1872'. *Continuity and Change*, vol. 9, part 2 (1994): 271–311.

Bailey, Molly, 'Never Say Die'. *Child Adoption*, no. 95 (1979).

Blom-Cooper, L. J., 'Historical Development of Legal Adoption'. *Child Adoption*, no. 20 (Autumn 1956).

Crutcher, Mary E., 'Eighty-Seven Years of Adoption Work'. *Child Adoption*, no. 19 (Summer 1956).

Dale, Pamela, 'Implementing the 1913 Mental Deficiency Act: Competing Priorities and Resource Constraint Evident in the South West of England before 1948'. *Social History of Medicine*, vol. 16, no. 3 (December 2003).

Fink, Janet, 'Private Lives, Public Issues: Moral Panics and "the Family" in 20th-Century Britain'. *Journal for the Study of British Cultures*, vol. 9, no. 2 (2002).

Frost, Ginger, '"The Black Lamb of the Black Sheep": Illegitimacy in the English Working Class, 1850–1939'. *Journal of Social History*, vol. 37, no. 2 (Winter 2003).

Halpin, Hilary, 'Why We Closed'. *Child Adoption*, no. 94 (1978).

Hugh Smith, Nancy, 'As It Was in the Thirties'. *Child Adoption*, no. 80 (1975).

Keating, Jenny, 'Struggle for Identity: Issues Underlying the Enactment of the 1926 Adoption of Children Act'. *University of Sussex Journal of Contemporary History*, issue 3 (Sep 2001). Online –http://www.sussex.ac.uk/history/documents/3._keating_struggle_for_identity.pdf.

Lewis, Jane, 'Adoption: The Nature of Policy Shifts in England and Wales, 1972–2002', *International Journal of Law, Policy and the Family*, vol. 18, no. 2 (August 2004).

Litten, John H., 'The Legalizing of Adoption', *Child Welfare Worker*, vol. 2, no. 8 (October 1921).

McCray Beier, Lucinda, 'We Were Green as Grass: Learning about Sex and Reproduction in Three Working-Class Lancashire Communities, 1900–1970', *Social History of Medicine*, vol. 16, no. 3 (December 2003).

Michaels, Dr Naomi, 'The Historical Development of the Law of Custody and Adoption', *Child Adoption*, no. 55 (1966).

Molloy, Val, 'Identity, Past and Present, in an Historical Child-Care Setting', *Psychodynamic Practice*, vol. 8, no. 2 (2002).

Pring, H. W., 'Pring on Adoption', *Child Adoption*, no. 47 (Summer 1965).

Ryburn, Murray. 'Secrecy and Openness in Adoption: An Historical Perspective', *Social Policy and Administration*, vol. 29, no. 2 (June 1995).

Seccombe, Wally, 'Starting to Stop: Working-Class Fertility Decline in Britain', *Past and Present*, no. 126 (1990).

Shaw, L. A., 'Following up Adoptions', *British Journal of Psychiatric Social Work*, no. 6 (May 1953).

Stanley Smith, A. E., 'The Adoption of Children Act 1926, The Benefit and Some Disadvantages of the Present Law,' *The Child Welfare Worker*, vol. 8, no. 29 (Spring & Summer, 1927).

Thane, Pat, 'What Difference Did the Vote Make? Women in Public and Private Life in Britain since 1918', *Historical Research*, vol. 76, no. 192 (May 2003): 273.

Workman, Joanne, 'Wading through the Mire: An Historiographical Study of the British Women's Movement between the Wars', *University of Sussex Journal of Contemporary History,* issue 2 (April 2001). Online – http://www.sussex.ac.uk/history/documents/2._workman_wading_through_the_mire.pdf.

Journals/newspapers substantially consulted

Charity Organisation Quarterly
Child Adoption (Adoption and Fostering from 1976)
The Child Welfare Worker
Daily Express
Guardian
Time and Tide
The Times

Websites

Department for Children, Schools and Families: www.dcsf.gov.uk
Home Office: www.homeoffice.gov.uk/webwork/hohist.htm
Human Fertilisation and Embryology Authority: www.hfea.gov.uk
National Statistics: www.statistics.gov.uk
Royal Free Hospital Archives Centre: www.royalfreearchives.org.uk
Welsh Assembly Government: new.wales.gov.uk/topics/statistics
10 Downing Street: www.pm.gov.uk

Index

Abbott, Mary 142
Abortion 207
Abstinence 198, 204
Adopted children – see Adoptees
Adopted Children Register 100, 102, 130, 145, 194, 202
Adoptees 4, 7, 51, 57, 75, 92, 98–102, 106, 109–113, 129, 130, 133, 135, 137–143, 179, 184–185, 188, 193–194, 195–196, 199–201
   Home Office 1928 statistics 123–125
   preference for girls over boys 50, 136, 176, 187, 203, 222 (note)
   right to copy of original birth entry 206
Adopters 4, 7, 47, 50–52, 55, 57, 75–76, 86, 99–101, 106, 108–113, 119, 129, 132, 135, 137–143, 155–162, 190–194, 195–196, 199–201
   contemporary debate over who may adopt 211
   Home Office 1928 statistics 123–125
   provisions of Adoption of Children (Regulation) Act 170–172
   single men adopting 111, 125, 141
   single women adopting 42, 51, 125, 138, 141–143, 194
Adoption
   adoption during Second World War 175–184
   adoption of British children overseas 146–147, 148, 163–164, 167–168, 171, 210
   adoption of children from overseas 201, 207–208, 209–210
   adoption outcome surveys 137–139, 158–159
   adoption prior to the 1920s 39–42
   adoption since 1950 205–212
   advertisements 146, 148, 165, 171, 177, 181
   assumption of parental rights by Poor Law Guardians 27
   attitudes towards 6–8, 69–71, 195–197
   baby farming advertisement 23
   baby farming 24
   case details in Bath 121–122
   concern about adoption societies' activities 144–153
   concluding discussion re its development 195–205
   1919 conference and report on its desirability 68–71
   cost of adoption order 121
   court procedures 120–126
   Curtis Committee 186–190
   decline in adoptions 207
   departmental conference 1921 90–91
   development after First World War 67–68
   early adoption Bill 24
   establishment of NCSS 'Gamon' Committee 186
   evidence of witnesses to Hopkinson Committee 72–83
   failed private members' bills 91–93
   further pressure for adoption reform 185
   growing pressure for legislation 67–71
   histories of 8–9
   Home Office 1928 report 123–125
   informal adoption 32, 39, 96, 121, 125, 154, 159, 171, 218 (note)
   legal position prior to 1926 28
   London County Council's role in organising adoption 130–136

NCUMC's opinion 65–66, 72–74
parliamentary debates over
  103–113
passing of Adoption of Children
  (Regulation) Act (1939)
  167–172
pressure to enact Adoption of
  Children (Regulation) Act
  (1939) 177–180
private adoptions 185–186,
  188–189, 197, 206
provisions of Adoption of Children
  Act (1949) 193–194
records 99
Report of Hopkinson
  Committee 84–86
Report of Horsbrugh
  Committee 154–167
Reports of Tomlin Committee
  96–103
step-parent adoptions 206, 207,
  238 (note)
Adoption Act (1950) 194
Adoption Act (1958) 206
Adoption Act (1976) 206
Adoption agencies – see Adoption
  societies
Adoption and Children Act
  (2002) 208, 209
Adoption of Children Act (1926) 66,
  89, 129, 130, 133, 144, 166, 168,
  171, 172, 191, 194, 198, 202
  court procedures 120–126
  effect of 117–120
  initial reactions 114
  legal queries arising from
    128–129
Adoption of Children Act (1949) 190,
  193–194
Adoption of Children Bill (1889) 24
Adoption of Children Bill (1925)
  103–104, 115, 128
Adoption of Children Bill (No.2)
  (1925) 105
Adoption of Children Bill (1926)
  debates on 105–113
  receives Royal Assent 114
Adoption of Children Bill (1949) 140
  debates on 191–193

Adoption of Children (Regulation)
  Act (1939) 167–172, 173, 188,
  196–197
  pressure to implement following
    delay 177–180
  request for its review after a year in
    operation 185
Adoption of Children (Scotland) Act
  (1930) 129–130
Adoption of Children (Summary
  Jurisdiction) Rules (1926) 120
Adoption of Children (Workmen's
  Compensation) Act
  (1934) 129
Adoption Register – see Adopted
  Children Register
Adoption societies 4, 5, 7, 36, 41–42,
  70–71, 85, 93, 96, 97–100, 102,
  107, 115, 116, 118, 135, 136,
  138, 174, 176, 178, 190, 191,
  192, 194, 195–197, 198, 199,
  200, 201–202, 205, 206–207
  concern about their activities
    144–153, 169
  Horsbrugh Committee Report on
    their activities 154–167
  provisions of Adoption of Children
    (Regulation) Act (1939)
    170–172
Adoption Society, The – see Church
  Adoption Society
Adoptive parents – see Adopters
Affiliation orders 64, 128
Affiliation Orders (Increase of
  Maximum Payment) Act
  (1918) 37
Alice, Princess, Countess of
  Athlone 48, 50, 58, 59–62,
  61(fig), 144, 151, 173, 174, 201,
  221 (notes), 249
Allen, Lady 186–187, 244
Anchorage Mission 183–184
Anderson, Sir John 94, 244
Anderson, Michael 14, 16,
  140, 204
Andrew, Miss Clara 6, 42–54, 44
  (fig), 57, 59–62, 76, 78–79, 81,
  82, 83, 137, 144, 172–174, 184,
  199, 201, 205, 221 (note), 244

Andrew, Sidney   42–43, 60–61
Ariès, Philippe   12
Associated Societies for the Care and Maintenance of Infants   68–71, 80
Astbury, Benjamin Edward   150, 153, 177, 188, 244
Athlone, Earl of   60
Astor, Lady   169–170
Atholl, Duchess of   92, 96, 244–245
Atholl, Duke of   92, 94, 130, 244, 245
Attlee, Major Clement   107
Attwell, Mabel Lucy   50
Austen, Jane   39
Australia   6, 7, 40–41, 85

Baby farming   23, 67–68, 102, 149, 161, 164, 196
Bachelor motherhood   36
Baldwin, Lucy   50, 144
Baird, Sir J. L.   83
Barker, Sir W. R.   96, 245
Barnardo's – see Dr Barnardo's
Bastardy Act (1923)   37
Bastardy Laws Amendment Act (1872)   37
Bath, Marquess and Marchioness of   55
Bedford, Adeline, Duchess of   68
Beesley, E. T.   126, 146, 149–150
Behlmer, George   8, 19, 25
Beier, Lucinda McCray   16
Belgian refugees   43–44
Berebitsky, Julie   204
Birkett, Sir Norman   177
Birth certificates – see Birth records
Birth mothers   4, 5, 7, 47, 55, 96, 97, 99–101, 109, 116, 119, 137–143, 144, 160–161, 168, 169, 188, 189, 190–194, 196, 197, 199–201, 204, 210
Birth parents – see Birth mothers
Birth rate   11–12, 20, 33
  illegitimate birth rate   32–33, 72, 175
Birth records   4, 6, 9, 129, 181, 188, 194, 202, 206

Births and Deaths Registration Act (1874)   24
Blackwell, Sir Ernley   90–91, 245
Blair, Tony   208, 209, 242 (note)
Board of Education   35, 90, 96
Boarding out, fostering   25, 26, 39, 40, 41, 74, 91, 127, 155, 182, 183, 187, 189, 197
Boards of Guardians – see Poor Law Guardians
Boer War   20
Bourke, Joanna   15
Brassey, Sir Leonard   91, 92, 245
Brassey, Lady Violet   92
Brixton   23
Brown, Ernest   145–146, 176, 179
Burnett, John   14–15
Burns, John   20
Butcher, Sir J. G.   72
Butler, Sir Geoffrey   103, 104, 115, 128, 245
Buttle, Rev. Frank   48, 54–55, 146, 162–163, 244, 245
Buttle Trust, The   163, 244

Catholic Rescue Society   126–127
Caldecote, Lady Augusta – see Inskip, Lady Augusta
Caldecote, Viscount – see Inskip, Sir Thomas
Cambridge   54
Campbell, Miss   76
Canada   40–41, 69–70, 85
Care of Children Committee, 1946 (Curtis Committee)   7, 186–190
Carlisle   26
Carp, E. Wayne   5–6
Carroll, In re   126–128, 160
Case committees   50, 52, 64, 151, 159, 170, 200, 201
Castlebar hostel, Sydenham Hill   58, 59, 60, 61, 223 (note)
Chamberlain, Neville   64, 72, 83, 89, 246
Chancery Division   28, 56, 95, 106, 191
Chapman, Allan   170

Chapman, Cecil M. 78, 149, 151
Charity Organisation Society 68, 149, 152, 153, 154, 177, 178, 188
Child's Garden of Verses, A 18
Child Adoption Committee 1924–25 (Tomlin Committee) 144, 145, 147, 150, 199–200
  establishment of 94–96
  First Report 96–101, 102, 117
  Second Report 101–102
  Third and Final Report 102–103
  Reports forwarded to Home Secretary 105
Child migration – see Emigration of British children
Child Study Movement 18
Child Welfare Council 63
Childhood, changing views of 18–22, 197, 199
Children Act (1908) 24, 25, 27, 54, 67, 91, 97, 102–103, 131, 147
Children Act (1948) 187
Children Act (1975) 5, 6, 204, 206
Children and Young Persons Act (1932) 147, 165
Children and Young Persons Bill (1931) 145–147
Children's homes 102–103, 149–150, 159
Children's Society – see Church of England Children's Society
Chinn, Carl 32
Church Adoption Society (formerly the Church of England Adoption Society and The Adoption Society) 54, 55, 146, 154, 162–163, 180
Church Army 68, 69
Church League of Women's Suffrage 54
Church of England Adoption Society – see Church Adoption Society
Church of England Children's Society (formerly Waifs and Strays Society, then Church of England Homes for Waifs and Strays, now Children's Society) 154, 176, 183, 197
Church of England Homes for Waifs and Strays – see Church of England Children's Society
Church of England Moral Welfare Council 178
Class 11–17, 18–19, 32, 51, 52
Cobb, Monica Mary Geikie 37
Cohen, Stanley 74
Committee on Child Adoption 1920 (Hopkinson Committee) 26, 40, 42, 51–52, 55, 69, 95, 99, 102, 105, 106, 116, 117, 153, 199, 201
  content of Report 84–86
  departmental conference about it 1921 90–91
  establishment of 72
  evidence to 72–83
  publication of Report 83
  reaction to Report 89–93
Common Law 28, 29, 80
Common law marriages 63
Compulsory schooling – see Education, Compulsory
Contraception 198, 204, 207
Corthorn, Alice 141
Cottage homes 25, 31
County Courts 81, 85, 90, 91, 92, 93, 106, 107, 110–111, 121, 125–126, 192
Court of Appeal 127–128, 129, 192
Court of Chancery 27, 28, 29, 63
Court of Wards and Liveries 28
Cox, Commissioner Adelaide 40, 74, 80
Crane, R. Newton 79–80
Crèches, day and residential nurseries 63, 64, 175, 183
Cretney, Stephen 89, 116, 187, 190, 193
Crichton-Stuart, Lord 112
Cripps, Sir Stafford 121
Crossick, Geoffrey 16
Crusade of Rescue 154, 165
Curtis Committee – see Care of Children Committee 1946
Curtis, Myra 187, 246

Custodianship 206
Custody 27, 28–30, 37
Custody of Children Act (1891) 24, 29
Custody of Infants Acts (1839) 29
(1873) 29

Davies, John Rhys 104
'De facto' adoption – see 'Adoption: informal adoption
Departmental Committee on Adoption Societies and Agencies 1936 (Horsbrugh Commmittee) 55, 102, 115, 136, 170, 188, 191, 196, 200
establishment of 153–154
passing of Adoption of Children (Regulation) Act (1939) 167–172
report 154–167
Departmental Committee on the Adoption of Children 1954 (Hurst Committee) 92, 205–206
Desborough, Lord 113
Diocesan Associations for Rescue and Preventive Work 69
Director of Public Prosecutions 150
Disability 157–158, 205
Disinherited Family, The 77
Domesticity 12–14, 88
Donor conception 210
Drawbell, J. W. 125–126
Dr Barnardo's 40–41, 63, 70, 83, 154, 176, 196, 197
Dunn, Edward 170
Dunnico, Rev. Herbert 103
Dutch Home Office 163
Dwork, Deborah 20

Ede, James Chuter 193
Education, compulsory 12, 18, 19, 23, 25
Eldon, Lord 28
'Elizabeth Ann' 177, 178
Elliott, William J. 148–149, 152
Ellis, Havelock 141
Emigration of British children 40–41, 69–70, 220 (note)
England, Mrs 45

Essex, Rosamund 142
Eugenics 21, 33, 36, 47, 158
Eugenics Education Society (Eugenics Society) 21
Evacuation 175, 178, 182, 183
Exeter 42–45, 173
Experiences from the Adoption Circle 7

F. B. Meyer Children's Home 126
Fairbridge Society 41
Family 195, 197, 203, 204
changing nature of 11–18, 197–198
size 11–12, 14, 21, 140, 198
Family allowances 77, 87
Family Endowment Society 77
Family Story, The 202
Fathers 12, 28–30, 36, 37, 181
Ferguson, Sheila 36
Fertility of Marriage Census (1911) 11
Filius nullius 37
Fink, Janet 199
First World War 21, 30, 33, 42, 62–63, 144, 175
Fisher, Lettice 64, 72–74, 167, 184–185, 246
Fisher, Mrs H. A. L. – see Fisher, Lettice
Fisher, H. A. L. 64, 246
Fitzgerald, Hilda 36
Fortescue, Lord 43
Fostering – see Boarding out
Foundling Hospital 31
Freud's 'family romance' theory 6
Frost, Ginger 32

Galbraith, James 105, 106, 111, 118, 129, 246
Gamon, Judge 186, 246
Gellhorn, Martha 142
Giles, Judy 15
Gilmour, Sir John 149
Gittins, Diana 13, 19
Gorell, Lord 95
Gould, Mrs Ayrton 191
Gray, Mrs Edwin 75, 197
Greer, Lord Justice 127
Guardian ad litem 101, 120–121, 125, 130, 131, 133–134, 159, 164–165, 187, 189

Guardianship of Infants Acts
  (1886) 29
  (1925) 29–30
Gwyer, M. L. 95, 98, 116, 147,
  202, 246

Hacking, Captain 112
Hall, W Clarke 63, 76–77, 79, 131
Harris, John Henry 153, 247
Harris, S. W. 90, 95, 98, 105, 116,
  129, 147, 152–153, 181, 247
Hardyment, Christina 18
Harkness, Janet 174
Hawtrey, Miss 178
Hayday, Arthur 104
Headlam, Lieut.-Colonel Cuthbert 108
Health visiting/health visitors 20,
  21, 155, 171, 178, 217 (note)
Helena Victoria, Princess 55
Henderson, Arthur 95
Hendrick, Harry 19, 25, 27
Heywood, Jean 19
High Court 24, 28, 29, 81, 86, 101,
  111, 119, 121, 122–123, 125,
  144, 165, 192
Hoare, Sir Samuel 167
Holden, Katherine 17, 142
Holland – see Netherlands
Hollyman, In re 192
Holtby, Winifred 87
Home Office 4, 9, 89, 90, 91, 93,
  94, 95, 103, 104, 118, 120, 123,
  128–129, 145, 147, 149, 153,
  174, 178–180, 181–182, 187, 198
Homeless Children's Aid and
  Adoption Society 126–127,
  146, 149–150, 154, 159
Homes, A. M. 7
Hopkinson Committee – see
  Committee on Child Adoption
  1920
Hopkinson, Sir Alfred 72, 73 (fig.),
  110–111, 114, 247
Horsbrugh, Miss Florence
  153–154 (fig), 168–170, 177,
  179–180, 205, 247
Horsbrugh Committee – see
  Departmental Committee on
  Adoption Societies and Agencies

Houghton Committee 206
House of Commons 103–113, 130,
  153, 190–193, 205
House of Lords 92, 113, 130, 191, 192
Housing 14–15, 215 (note)
Hubback, Eva 118
Hudson, Dr Margaret 40
Hurst Committee – see Departmental
  Committee on the Adoption
  of Children 1954 (Hurst
  Committee)
Hurst, Sir Gerald 91, 92, 115,
  205–206, 247
Human Fertilisation and Embryology
  Authority (Disclosure of Donor
  Information) Regulations 210
Humphries, Steve 34

Illegitimacy 2–3, 30–38, 46–48,
  62–66, 72, 78, 90, 106, 115,
  125, 128–129, 140, 158, 172,
  176, 183, 189, 195, 203, 207,
  218–220 (notes)
  in USA 5
  see also Birth rate
'In Loco Parentis' 186
Infant Life Protection Acts
  (1872) 23, 24
  (1897) 24, 27
Infant Life Protection Society 24
Infant mortality 12, 20, 22, 32, 62,
  72, 204
Infant welfare movement 20, 21
Infertility 139–140, 210
Inskip, Lady Augusta 59–62,
  184–185, 247
Inskip, Sir Thomas 50, 59–62, 92,
  103, 110, 128, 145, 192, 248
Insurance companies 114
Intercountry adoption – see Adoption
  adoption of children from overseas
Interdepartmental Committee on
  Physical Deterioration 20
Intestacy 38, 86, 102, 110, 194, 202
Isaacs, Dr Susan 186

Jackson, Alan A 14
James, Mrs, owner of Redhill nursing
  home 178, 188

Jewish Association for the Protection of Girls and Women (also known as the Jewish Association for the Protection of Women and Children) 74, 155
Jewson, Dorothy 96, 248
Josephine Butler House 151
Joynson-Hicks, Sir William 105, 107–108, 110, 128, 248
Juvenile Courts 27, 120–125

Kensington, Bishop of 48, 50
Kenworthy, Lieut.-Commander 103, 112
Kiernan, Kathleen 31, 63
King, Joseph 63
Kornitzer, Margaret 9

Lambeth Board of Guardians 27
Lancashire and Cheshire Child Adoption Council 184
Land, Hilary 31, 63
Legitimacy Act (1926) 37–38, 89
Legitimation of illegitimate children 37–38, 89, 91
Lennon, John 181
Levy, Benn 192–193
Lewis, Jane 12, 31, 63
Lloyd, Geoffrey 170
Lloyd George, Mrs 52, 144
Local authorities 103, 120–121, 125, 130, 155, 165–166, 178, 179, 180, 182, 189, 206, 207, 208
provisions of Adoption of Children (Regulation) Act (1939) 170–171
Local Government Act (1929) 132
Local Government Board 43, 45, 46, 48
Locker-Lampson, Godfrey 104
London County Council 60, 130–136, 151, 153, 154, 162, 165, 180
Lord Chancellor's Office/ Department 89, 90, 91, 93, 94, 95, 105, 118, 152, 181–182, 198
Lovat-Fraser, James 145, 147
Lucan, Earl of 130

Maclachlan, A. B. 145–146, 150, 248
Macnaghten, Sir Malcolm 92, 105, 248
Magistrates' courts 81, 93, 101, 106, 107, 120
Magistrates' Association 146–147
Mallon, J. J. 153, 248
Mamhead, Lord – see Newman, Sir Robert
Manning, Brian 153, 164, 248
Many-Sided Triangle, The 7
Marx, Eleanor 141
Mary, Queen 48, 58, 60
Mass Observation 14–15
Maternal and Child Welfare Act (1918) 22
Maternity and child welfare clinics 21, 217 (note)
Mathers, George 129–130
Matrimonial Causes Act (1857) 29
Maugham, Lord 168
McEwan, Ian 181
McKibbin, Ross 140
McLeod, Hugh 17
McWhinnie, Alexina 9, 138, 142
Meath, Earl of 24
Mental deficiency 31, 33–34
Mental Deficiency Act (1913) 33–34
Menzies, Dr Frederick 74, 76
Middleton, Nigel 26
Milburn, Alan 1
Milne, Kenneth 91
Mind – see National Association for Mental Health
Ministry of Health 22, 45, 48, 53, 54, 55, 76, 90, 91, 93, 95, 176, 178, 180, 182, 183, 198
Ministry of Pensions 26, 90, 91, 176
Mission of Hope 146, 150, 154
Mitchison, Naomi 15
Morant, Sir Robert 76
Morgan, Patricia 208
Morris, Temple 153
Morrison, Herbert 179, 187
Mother and baby homes and hostels 30, 65, 74, 182–183
Mothers' pensions 76–77, 104

Muir Mackenzie, Lord 113
Musson, Susan 114, 178

NCH – see National Children's Home and Orphanage
Napier, A. E. A. 118
National Adoption Society (NAS) 42, 48, 54–57, 68, 69, 70, 81, 92, 99, 119, 128, 144, 146, 150, 154, 158, 162, 181, 184, 185–186
National Association for Mental Health (later Mind) 137
National Baby Week 22, 46
National Children Adoption Association (NCAA) 4, 42, 46–55, 56, 57, 58–62, 68, 69, 70, 71, 79, 82, 83, 92, 93, 105, 118, 129, 137, 142, 144–145, 146, 151, 152, 154, 172–174, 177, 178, 184–185, 186, 192, 198, 199, 200–201, 207
National Children's Home and Orphanage (later NCH) 39, 57, 118, 138–139, 154
National Council for One Parent Families – see National Council for the Unmarried Mother and Her Child
National Council for the Unmarried Mother and Her Child (NCUMC, later National Council for One Parent Families, then One Parent Families) 35, 36, 62–66, 69, 73, 114, 116, 152, 154, 177, 178, 183, 184–185, 196, 197, 203, 224 (note), 246
National Council of Social Service 186
National Council of Women (see also National Union of Women Workers) 71, 75, 82, 152, 197, 225 (note)
National Federation of Institutions for the Unmarried Mother and Her Child, Holland 163
National Relief Fund 63
National Society for the Prevention of Cruelty to Children (NSPCC) 24, 25, 63, 75, 82, 83, 85, 90, 91–92, 119, 122, 125, 148–150, 152, 154, 159, 196, 241 (note)
National Union of Societies for Equal Citizenship 118, 231 (note)
National Union of Women Workers (see also National Council of Women) 64
Natural parents – see Birth mothers
Netherlands 163–164
Newman, Sir George 76
Newman, Sir Robert (Lord Mamhead from 1931) 111, 113, 152
New Zealand 6, 41, 85
Nicholson, Reginald 91, 92, 249
Nield, Basil 140, 190, 248
Norman, Mrs (later Lady) Priscilla Montagu 153, 158, 249
Norman, Lady Priscilla 72, 79, 249
Northcote, Lady 48
Northern Ireland 112
Norwood School 27
Notification of Births (Extension) Act (1915) 22
Nurseries – see Crèches, day and residential nurseries
Nursing homes 164, 178, 188

Official Solicitor 122–123, 125, 137, 144
O'Neill, Dennis 187
One Parent Families – see National Council for the Unmarried Mother and Her Child
Orwell, Eileen 185
Orwell, George 185

Palin, J. H. 108
Pankhurst, Sylvia 36
Parental rights 27–30, 37–38, 80
Parr, Joy 40
Parr, Robert J. 83, 91–92
Parry, Edward Abbott 80
Peacock, Mrs Katherine 58–62
Peake, Osbert 178–179
Peg's Paper 13

274 *Index*

Percival, Tom (Tynemouth Poor Law Guardians)   26, 75
Peter Pan   18
Pethick-Lawrence, Frederick   108
Peto, Miss R. S. M.   42, 79, 82
Pfeffer, Naomi   139
Pimlott, J. A. R.   153, 249
Plows-Day, Miss   48
Plummer, Mrs   174
Poor Law Act (1930)   132–133
Poor Law Amendment Acts (1834)   23
   (1889)   25
   (1899)   25
Poor Law Guardians   23, 24, 25–27, 31, 37, 69–70, 83, 90, 91, 103, 108, 125, 132, 217 (note), 218 (note)
Poor Relief Act (1601)   23
Postponement of Enactments (Miscellaneous Provisions) Act (1939)   172
Prevention of Cruelty to, and Better Protection of, Children Act (1889)   24–25
Pringle, J. C.   149
Professional Classes War Relief Fund   21
Public Health Act (1936)   165
Pugh, Martin   13, 88
Puxley, Miss Z. L.   48, 49, 55, 57, 76, 83, 174, 249

Radcliffe, F. R. Yonge   81
Rathbone, Eleanor   77, 87
Registrar General   102, 202
   report of 1939   17
Religion   52, 86, 112, 126–127, 212, 240 (note)
Relinquishing mothers – see Birth mothers
Renier, Olive   141
Rentoul, Sir Gervais   106
Respectability   3, 12, 15–17, 32, 34, 127, 173, 176, 201
Richardson, Mary   142
Rhondda, Lady   87
Rhondda, Lord   45
Roberts, Elizabeth   16, 17, 31, 32, 34, 137, 182

Roberts, Gwyneth   54
Rose, June   41
Rose, Lionel   25
Ross, Ellen   12
Rosser, Miss Enid   95
Rover, Constance   36
Russell, Geoffrey W.   96, 153, 164, 167, 250
Russell, Lilian   72, 82, 250
Ryburn, Murray   4–5

Sark, Dr   163
Salvation Army   36, 40, 69, 74, 82–83, 154, 155, 165
Samson, Lt-Col Rhys   60
Samuel, Sir Herbert   145
Savage, Gail   116
Sayers, Dorothy L.   35–36, 140–141
Scandinavia   85
Schreiner, Olive   141
Schuster, Sir Claud   90, 94, 114, 152, 250
Schuster, Ernest J.   81,
Scotland   9, 112, 129–130, 137, 138, 194, 202, 241 (note), 242 (note)
Scott, Miss Amelia   75
Scrutton, Lord Justice   127, 160
Second World War   4, 36, 139, 172, 175–184, 190
Secrecy   3–6, 32, 52, 78–81, 93, 98–100, 106, 107–108, 109, 110–111, 115, 116, 118, 129, 130, 140, 144–145, 159–161, 174, 192–193, 198, 201–203, 205, 210, 212
   adoptees' right to copy of original birth entry   206
   birth parents' right to contact their children   210
   serial numbers replacing adopters' names   191, 193, 194
Seddon, James A.   72, 82, 250
Select Committee on Protection of Infant Life   24
Separation allowance   63
Sex Disqualification (Removal) Act (1919)   30, 88

Sexuality   17, 34, 139
Shaw, George Bernard   186
Sheffield and District Adoption Committee   188
Sherwood, Frederick   72, 250
Shortt, Edward   71–72, 83, 89, 250
Simon, Sir John   152, 153, 168
Singer, Charles   79
Six Point Group   87–88
Slater, Elliot   139
Slesser, Sir Henry (Lord Justice)   103, 105, 128
Smith, Mr Stanwell (Southwark Poor Law Guardians)   26
Snowden, Mrs (later Viscountess) Ethel   144, 173, 238 (note)
Social Purity and Hygiene Movement   33
Social Welfare Association   63
Social work/social workers   8, 151, 156, 158, 208, 209
   in US   6
Soldiers', Sailors' and Airmen's Help Society   183
Somerset, Lady Henry   1, 42, 75, 83
South Africa   58
Standing Conference of Societies Registered for Adoption   142, 174, 207, 242 (note)
Stevenson, Miss   178
Storks, The   42
Stutchbury, H. O.   45, 91, 116, 250
Sunday Dispatch Wartime Aunts Scheme   177
Szreter, Simon   11

Tate, Mrs Mavis   145, 147, 251
Taylor, A. J. P.   87
Thane, Pat   22, 88
Thomas Coram Foundation   158
Thomson, Matthew   33
Thurtle, Ernest   193
Time and Tide   69, 87, 89
Tinker, John Joseph   169
Tomlin, Mr Justice   95, 98, 251
Tomlin Committee (see Child Adoption Committee 1924–25)

Tower Cressy hostel, Kensington   48–49, 49 (fig), 50, 51, 58–62, 76, 172, 174, 221 (note)
Trade union movement   12
Triseliotis, John P.   9, 130, 137
Toynbee Hall   153
Truby King, F.   204

United States of America   5–6, 18–19, 22, 85, 169, 204
   babies sent there   56, 146
Unmarried mothers   5–6, 30–38, 48, 53, 62–66, 70, 72–74, 76–78, 84–85, 93, 116, 119, 140, 165, 172, 182–185, 190, 194, 195, 196, 197, 203–204, 207, 209

Voting rights for women   87, 88

Waifs and Strays Society – see Church of England Children's Society
War Cabinet   179
Ward, Miss Irene   178, 179, 251
Wardship   27, 28
Wasserman test   157, 188
Waters, Margaret   23
Wells, H.G.   35, 141
West, Rebecca   35, 140–141
Wethered, Mrs R.P.   80
White, Cynthia   13
'Whose Children?'   187
Widows', Orphans' and Old Age Contributory Act (1925)   77
Wilkinson, Ellen   108–109
Williams, Herbert G.   109, 168
Wilson-Fox, Mrs Eleanor   96, 251
Women
   adoption and women   203–205
   domestic role   12–14
   feminist activists   87–89
   infertility   139–140
   lack of senior women in Civil Service   230–231 (note)
   magistrates   146
   married in paid employment   13, 140, 203, 234 (note)
   married, with illegitimate children   175, 180–182, 193, 239 (note)
   mothercraft   22, 205

Women (*continued*)
  motherhood 14, 21–22, 204–205
  mothering skills 20, 204–205
  unmarried/spinsters 17–18,
    169–170, 172
  unmarried women adopting –
    see Adopters, single women
    adopting
  voting rights 87, 88
Women's Local Government
  Society 64
Women's magazines 13
Women Power Committee 178
Womersley, Sir William 176

Woodcock, H. B. Drysdale 81, 99
Woodside, Moya 139
Woolwich Arsenal 43, 63
Workers' Education Association 64
Workhouses 23, 25, 30, 31, 32, 39,
  65, 82, 109, 126
Workman, Joanne 87
Workmen's Compensation Acts 80,
  81, 106, 129

Younger, Kenneth 192
Younghusband, Eileen 151

Zelizer, Viviana A. 18–19